History 5–11

Now in its third edition, *History 5–11* aims to make teaching about the past exciting and stimulating for both teachers and children. Focusing on the English National Curriculum for History (2013), and with an emphasis on the importance of learning about the past through the processes of historical enquiry, *History 5–11* contains case studies, lesson planning guidance and methods to develop pupils' historical understanding. It offers creative and innovative ways to teach the subject of history, refreshing teachers' confidence in teaching the 2013 curriculum, and is illustrated by new case studies and research.

This fully updated third edition includes:

- References to the 2013 National Curriculum, its aims and purposes, and its content and processes for Key Stages 1 and 2

- Guidance on making local, national and global connections between societies over time

- Planning for assessment and progression

- New research and illustrative case studies

- New sections on local history and links to oracy

- Updates to all existing chapters

- Reflection on practice and research: undergraduate, Masters level and PhD.

This textbook is an invaluable resource to all trainee and practising primary teachers interested in teaching history in an accessible, dynamic and, above all, enjoyable way.

Hilary Cooper is Emeritus Professor of History and Pedagogy at the University of Cumbria, UK. She has published numerous books on history teaching and is an internationally renowned keynote speaker.

The 5–11 series combines academic rigor with practical classroom experience in a tried and tested approach which has proved indispensible to both trainee PGCE students and to practicing teachers. Bringing the best and latest research knowledge to core subject areas, this series addresses the key issues surrounding the teaching of these subjects in the primary curriculum. The series aims to stay up to date by reflecting changes in government policy and is closely related to the changing curriculum for the primary core subjects.

Each book contains lesson planning guidance and methods to develop pupils' understanding as well as offering creative and innovative ways to teach subjects in the primary classroom.

Titles in this series include:

Physical Education 5–11, Jonathan Doherty and Peter Brennan

History 5–11, Hilary Cooper

Modern Foreign Languages 5–11, Jane Jones and Simon Coffey

English 5–11, David Waugh and Wendy Jolliffe

Science 5–11, Alan Howe, Chris Collier, Dan Davies, Kendra McMahon and Sarah Earle

History 5–11

A Guide for Teachers

Third Edition

Hilary Cooper

Routledge
Taylor & Francis Group

LONDON AND NEW YORK

First published 2018
by Routledge
2 Park Square, Milton Park, Abingdon, Oxon OX14 4RN

and by Routledge
711 Third Avenue, New York, NY 10017

Routledge is an imprint of the Taylor & Francis Group, an informa business

British Library Cataloguing in Publication Data
A catalogue record for this book is available from the British Library

Library of Congress Cataloguing in Publication Data
Names: Cooper, Hilary, 1943– author. | Cooper, Hilary, 1943– History 3–11.
Title: History 5-11 : a guide for teachers / Hilary Cooper.
Other titles: History five–eleven
Description: Third Edition. | New York : Routledge, 2018. | Previous edition: 2012.
Identifiers: LCCN 2017030961| ISBN 9781138720817 (Hardback) |
ISBN 9781138720831 (Paperback) | ISBN 9781315194875 (Ebook)
Subjects: LCSH: History—Study and teaching (Elementary)—Great Britain.
Classification: LCC LB1582.G7 C66 2018 | DDC 372.890941—dc23
LC record available at https://lccn.loc.gov/2017030961

ISBN: 978-1-138-72081-7 (hbk)
ISBN: 978-1-138-72083-1 (pbk)
ISBN: 978-1-315-19487-5 (ebk)

Typeset in Bembo and Helvetica Neue
by Florence Production Ltd, Stoodleigh, Devon, UK

Contents

Figures

Tables

Acknowledgements

The third edition of *History 5–11* draws on examples of practical, school-based research into the teaching and learning of history, case studies applying research to practice and case-study examples of innovative and creative approaches. I am therefore very grateful to teacher educators, whose work I have referred to. The work of the late Hilary Claire, made a lasting contribution to our understanding of how to encourage young children's understanding of controversial questions, and of issues of social, justice, diversity and equality, through teaching history. The late Anna Craft was enormously influential in defining what we mean by creativity in education and enabled us not only to justify creative approaches to teaching history but also to argue that good history teaching is essentially creative. I also refer to the work of the late John Fines, whose recognized expertise in the teaching of history was based on extensive classroom experience, an expert on the teaching of history. Other valued colleagues whose work is referred to include Jon Nichol, Penelope Harnett, Pat Hoodless, Peter Vass, Hugh Moore, Linda Cooper and Sue Temple, who have contributed to this book and others, and Peter Lee, who supervised my doctoral research, and – more importantly – led the Concepts of History and Teaching Approaches at Key Stages 2 and 3 (CHATA) Research. Thank you to all of them.

Through working with Jon Nichol on the *International Journal of Historical Learning, Teaching and Research* (IJHLTR) and the related annual History Educators International Research Network conferences (HEIRNET) I have made many friends internationally; the English approach to primary history education is increasingly regarded as important. The research of some of these colleagues is found in IJHLTR and referred to in this book. They include Helena Pinto (Portugal), Hideo Sugao (Japan), Yvonne Vella (Malta), Sunjoo Kang (South Korea), Maria Schmidt and Tania Garcia (Brazil), Keith Barton (Indiana), Alan McCully, (Northern Ireland), Gail Weldon (South Africa), Jocelyn Letourneau (Canada), Laura Capita (Roumania), Andrei Sokalov (Russia). I also quote workshops I had the pleasure of doing with some of their students.

Many examples of good practice in this book have been provided by articles in the Historical Association of Great Britain's publications, *Primary History* and *Teaching History*, which constantly examine issues of current concern in history teaching and provide interesting, practice-based suggestions. Contributors to these journals, whose work is quoted, include Jane Card, Gerraint Brown and Andrew Wrenn, Bev Forrest and Stuart Tiffany, Matthew Sossick, Christine Counsell, Karin Doull, Pat Lewis, Ilona Aranovsky, Paul Bracey, Tim Lomas and Ian Dawson.

Investigating practice, of course, must be carried out in schools. In England most schools welcome researchers, and we must value this spirit of trust and openness, because it is not usual in many countries, where schools are seen as 'private' and so research into new ideas and practices is neither welcome nor possible. Collaboration with Stramongate School, Kendal, and Greenvale School, Croydon, on some case studies was appreciated.

Of course we are all grateful to the professional researchers and historians, who constantly challenge out preconceptions, making history constantly dynamic and surprising, and provide role models for the discipline of historical enquiry and the new accounts it precipitates, on which vibrant history teaching depends. For example, Linsay Allason-Jones (2011) has shown convincingly how much we can learn about the material culture of Ancient Rome, through asking the questions that Collingwood originally posited about how the enormous number of surviving Roman artefacts were made and used. They have developed the methods we have learned to use with children at an adult level. Similarly Anne Gerritsen and Giorgio Riello (2015), touching on archaeology, art history, literary studies and anthropology, have developed our understanding of the relationship between artefacts and historical narratives at the level of academic scholarship, which it will be fascinating to modify, in work with children. Von Prezinger's research (2016) into communication between peoples, over vast areas and periods of time during the Stone Age, really challenges existing academic understanding and will stimulates the imagination of children.

And finally, I am grateful to those who, like Professor Richard Evans, fought for a redraft of Michael Gove's February 2013, 'pub quiz' National Curriculum for history, what Simon Shama described as '*1066 and All That*, without the jokes' (Hay Festival 30.05.2013) https://media.education.gov.uk/assets/files/pdf/n/national%20curriculum%20consultation%20-%20framework%20document.pdf

Their energetic criticisms resulted in the revised September version (DfE 2013) which emphasizes the processes of historical enquiry, and 'The Big Picture' and encourages its interpretation and assessment at the highest level, by respecting the professional judgments of teachers.

Introduction

The history of *History 5–11*

In 1992 I was teaching in a London primary school. I had just completed a doctorate on 'Young Children's Thinking in History' using data from the classes I taught, and the first National Curriculum for history had been published the previous year. David Fulton invited me to write a book for teachers on teaching history in primary schools, relating theory to practice. Since my head was buzzing with 'theory and practice' I wrote *The Teaching of History* quite quickly and, although modesty should forbid me to say so, it became Fulton's bestseller that year. This was because, before the National Curriculum, there was no requirement to teach history in primary schools. In some classes, with an enthusiastic teacher, it was well taught; sometimes teachers used books such as *From Cavemen to Vikings* (Unstead 1953, second edition 1961). The section on the Romans (pp. 40–41) tells us that

> The boys had to learn many of the things we do, also to ride a pony and to use a little sword. The girls learnt to sew and to keep house. They played with dolls and balls and a game called knuckle bones. They always obeyed their father.

In most primary schools history was not taught. The Plowden Report (1967) had endorsed the view that history is remote and abstract, concerned with the affairs of adults and too difficult for children to become actively involved in.

In the 1970s deadening, didactic history teaching in English primary schools was challenged by two pamphlets, *Educational Objectives for the Study of History* (Coltham and Fines 1971) and *The New History, Theory into Practice* (Rogers 1979). Cannadine *et al.* (2011) critically analyse ways in which the pamphlets drew on generic hypotheses about progression, drawing on the work of Elton (1967), Bruner (1963, 1966) and Bloom (1956) and gave rise to such competences as asking questions, working on sources, understanding differing viewpoints and interpretation in a range of genres. These pamphlets initiated the complex task of analysing what is involved in learning history.

Schulman's (1986) 'discovery' of procedural knowledge and school history reflected the work of Coltham and Fines (1971) and of Rogers (1979), which claimed that school history, at appropriate levels, can be linked to the processes used by academic historians, if it is grounded in theories of learning and the philosophy of history, a claim not understood in all European countries.

In the 1970s philosophers (Lyotard 1979, White 1992, Olafson 1979), in response to the increasing variety of historians' writing, also analysed the reasons why history as a 'Grand Narrative', consisting of a sequence of stories about a society's emerging identity and unquestioned values, was simplistic. They made the case that understanding that the past is complex and controversial and depends on debate and dialogue.

These influences on history education, the changing scope of academic historians and the changing philosophy of history, impacted on practice and informed the structure of the 1991 National Curriculum.

For the first time, the 1991 National Curriculum (DES 1991) required children, from Year 1 to Year 6, in increasingly complex ways, to find out about the past through making deductions and inferences from sources and to use time concepts such as continuity, change, cause, effect, similarity and difference. Teachers were expected to plan for learning outcomes and assess children's progress using 'Attainment Targets'. For many teachers this was a considerable challenge and in the 2013 National Curriculum for history targets and levels were seen to be unhelpful and removed.

Yet I find that I wrote in the introduction to the second edition, *The Teaching of History in Primary Schools: Implementing the Revised National Curriculum* (Cooper 1995b: vii), 'In history, the sea change in 4 years has been amazing. In schools all over the country we find school museums, displays of 'old things', presentations of local and family investigations, pictures and models made after visits to museums galleries and Living History reconstructions . . .' Key Stage 1 teachers, after their initial scepticism, found that history could be an appropriate and enjoyable subject for young children. The third edition of *The Teaching of History in Primary Schools* (2000) was followed by *History 3–11* (2007) and *History 5–11* (2012). Each edition introduced new case studies and ideas which attempted to retain both time for history and the integrity of history, within a curriculum increasing overcrowded by the Literacy and Numeracy Strategies (DfE 2008–11) and countless subsequent policies. And teachers continued to teach history well. History was regarded as good or very good and enjoyed by teachers and pupils in almost all the schools visited by Ofsted (2011).

The Cambridge Primary Review and the 2013 history curriculum

History is central to the advancement of a number of aims proposed in the Cambridge Primary Review (CPR) (Alexander 2010). These include local, national and global citizenship, culture and community, the shaping of consciousness and identity and the lessons history offers to our understanding of present and future (p. 272). Yet, it is argued, the initial promise of a broad and rich curriculum has been sacrificed in pursuit of a narrowly focused 'standards agenda', of which the humanities are a casualty, as is generic learning across the whole curriculum. This requires time for thinking, talking, problem-solving and in-depth exploration which engages children and which they find meaningful. A parallel sacrifice has been reflective and interactive pedagogy which advances children's understanding in 'the basics', no less than in other subjects (p.237). Yet children's submissions to the Review singled out history as enjoyable, because it offers them opportunities to be actively involved in learning, to use imagination and explore what seems curious (p. 213).

Relevant extracts from the Cambridge Review are included throughout the book. This is because the National Curriculum for History (2013) remains a contested curriculum, which can be marginalized, because of the accountability invested in English and mathematics and so interpreted merely as a transmission of facts. However, the Review presents pressing arguments for a pedagogy in which history is among those subjects regarded as central to the curriculum. *Children, Their Lives, Their Education: Final Report and Recommendations of the Cambridge Primary Review* (Alexander 2010) is a powerful reminder that history remains in need of public, professional and political recognition. We must grasp the opportunity that the English history curriculum allows us to decentralize control of the past. Perhaps it is democratically essential for individuals to develop individual historical voices. This book will argue why.

The scope of the 2013 National Curriculum

This edition of *History 5–11* is different from previous editions because, although the processes of enquiry remain the same, the current National Curriculum for history is different, in key ways, from the previous curriculum. It is different in its purposes, scope and aims, in its units of study and in its approach to assessment. The most significant development is on children learning to build up a 'Big Picture' of the past.

- The focus of the current curriculum is on making connections: links between, and similarities and differences between places, over time. The aim is for children to apply the processes of historical enquiry both in depth and across long periods of time, to construct a coherent 'Big Picture' of the past.

- There is therefore greater emphasis on chronology and concepts of time. Britain is seen as connected with many other places, in different ways and at different times.

- Coherence and breadth is created by British study units which are sequential (although they need not be taught sequentially), starting with the Stone Ages, with earlier European Societies, ancient civilizations which preceded Ancient Greece and Rome, and themed breadth studies which may extend as far as the present. Key Stage 1 can be planned in ways that integrate it with Key Stage 2.

- For the first time, methods of assessment and recording of pupils' progress are decided by individual schools and their teachers.

What is new in this edition?

This edition aims to support teachers in encompassing all the new dimensions of the 2013 National Curriculum listed above: 'The Big Picture'.

■ Throughout, examples are related to new study units in the 2013 curriculum.

■ There is an emphasis on discussing concepts of time over long periods, related to places, local, national and global, with coherence across Key Stages.

■ Innovative methods are introduced for comparing continuity, causes and effects of changes, similarities and differences, between societies in English National Curriculum Programmes of Study and in making international and global connections between Britain and the rest of the world and between the ancient civilizations in the National Curriculum.

■ The inter-relationship between planning for the 2013 curriculum and assessing pupils' progress without using pre-planned level criteria is considered, with an emphasis on formative assessments and an innovative strategy for summative assessments.

■ There has been a lot of research into both the teaching and learning of history and in academic history, since the previous edition; this is integrated throughout the book.

■ Many new websites are referred to, which support the research of both children and teachers.

■ This edition required significant new writing, in response to the 2013 curriculum and so aims to be more coherent and cross-referenced than previous editions.

■ It aims to be useful for a wide range of readers from Initial Teacher Training Students to experienced teachers, including those taking postgraduate qualifications, because the questions it addresses can be answered at many levels and because of the extensive references, which support further study.

Building up 'The Big Picture'

Neil McGregor, the previous director of the British Museum, focused on the stories of *things* to tell 'The Big Picture', The History of the World in 1,000 objects. Dr Hartwig Fischer, the recently appointed director of the British Museum, has said (2017) that he aims to overhaul the permanent collections so that visitors move directly between galleries displaying closely linked cultures, guided by digital applications. 'We want to give them the idea of what humankind shares despite all the differences. A walk around the museum should be like a journey. You should be able to cross the border very easily, into another culture and understand that they inspired each other', he said. Other parts of the museum may be arranged thematically. His philosophy reflects the aim of the National Curriculum, to encourage us to make connections between times and places, and this is the rationale of this book, focused on in depth in Chapter 8. Fischer evocatively explains his love of 'The Big Picture' and the parallels it recognizes between the old and the new. 'You happen upon something in a museum and you realize that these were human beings like you and they had to think about the sky and the stars and the gods and work out how to make their family survive and how to live in a society' (*Times 2*, 21.04.2017 2: 4).

Structure of the book

Part I Teachers' pedagogical knowledge: understanding the processes of historical enquiry

Chapter 1, 'Changes in the teaching and learning of history', gives examples of the ways in which the scope of history and the processes of historical enquiry have evolved and how, as a result, approaches to teaching history in primary schools have changed over the last twenty-five years. It argues that children, from their earliest years, have an awareness of past times and that they should learn history by learning to ask and answer questions about the past and that there are many exciting sources which can enable them to do so.

Chapter 2, 'Historical sources', discusses the range of interesting historical sources available to primary school children, including exciting recent discoveries relevant to the National Curriculum. It explains the questions children should ask about sources, some of the complexities that may arise and how children can respond to them in surprisingly sophisticated ways. It shows how these thinking processes are embedded in constructivist theories of learning and describes recent international research into children's use of a variety sources.

Chapter 3, 'Interpretations and accounts', explains why accounts of the past may be different, but equally valid. It considers different accounts of the past children can discuss (information books, re-enactments, films, reconstructions and museum displays) and ways in which children construct their own interpretations through writing, drama, art and models. It gives examples of different Anglo-Saxon accounts and how children could compare, explain and evaluate them. There are case studies of international research showing children's ability to explain and evaluate different interpretations.

Chapter 4, 'Chronology, time concepts and other key concepts', explains the reasons why chronology is important. The importance of using timelines to explore questions involving concepts of sequence, cause and effect, similarity and difference, continuity and change and duration is emphasized. Relating the National Curriculum for mathematics and for history, the ways in which this can be done and the ages at which number, calculation and statistics can be used in timeline enquiries are discussed. Case studies illustrate innovative uses of timeline enquiries and research studies show how children's chronological understanding can be progressed, accelerated and assessed.

Part II Connecting with the past

Chapter 5, 'What makes history enjoyable?', suggests that children make connections between challenge, working with others and enjoyment. They say that they like to be questioned, challenged, argue different viewpoints and have their opinions treated with respect. Case studies about the Stone and Iron Ages and the Anglo-Saxons are analysed to identify ways in which teachers do this.

Teachers say they enjoy 'hands-on' activities. Case studies analyse connections between 'hands on activities and children's learning in history, between inclusive connections with local communities, families and parents, and connections between enquiries and children's ownership of them.

Chapter 6, 'Connections between historical enquiry and creativity', analyses the relationship between the discipline of history and creativity. It is argued, based on recent research into the characteristics of creativity and on neuroscience, that the processes of historical enquiry and creativity are interdependent. Examples of enquiries illustrating this interdependence include collaborative enquiries such as drama and model-making, which generate new ideas through team-work and discussion; historical imagination generating hypotheses and probability thinking; risk-taking, suggesting probabilities which have to be defended. There are many examples of pupil-initiated creativity. A distinction is explained between teaching creatively and teaching for creativity.

Chapter 7, 'Connections between history and other subjects', explores ways in which other Programmes of Study can contribute to units in the history curriculum. It discusses contexts for spoken language, reading, writing and vocabulary and procedural language with examples. In mathematics, opportunities for applying geometry, statistics and time calculations are linked to appropriate year groups. There are suggestions for linking history and geography at Key Stages 1 and 2 through local, national and global events and contacts. Connections are also discussed between history and information technologies, and history and art are considered.

Chapter 8, 'Local, national and global connections over time', considers the reasons for making such links and ways in which this can be done at Key Stages 1 and 2, in order to give children an increasingly coherent understanding of the variety of interactions and influences between local, national and global societies, during each of the National Curriculum history study units. It shows questions which can be asked in order to explain changes and patterns over time, with some innovative approaches for doing this, drawing on fascinating information from recent research.

Part III Planning, assessment and recording

Chapters 9, 10 and 11 are essentially inter-related and should be read together. Chapter 9, 'Whole-school planning', discusses the areas in which the whole school should make collaborative decisions, in order to have a shared understanding about how to teach history and why: consistent implementation of the purposes and aims of the National Curriculum, the implications for history of the school philosophy, the implications for history of values education, the decisions to be made in sequencing units of study, how to plan for and assess progression and the relationship between history and the advantages and possible problems of cross-curricular approaches. The chapter explains a theme running through the book: how teaching key concepts, which underpin all societies, makes it possible to plan for continuity and coherence between and across all the study units, at both stages.

Chapter 10, 'Medium-term planning', explains the limitations of unmodified, down-loaded plans and the elements necessary in a medium-term plan (MTP). The essential aspects of medium-term plans are discussed, including planning for breadth and depth studies, planning links between societies over time and place and making cross-curricular links. Exemplar medium-term plans for the Stone Age, Roman Britain and the Anglo-Saxon and Viking struggle for the kingdom of England are offered, for discussion and evaluation. The translation from medium-term plans to lesson plans is discussed.

Chapter 11, 'Assessment, monitoring and recording pupils' progress', explains the purposes of assessment, discusses the reasons why there are no national assessment levels and the advantages of this. Mastery assessment is discussed in relation to history. There are examples of how teachers can approach assessment which progresses learning in meaningful and manageable ways. There is a focus on different methods of formative assessment, supported by examples and on the importance of classroom ethos in doing this effectively. It is argued that excellence is most likely to be demonstrated by imagination and creativity and result from children's motivation, self-evaluation and ownership of their learning. There are examples of summative assessment which meets practitioner research statutory requirements and of what is required to meet Ofsted expectations.

Part IV Practitioner research

Chapter 12, 'Doing research into the teaching and learning of history', refers to the many interesting research projects throughout the book undertaken by practitioners. It shows how research can emerge from teaching and, in turn, inform teaching. It discusses the reasons for doing research at undergraduate, Master's or doctoral level and the benchmarks for each level. The reader is then taken through the stages of doing a research project, illustrated by examples at each stage. Professor Bodo von Borries, an eminent German professor of history education who led a very large research study on comparative history education in twenty-seven European countries (Angvik and Von Borries 1997), told me he thought that small case studies, undertaken by practising teachers, reveal far more than the extensive study he had managed. It depends whether you are looking for a little information about a lot of people or in-depth studies which might change practice.

Aims of the book

This book is not a book of recipes for complying with the statutory curriculum for history. It aims to provide practical insights and guidance into how the statutory curriculum can be taught in ways that are both challenging, transforming and exciting for both teachers and their pupils, that make us all realize that learning about the past is very important because it is a continuum of human experiences, in all their vicissitudes, and that we are an integral part of that continuum – of the past as well as of the future. Our histories are part of who we are and of how the future can be. I hope you find as much stimulation and pleasure in teaching history to young children as I have done. For, as Bruner said (1966: 22),

> We teach a subject not to produce little living libraries, but to consider matters as an historian does, to take part in the process of knowledge.

Teachers' pedagogical knowledge

Understanding the processes of historical enquiry

Changes in the teaching and learning of history

This chapter considers how the history people have learned has changed over the years. First it illustrates this through a focus on King Alfred (849–899), since he is a significant figure in the current history curriculum. He first became known as 'Alfred the Great' in the sixteenth century, because his piety and his emphasis on 'the English' made him seem like a precursor of the Protestant Reformation. The Hanoverian kings promoted him because they shared his Saxon roots. In Victorian times, the English believed they could trace their laws back to the fifth century, when they defeated the Romans. So Alfred, because of his Constitutional Code, piety and sense of duty, (recorded in the biography which he commissioned himself, from Bishop Asser), was rediscovered as the perfect king. It was felt that Alfred represented positive facets of the national character, which enabled the English to rule those less fortunately endowed (Yorke 1999). In the millenary celebration of Alfred's birth, at Wantage in 1849, 8,000–10,000 people enjoyed traditional games, an ox roast and the following jubilee poem.

> Anglo-Saxons! – in love are we met
> To honour a name we can never forget!
> Father, and Founder, and King of a race
> That reigns and rejoices in every place,
> Root of a tree that o'er shadows the earth
> First of a family blest from his birth
> Blest in this stem of their strength and their state
> Alfred the Wise, and the Good, and the Great!

(Martin Tupper 1849)

In *A Child's History of England* (1851–1853), Charles Dickens represents many examples where Alfred was used to demonstrate the best of the English character:

> The noble king . . . in his single person, possessed all the Saxon virtues. Whom misfortune could not subdue, whom prosperity could not spoil, whose perseverance,

nothing could shake. Who was hopeful in defeat, and generous in success. Who loved justice, freedom, truth and knowledge.

(Dickens 1905)

This tradition continues in *Our Island Story* (Marshall 1905), reprinted by friends of *The Daily Telegraph* in 2005, for distribution to schools. It represents the view of the past, as generally taught in elementary schools from about 1905–1965. Marshall illustrates a reference to one of Alfred's sea battles against the Danes with this rousing song, actually written eight centuries after King Alfred.

> Ye mariners of England
> That guard our native seas,
> Whose flag has braved a thousand years
> The battle and the breeze,
> Your glorious standard launch again
> To match another foe
> And sweep through the deep,
> While the stormy winds do blow;
> While the battle rages loud and long
> And the stormy winds do blow . . .

(Thomas Campbell (1774–1844))

But now, with the marvels of new technology, you can sing along to 'Ye mariners of England' on YouTube (www.youtube.com/watch?v=23pPQDJiCm4).

The experience of such history lessons was brilliantly satirised by Sellar and Yeatman (1930: 18):

> Alfred noted that the Danes had very long ships, so he built a great many more much longer ones, thus cleverly founding the British Navy. From that time onwards foreigners, who, unlike the English, do not prefer to fight against long odds, seldom attacked the British Navy. Hence the important International Law called the Rule Britannia, technically known as the Freedom of the Sea.

And if you do not think that is funny – good! You did not experience that sort of history teaching. (Table 10.3 offers a modern take on learning about King Alfred, inviting children to investigate the question 'Was Alfred Great?')

Anyone who was in primary school between 1967 and 1991, following the recommendation of the otherwise progressive Plowden Report, probably did not learn history at all:

> History, it is said, again and again, is an adult subject. How can it be studied by children without being so simplified it is falsified? There is first the problem that it is not until the later years of primary school that some children develop a sense of time. . . . Yet we visited an Infant school where one exceptional child had memorised the dates of the Kings and Queens of England.

(Plowden Report 1967, paragraph 620)

Rethinking primary history: a personal perspective

Only since the 1980s, have we identified what exactly is involved in finding out about the past and explored ways in which young children can actively engage with this process, in ways which develop critical and discursive thinking, rather than brainwashing. I read history at university, but found teaching young children, in the Plowden tradition, much more interesting than teaching history in the sort of high school for girls that I had attended. After some time I was seconded to take an Advanced Diploma in Child Development, at the Institute of Education in London. There I realized that no one had ever systematically tried to apply theories of constructivist learning to the processes of historical enquiry, so I made this the subject of my dissertation. When I returned to school, I used my work as a Year 4 class teacher to collect empirical data that informed my PhD on 'Young Children's Thinking in History' (Cooper 1991). The *International Journal of Historical Learning, Teaching and Research* (www.history.org) illustrates how history educators around the world, ranging from previously Communist countries of Eastern Europe to previously fascist countries of Western Europe and South America, have also begun their own researches into the teaching of history to young children, in their own contexts, which engage children in active enquiry rather than giving them a simple 'story of the past', which can be politically manipulated.

For, of course, young children are aware of times before their own, although their understanding may be incomplete and even stereotypical, if not mediated through education. From their earliest years, children have some awareness of 'the past' through illustrations of traditional stories and rhymes, family photographs, old buildings, then later through film, television and heritage sites. But to begin to understand the past children must learn, from the beginning, the questions to ask and how to answer them.

The evolution of history as a discipline

Content

Originally the story of a society's past was handed down orally, and in some societies it still is. In others, it was written down: by the Greeks as epic poetry, in *The Odyssey*; by Medieval monks as chronicles, lists of events, of battles lost and won; in Shakespeare's histories as the story of a nation's kings. The story was always told for a particular audience and a particular reason.

Over the past 150 years, history has become recognized as an academic discipline and its scope has broadened. Frederick Maitland (1850–1906) justified history as the study of the law, in any society. Marc Bloch (1886–1944) drew on new disciplines to study human settlement: place-name study, technology and social sciences. Lewis Namier (1888–1960) analysed political life, and Mortimer Wheeler archaeology. Fernand Braudel (1902–1985) linked geography and history, making connections over time and space and exploring the role of large-scale, socio-economic factors in finding out about the past.

A history then may be broad or in-depth. It may be about an individual, about social groups, economic or political movements, local, national or global. Historians have their own interests: women's history, black history, the history of childhood, the history of a particular class, left-wing or right-wing perspectives. And since history is an umbrella subject that includes all aspects of life there are histories of music, art, science, religion, geographical histories and sports history.

Selecting content

Within the statutory requirements of the National Curriculum there are vast opportunities to plan content creatively. But no teacher can have a comprehensive knowledge of every period of history, in every civilization, so it is important to do your own research in planning a topic and also to engage with the children in their enquiries. Children need to understand that teachers do not know all the answers and it is good to see teachers modelling the enquiry process and getting as involved in, and as excited by it, as their pupils. For if they do not find it interesting why should anyone else?

Books and websites for adults, for example websites for art galleries and museums, frequently have good illustrations and photographs that can be projected as a PowerPoint® presentation and that children of any age can use as sources, although seeing sources first hand, whenever possible, conveys a far more exciting connection with the past. Your local history librarian and archivist will offer invaluable support for local history.

The process of historical enquiry

The process of enquiry, too, has evolved gradually. Leopold von Ranke (1795–1886) studied records. How did this document come into existence? How has it come down to us? How do the answers to these questions influence its trustworthiness? How do they explain the differences between two accounts? For Marc Bloch, clarity of analysis and asking the right question were consistent criteria. What do we know? What can we know? How do we know? How can we communicate that knowledge? Herbert Butterfield (1900–1979) employed imaginative sympathy in describing characters and events.

R.G. Collingwood clarified the process of historical enquiry in his *Autobiography* (1939). He saw historical enquiry as beginning with a complex of ordered, specific questions in the tradition of the great philosophers, such as Plato, Bacon, Descartes and Kant. He said that, just as philosophy had found it necessary to accommodate a revolution in thinking about the natural world, based on empirical observation and deduction in the seventeenth century, it must encompass a similar revolution in the way it studied man in constantly changing societies.

Collingwood worked out this philosophy of history through constant practical application in archaeology. He proceeded from specific questions about sources, the significance and purpose of objects, whether they were buttons, dwellings or settlements, to the people who made and used them. The sequence proceeded from what can be known about an object, then what can be 'guessed', then, finally, what he would like to know, in order to support, extend or contradict his guesses. For instance, he knew from concrete evidence that a Roman wall from the Tyne to the Solway existed.

He guessed that its purpose was to form a sentry walk with parapets as protection against snipers. He wanted to know if there were towers as a defence against vessels trying to land between Bowness and St Bees, in order to support his guess. A resulting search revealed that towers had been found but their existence forgotten, because their purpose was not questioned. History, then, involves interaction between the known content and the process of enquiry, in order to try to make sense of it. First, then, we need to find out how historians use sources and how we can use them with children.

Planning for enquiry

History is not just a story or a list of events. Whatever content an account of the past may focus on, it must be investigated through the process of historical enquiry. It is important to remember that children need to understand the process of historical enquiry and how to integrate content with process, if they are to learn history, to understand why there are different perspectives and interpretations and not simply to learn what Charlotte Mason, an innovative educationist writing in the nineteenth century, called 'miserable little chronicles of feuds, battles and death which are presented as "a reign"' (Mason 1993, vol. 1: 281).

Different strands of the processes of historical enquiry are addressed in the following three chapters. However, it is important to read them together as the processes described are interdependent.

2

Historical sources

At Key Stage 1 'children should understand some of the ways in which we find out about the past' and at Key Stage 2 they are expected to 'use a range of historical sources' (DfE 2013). Historical sources are any traces of the past that remain. They may be written sources: documents, newspapers, laws, literature, advertisements, diaries, place names. They may be visual sources – paintings, cartoons, film, video, maps, field patterns, plans – oral sources or music. They may be artefacts, sites or buildings.

Children enjoy working with all kinds of sources, but particularly with artefacts, visual sources, sites and buildings (Cooper 1991). These are exciting because they were made with another person's hands and touched and looked at by people, many years ago, yet we too can touch them. This frisson makes us reflect on how something was made and used and its impact on the people who made and used it. It can lead us to consider its economic, political and cultural significance.

Exciting recent discoveries

Reflective transformation imaging

Reflective Transformation Imaging (RTD) enables us to read the Vindolanda birch tablets which tell us about life on Hadrian's Wall, from CE 92 to 103. They would crumble to dust if they were touched but can now be read. RTD uses computers to build images of objects from dozens of different angles and faint graffiti in stone. These letters include letters requesting more beer at the garrison, information about the roles of the keeper of the bath house, shoe makers, construction workers, medical doctors, maintaining wagons and kilns. Sophisticated X ray scanning also enables us to virtually open scrolls charred by Vesuvius in 79 CE, Native American copperplates that have fused together, the Egyptian Book of the Dead and Medieval documents.

Recent archaeological discoveries

New discoveries are continually recorded on television and in newspapers, sometimes by amateurs. This can help children to understand why there is still so much we do not know, why historical accounts are constantly changing, why history is dynamic. The following examples change our thinking about National Curriculum topics.

The Stone Age and gender issues

Should you want to do a linear study of the changing roles of women you might like to start with the Stone Age. Research suggests that women and children could hunt with weighted sticks to throw light spears or darts (atls) quite as effectively as men, but after bows and arrows were created, about 1,000 years ago in Europe, women did not have sufficient upper body strength to hunt alongside the men, and that this changed the status of women, which persists in societies today. The bow and arrow was faster to reload and more accurate so that hunters could target smaller game, which allowed a broader diet and freed people from having to hunt together for safety. But it is also argued that, although the bow may have led to an increase in human conflict, it also allowed individuals and groups to have power over a greater area and so create organized societies – in which the macho men went after the 'higher risk' calories while the women remained gathering safe, reliable resources such as plants and shellfish (Grund 2017).

Bronze and Iron Age discoveries: new sites, new transport

Patterns are made when crops ripen at different times because water is retained in ancient walls and paths. Aerial photography reveals several hundred new Bronze and Iron Age sites in Britain every year (*The Times* 28.06.2016).

Archaeologists' ideas about how advanced early British communities were in about 1,100 BCE were challenged in 2016, by the discovery of a large Bronze Age wheel, which must have been a symbol of wealth for a family living on the outskirts of the Fenns. The community lived in houses built on stilts above the River Nene, and suggests to archaeologists that the owners were at home on water and land (boats 3,000 years old were also discovered), and that they would travel long distances with their belongings and livestock. Archaeologists said that probably the dwellings had a short life and were deliberately burnt down before the community moved on (*The Times* 02.19.2016: 17). An Iron Age chariot and horses, dating back to 500 BCE, described by archaeologists as of 'international significance' was found in February 2017 beneath a housing development in Pocklington, East Yorkshire (*The Times* 31.03.2017: 23).

The sequence of inferences about the wheel and community is exactly the same as the one we teach children, based on the work of Collingwood (1939), as you will see below. It is a wheel (fact); *therefore* the family were wealthy (based on knowledge of the period). They had boats, their homes were built on stilts and they had carts; *therefore* they lived on land and water. The community *probably* burnt their houses and moved on *because* they had transport and their houses would not last long. A statement, followed by an argument, followed by a hypothesis.

Romans: a new Roman road

David Ratledge had spent his weekends for 50 years looking for a Roman road, part of a network built to conquer northern England. Archaeologists knew there was a Roman road leading from Ribchester to Lancaster but had been looking for it in the wrong place. The Environmental Agency had been using light detection and lidar technology to detect areas liable to flood and their maps were available to the public. Ratledge, using the lidar maps, found slightly raised strips of ground, lined them up and found the lost Roman road. The Romans had not gone directly but used a dog-leg route to avoid the steepest hills! (*The Times* 01.01.2016). The process of this discovery is the same as the way in which Collingwood (1939) discovered Roman defensive towers at Bowness and St Bees. He *knew*, from evidence that a wall from the Tyne to the Solway existed. He *guessed* that its purpose was to form a sentry walk with parapets as protection against snipers. He *wanted to know* if there were towers as a defence against vessels trying to land between Bowness and St Bees, in order to support his guess. The resulting search revealed the towers.

The Saxons: a town King Alfred knew

In 2011 a metal detector discovered an entire, previously unknown Saxon town, in the Lincolnshire marshes, near the village of Little Carlton. It was only 1 foot beneath the surface. It is a large site of international importance, thought to have been a burgh, a fortified Saxon town. The town appears to have flourished through the eighth century. Finds include a silver stylus and ornate writing books, evidence of literacy and so wealth. 'Cudburg' a woman's name was inscribed into a lead plaque, suggesting that this woman had status. But this town disappeared suddenly in the ninth century, when the Vikings began to plunder and pillage the north-east coast. (*The Times* 02.03.2016: 22).

Yes, I do read *The Times*, but each of these discoveries in 2016 was recorded in most newspapers and further details can be found on Google. Children can be involved in the dynamism of historical enquiry, finding out about such newly discovered sites. Of course amazing discoveries need to be regarded critically. *The Times*, (News 28.03.2017) reported that Edward VI (1537–1553) owned a Daimler. On 29.03.2017 *The Times* apologized. The vehicle in question belonged to Edward VII (1841–1910).

Questions to ask about sources

The questions we ask about sources are valid if they lead somewhere. Collingwood (1939) identifies key questions: How was it made? Why? How was it used? By whom? Were there others? What did it mean to the person who made and used it? How was a Roman shoe found at Vindolanda made and who used it? It is a superior example of a Roman shoe (the equivalent of one made by Gucci or Lobbe today). What does this tell us about the person who wore it? It tells us that people of high *social status* were stationed at Vindolanda. It tells us something about the *economic* status of the fort and about its communications with sophisticated parts of the Empire; probably it was made in Rome. A letter from a first generation 'Dutch' Roman at the fort tells us something about the person who wrote the letter; he was a member of a 'Dutch' tribe and such people were cold. They wore Roman-style socks and pants, which they had sent from Rome and were *probably* happy to consider themselves culturally Roman. It is the graffiti on the door of Newgate Prison or the Robert Burns song scratched into the glass of a casement window that quickens the pulse – tangible links with other people who lived in other worlds.

- A fascinating and highly academic book on *Artefacts in Roman Britain* (Allason-Jones 2011) reiterates and develops Collingwood's questions to ask about an artefact, with references to recent archaeological finds. Allason-Jones adds four supplementary questions. Appearance: what does it look, feel, smell like and has it been broken, used, repaired? Design: has it been decorated and if so how, why and is this functional or aesthetic? Significance: is it symbolic or practical, of sentimental or social significance and does it provide any clues to its owner's economical and social status or gender? Context of discovery: does this indicate its use? Interestingly the answers to Collingwood's questions, which children give in case studies in this book, take these questions into account. Never underestimate children.

- Another recent book I love (Gerritsens and Riello 2015) shows how artefacts, (now called 'material culture') extend the scope of historians, who have tended to rely on written sources. Everyday objects, they say, provide evidence that history can include the perspectives of ordinary 'unseen' people, seldom referred to in documentation, and they tell of global interactions. Traded artefacts allow people to visualize life in distant places and, of course, to modify them, whether weapons or pottery. Artefacts can tell us about the sounds people heard in the past. Artefacts are not just a way into history for young children.

Both of these books delight me because, in 1993, when a member of the Schools Curriculum and Assessment Authority (SCAA), the first government attempt to control assessment, I was patronized for suggesting that A-level sources could include discussion of artefacts as sources: I was told that these were intelligent, mature people.

Problems with sources

What makes sources intriguing is that they do not yield their secrets easily (note *probably*, above). We usually have to hypothesize, to 'guess' what they may be telling us, based on what else we may know. There may be more than one possible inference to make about a source. Children particularly enjoy 'guessing' about a source, justifying it, arguing with other interpretations, when no single 'correct' answer may be known. Even if their hypotheses seem unlikely, they are learning to engage with the process of historical enquiry. With maturity and greater knowledge children's 'guesses' become more valid, in that they conform to what is known about the period, what is likely and whether there is contradictory evidence. With experience and maturity they become more aware of the factors to take into account in asking questions about sources.

Asking questions about sources

- Sources may be of varying status, because they were created for different purposes: a diary, a newspaper account, an advertisement; portraits of, for example, Elizabeth I, are masterpieces of propaganda, often conveyed through the symbolism of power and ambition.

- Sometimes new evidence comes to light. Harlow (1996) describes the discovery of the site near St Paul's Cathedral of a 'forgotten' battle between Normans and Saxons, which took place three months after the Battle of Hastings and was actually the point when the Normans conquered England. Norman propagandists wanted to portray William as a military genius capable of overwhelming the Anglo-Saxons with one overwhelming blow at Hastings so they forgot about this final bloody confrontation. But other contemporary sources, such as William Jumieges, a French monk, dedicate as much space to this battle as to the Battle of Hastings, and Guy de Amiens describes how Duke William of Normandy took the battle so seriously that he constructed siege engines and battering rams.

- Sources may be reinterpreted as society changes. In Monte Alban, the great abandoned city of pre-conquest Mexico, in tomb seven, the focus of the 500 precious grave goods was said to be a priest associated with the god Xollotl. However, this was because, in archaeology, figures associated with wealth and power are generally assumed to be male. Dr Sharisse McCafferty (in Burne 1995) has not come up with any new evidence but applied a modern feminist perspective to the grave goods. The weaving battens are a badge of femininity, which boys were prevented from touching. There is also spinning equipment. What were originally thought to be false fingernails are, in the new interpretation, thought to be thimbles (Burne 1995). The skeleton, McCafferty argues, is therefore female.

- Sources may be cult or ceremonial objects that we do not understand. The Iron Age 'Waterloo Helmet' in the British Museum or the Uffington chalk horse in Berkshire may represent ideas or social practices about which we can only surmise. The recorded discussion of my Year 4 class about the meaning of the Uffington horse involved geology and the social organization needed to make it and its practical and symbolic significance. They follow through and weigh each other's points of view, form imaginative ideas into logical arguments and use abstract concepts: co-operation, community, ceremonies, beliefs and customs. Here is a short extract.

  - It looks like a bird.
  - It's a horse.
  - They could draw horses.
  - So they had horses.
  - They were hard workers . . . skilful . . . artistic . . .
  - There must be a lot of chalk under the surface.
  - So there won't be trees like oak trees – not many trees.

- They could live on the chalk; it's well-drained – the water would run away.
- The soil would be thin – it's easy to plough.
- Whatever tools they used it must have taken a long time. They must have co-operated. They lived in a community.
- It's not an ordinary horse. It's much more different from the ones we see.
- It must be a special one or they wouldn't go to all that trouble.
- It's probably a symbol for something – a clue.
- To bring a good harvest?
- A symbol of strength?
- To an enemy? Perhaps the horse brought bad luck so they stayed away.
- Perhaps if someone was ill they prayed to it. It gave them power when they were ill.
- Or perhaps they just had fun.
- Maybe they danced around it – or put fires on it and burnt something, maybe for the chief's birthday.
- I don't think they had birthdays.
- But they had beliefs and ceremonies . . .

■ We have to accept that sometimes we cannot know. A recently unearthed pot of Roman face cream has been described as showing the 'finger marks of the woman who used it' – but is this merely a stereotypical assumption? What had happened to the fifty-six, taller-than-average Romans, all prime-of-life males, whose cleanly beheaded skeletons were found in York in 2004? Were they legionaries killed in battle, the result of a pagan ritual, victims of each other as gladiators, punished as a unit found guilty of cowardice, loyalists of the Emperor Caracalla's brother? The opinions of experts vary. What is *certain* is that they died horrible deaths, were a mix of nationalities, that they were of high social status. What is *probable* is that they were the elite victims of military persecution. What is *possible* is that they were killed for disloyalty or cowardice. The rest we can probably never know (Girling 2006 *The Sunday Times Magazine*, 2006: 14–18).

■ Traces of the past may tell us something of people's actions, but we can never know the thoughts and feelings that underpin those actions. We cannot even know what a contemporary may be thinking and feeling. Sarah Wheeler, writing about historical biography, asks,

> 'What is motivation? . . . Which of us can say that we understand the tangled skeins of fears and desires that control our own behaviour, let alone those of a husband or wife, letting even more alone that of a long dead stranger'.
>
> (Wheeler 2006)

Collingwood (1939) attempted to clarify the relationship between interpreting evidence and the thoughts and feelings of people. Historical evidence, whether it is an artefact, a building, a picture or writing, is the result of an action. An action is the result of rational thinking. Rational thought has its roots in feeling and imagination. Feelings and thinking only continue to exist to the extent that they are represented in the action, in the evidence. Collingwood says, for example that we *know* that Julius Caesar invaded Britain in successive years, we can *suppose* that his thoughts may have been on trade or grain supply or a range of other possibilities and his underlying feelings *may have included* ambition or career advancement. Collingwood points out that a historian can share the thoughts of someone in the past because he has experienced similar feelings and thoughts within his own contexts through shared humanity but that, nevertheless, they are different thoughts because the person was thinking them in response to a particular, ongoing situation at the time.

■ It is necessary to understand societies in the past from the standpoint of a person living at the time, in a society that may have had different attitudes, values and beliefs from our own. Collingwood (1946) says that man does not live in a world of hard facts, to which thoughts make no difference, but in a society with moral, economic and political structures and rules, as the structure changes, man's thoughts and behaviour change too. People may have had different values and beliefs from our own, because they had different knowledge bases. We need to try to see the world from the standpoint of other times to try to understand why the Saxons relied on immersion in water to determine guilt or innocence; why sixteenth-century people thought the plague was a punishment from God; why Victorian children worked in factories or were sent to the workhouse.

■ New evidence may be discovered, as discussed above. The Mildenhall Treasure in the British Museum, (a hoard of Roman silver plate dug up in 1943 in East Anglia), was thought by the farmer who discovered it to be pewter and he put it on his mantelpiece. When it was identified later by a visitor as Roman silver and examined by experts in the British Museum, historians were forced to reassess their ideas about the quality of silverware used in Eastern Britain in the fourth century CE. (www.britishmuseum.org_Explore_Highlights)

■ Evidence is often incomplete. Historians need to use imagination in order to do what Elton (1970) calls 'filling in the gaps' in a narrative, when evidence is incomplete. Ryle (1979) sees this as cashing in on the facts and using them: ammunition shortage and heavy rain before a battle cause the historian to wonder about the hungry rifleman and delayed mule trains. But historical imagination is not free floating. It needs to be based on the most likely explanations of what is known.

For all these reasons, several hypotheses about a source may be different but equally valid. Making inferences about sources involves giving reasons for your argument, listening to the views of others and being prepared to change your mind, or to accept that often there is no single, correct answer. This skill is important in social, emotional– and cultural–development.) We have to make reasonable hypotheses about what we can infer. Such 'guesses' are valid if there is no contradictory evidence, if they are reasonable and if they fit in with whatever else is known about the period.

Impact of learning theories on children's use of sources

The key constructivist theorists are Piaget, Bruner and Vygotsky. Their work has been both modified and developed over the years by many others, but essentially their contributions to our understanding of learning remain central.

Inferences about sources

Piaget offers some insights into the progression in children's ability to make inferences from sources. His work suggests a sequence in development in which, at first, children's thinking is dominated by intuitive trial and error, by the child's own experiences and feelings. Wood and Holden (1997) found, in discussing old domestic objects with Key Stage 1 children, that the younger children drew *randomly* on their experience, including factual and fictional knowledge, although they were able to use this knowledge to make informed suggestions about how the artefacts were used; one child drew on his knowledge of Mrs Tiggy-Winkle. The older children's knowledge was more organized, and they were increasingly able to draw on relevant information from their home and school experience.

When they are capable of 'concrete operations', Piaget found that a child can take in information from the tangible and visible world, fit it into existing mental patterns, adjusting these when necessary to accommodate new information, and so store it, in order to use it selectively to solve problems. A child is able to form a reasoned premise and support it with a logical argument. In Chapter 12, we see how children retain vocabulary they have learned in one context and transfer it to new contexts. They interpret evidence in a previously unseen map by drawing on a field visit to a similar area, on previous class discussion and also on their own ideas. They transfer the thinking skills they have learned in whole-class lessons to group discussion when no adult is present.

When someone is capable of formal operations, she can think in terms of abstract and negative propositions (if . . . then; either . . . or; when . . . is not; both . . . and) and weigh all the possible variants in an argument.

Argument

Piaget's work on language (1926, 1928) suggests that a young child is able to communicate a valid statement of fact or description. This is followed by a stage of 'primitive argument', in which the statement is followed by a deduction going beyond the information given but the explanation is implicit. Next a child attempts to justify and demonstrate an assertion using a conjunction (since, because, therefore), but does not succeed in expressing a truly logical relationship. The child eventually arrives at 'genuine argument' through frequent attempts to justify an opinion, and is able to use 'because' correctly. An example of this is found in the archaeologist's report sheet on page 232. However, in history this sequence depends on the complexity of the evidence and the questions asked. Donaldson (1978) recognized that children's ability to reason depends on what the question is, how it is relevant to a child's concerns, the child's expectations of the questioner, the extent to which they concentrate on language and that language is related to non-verbal cues. She concludes that young children must develop their ability to reason and make inferences as early as possible by receiving the right kind of support.

Rules

Piaget (1932) suggested that children at first see no reason for rules. Later they think that rules must be rigidly obeyed, then finally they recognize that there are circumstances in which they should be challenged or changed. In a historical context, children initially see people's behaviour as idiosyncratic. Then people are seen as good or bad, heroes or villains, friends or enemies. Later children can begin to discuss the reasons for people's behaviour, in a society different from their own, with different knowledge bases, and to understand why perspectives differ. There are resonances here with current culture clashes. One 6-year-old told me that he had learned that, in India, 'which was once part of Britain', there are sixty children in a class, but in England you can only have thirty children in a class. How can that be? I explained that when I was in primary school we had fifty-eight children in my class. Lesson: rules can change with circumstances.

Probability

Piaget's work on probability (Piaget and Inhelder 1951) also shows that at first children cannot differentiate between chance and non-chance, but at a concrete level they have an increasing understanding of what we can know and what we can guess. Eventually, they can differentiate between what is certain and what is probable.

Teaching approaches and progression

Bruner (1963) introduced the notion of a 'spiral curriculum', precursor of the English National Curriculum. He set out the processes whereby a discipline may be structured so that the thinking processes which lie at the heart of a discipline can be tackled from the very beginning in their simplest form, then in increasingly complex ways. He said that this involves translating a subject into appropriate forms of representation that place emphasis on 'doing', on appropriate imagery, and on a set of rules for making deductions and inferences. Problems, he said, must involve the right degree of uncertainty in order to be interesting, and learning should be organized in units, each building on the foundations of the previous one. He also said that we should define the skills children need in order to extrapolate from particular examples, from a memorable specific instance, to the general, in order to transfer the thinking processes learned to other similar problems; this gives confidence and avoids 'mental overload' of facts. Children learn, in whole-class lessons, how to ask and answer questions about sources, then are able to transfer this process to new sources. They need opportunities to answer questions about tactile, visual and symbolic sources.

This approach is employed in the case study in Chapter 12. Each period (Stone Age, Iron Age, Romans and Saxons) was explored through sources: artefacts, pictures, diagrams, plans and written sources, supported by a site or museum visit. Observations were recorded in a variety of cross-curricular ways: kinetic, iconic and symbolic approaches; through art techniques (painting, embroidery, lino cuts and silkscreen prints and pottery), through science experiments (dyeing, firing clay and cooking food), through technology (building a model Roman kiln, an Iron Age hut), through writing in different genres (notes, poems, fiction and reports) and tape-recorded discussions.

Bruner described the role of the teacher as 'scaffolding' children's learning, for example by questioning, cueing and providing resources. This was part of the whole-class lessons and is also exemplified in the structure of the archaeologist's report (p. 232), which aimed to structure thinking by developing causal thinking, differentiating between what is known and what can be 'guessed' and what cannot be known, and by encouraging the use of abstract concepts to reach conclusions – 'hard words'. In this case study children were taught about four sequential periods. In each period they were taught and learned to apply the same thinking processes in interpreting sources.

Discussion

Vygotsky made two contributions to our understanding of children's ability to make deductions and inferences about sources. First, he demonstrated the importance of social interaction and trial and error through discussion, forming a point of view, listening to others, modifying the original viewpoint (1962). Second, his work on the 'zone of proximal development' (1978) showed how, by working with an adult or more competent peer, children's thinking can be taken forward. Both aspects of Vygotsky's work, discussion and concept development, are illustrated in Chapter 12.

Recent research into children's use of sources

Attitudes and values

Bage (2000: 26) says that leading learners willingly into worlds different from the societies in which they exist is a moral and creative act of the highest order. Barton (1996) found that children often seem to feel impelled to respond to the challenge of explaining attitudes and values in the past. For example, younger children (Ashby and Lee 2001) suggested that the Romans executed slaves 'because they did not know about God and Jesus'; Saxons resorted to deciding guilt by oath-taking because 'They did not know about police courts – or medicines – or about floating and sinking', or 'because it was their religion'. Older pupils tried to unpack the values and beliefs behind the institutions, referring to culture and norms. However, it is important to notice that some Year 2 children responded in ways characteristic of 14-year-old children. They behaved as if they believed that even puzzling institutions could be made intelligible by understanding how people saw their world, not by reference to our world.

Distinguishing between validity and truth

Ashby (2004) investigated the development of the ability of pupils in Years 3, 6, 7 and 9 to grasp the difference between a true and a valid statement. She asked them how they could decide if the claim by the Welsh monk Nennius, that 'Arthur killed 960 Saxons at Mount Badon', was true. Their answers illustrated progression. The younger children wanted to find out from an authority, an adult or a book. They did consider the credibility of the author; 'monks would write the truth' (hem!). By Year 7, pupils recognized that books may differ, in which case they would see what most books say. Most Year 9 pupils questioned the author's claim on the basis of his ability to know. They recognized that inferences could be made from sources and considered whether these were likely.

Developing historical imagination

Vass (2004) described a way of developing historical imagination through story. He based his approach on the view that the outcome of the historian's labours is 'any patterned account, intended to be true, of any past happenings involving human intention or doing or suffering' (Hexter 1971: 3). He gave pupils artefacts from the Second World War (e.g. blackout curtain, ration book and gas mask) and invited them to 'fill in the gaps' to make their own stories, set in London in the Blitz. They used event framing. This enabled the stories to take place within a given chronological framework. One child, evaluating the stories, concluded that, 'I think Jodie's story is more like it was than mine. There is more evidence.' She was, Vass reflects, 'discovering that historical evidence is not as tangible or obvious as imagined'. Children decided on a 'key factor' that determined the origin of the stories (e.g. the ration book was lost in the dark). This gave rise to interesting discussions about 'unique events' – 'No two stories are ever the same, even in history books . . . It depends on who is writing the story' – and to discussion about chance: 'Most things happen by chance . . . this, therefore that . . . There was a good chance of an air raid during the war but you never know do you, if that was how the ration book was lost?' Second, Vass drew on the work of Ferguson (1997), who argues for a 'chaotic' model of historical forces, where the actuality of the past is seen as only one of many possible outcomes; he claims that this helps historians to understand better what actually happened and why. The children constructed 'counterfactual histories', beginning with a Bethnal Green air raid in 1943 and ending, via six event frames, with the commemoration of the victims thirty years later. One child's perceptive conclusion was that 'It was the rockets that did it [caused panic in which people were crushed to death]. The sirens worried people but it was the rockets going off that caused the panic. They were new. People had never heard that sound before. It was the rockets that did it.'

Distinguishing between what is known and what can be guessed

A group of 8-year-old children (Cooper 1991) who had been learning about the Saxons through class lessons that involved making deductions and inferences (good guesses) about a variety of sources were given previously unseen sources to discuss. One of these was a slide of a replica of the Sutton Hoo sceptre. They interpreted this within the framework of the knowledge acquired through their sequence of lessons.

1   Where did the Saxons come from, where did they settle, when and why? This lesson was based on Saxon artefacts (wrist clasps, brooches, etc.) linked to maps showing where the artefacts had been found, written evidence of the Roman withdrawal and Saxon records of where they settled (www.vortigernstudies.org.uk; Bede (2008); *Anglo-Saxon Chronicle* (Swanton 2003).

2   Inferences about Saxon life based on extracts from *Beowulf* (Heaney 1999).

3   Map of the seven kingdoms in AD 700, information about kingship from Bede (2008) and the *Anglo-Saxon Chronicle* (Swanton 2000), and some seventh century Anglo-Saxon laws in Kent and Wessex.

4   Evidence of the spread of the Roman church and the Celtic church from Bede, linked to a map.

5   A local visit to Coulsdon to trace evidence of Saxon settlements from spring line, place names and hedge dating.

Here are some of the children's (written) responses to the questions: what do you know, what can you guess and what can't you know about the Sutton Hoo sceptre?

■   I know: They had kings. Therefore they must have had to be obedient, they must have had to be loyal. They had a sceptre with an animal on it (deer). Therefore it must have been a symbol. It was precious. It took a long time to make. Therefore it must be unique.

■   I can guess: The gold sculpture deer may be saying 'save our lives or where we live'. Therefore the sceptre may mean 'Kill us and be warned; you'll die'. That might be why the ruler carries it; to show he is the ruler for God on earth.

■   I'd like to know: Why it's made out of stone because it must be heavy and why there is no picture of himself on it, because it could tell us what sort of a king he was.

These 8-year old children are discussing an artefact and applying information and thinking learned in the previous three units to a new source (Bruner 1963). They are distinguishing between what they know, what they can guess and what they would like to know (Piaget and Inhelder 1951). They are using 'because' and 'therefore' to justify their statements about how it may have been made and used (Piaget 1926) and what it may have meant to the people who made and used it (Collingwood 1939). There are also attempts to consider the possible thoughts and feelings of these people (Collingwood 1946) and understanding that they probably had different values and beliefs as represented by the 'symbol'. Children were using their imagination, based on what they knew, and learning to make suppositions. The more they make, with maturity, the more valid these will become.

Inferences from images

In an interesting study with 7-year-old children in Malta, Yvonne Vella (2004) describes a series of activities that were designed to help pupils to make inferences from pictures. At first the children were shown a painting and asked to 'say anything you wish about this painting'. The discussion was video-recorded. Activities followed that were intended to accelerate the children's ability to interpret visual sources.

■ An early-twentieth-century photograph of a milk seller with goats was shown. Children were asked what they thought was going on. Then the photograph was divided into four using two strips of paper and the children were asked to look at specific areas of the picture and were asked much more specific questions.

■ The children were given a magnifying glass to look at a small eighteenth-century picture of a toddler in a baby walker made of cane. This picture was part of a larger painting, which was later uncovered. The children could see whether they had been correct in their first analysis.

■ Using a nineteenth-century painting of sailors looking out from a boat, the children were asked to play a game in which the paper was lifted for a brief moment. Each time they were asked to say what they had spotted.

■ Children were shown a nineteenth-century picture of a Maltese lady and were asked, 'Do you think this lady really looked like this?'

Then the children returned to the original picture. Again their discussion was recorded. They focused much more on the detail in the picture and the points they made were more complex.

Student teachers investigate children's inferences about sources

Paula Andrews wondered what sorts of questions her Key Stage 1 class should be encouraged to ask and what was the teacher's role. Is there progression from Year 1 to Year 2? What artefacts stimulate the most questions and why? She found that the youngest children made observations but needed help in turning these into questions. As they got older they were able to formulate their own questions and increasingly asked open questions that led to discussions: how things were made, how they were used and why. The artefacts that stimulated the most interest and discussion were things that worked and could be explored through manipulation.

Beverley Wright used a literacy session on adjectives to ask her Year 3/4 class to make inferences about the people depicted in Tudor portraits. She, like Claire (1996), found that children attributed strengths and weaknesses to male and female portraits, respectively. Beverley used the plenary session to discuss this with them and challenge their assumptions.

Some ideas for practical activities using sources to engage you in reflection on your own practice

■ Portraits: Put a portrait in the middle of a sheet of paper and invite children to make a spider graph of what they can infer from the portrait. Can they divide their ideas into categories; what categories? Do children get better at this activity with experience? In what ways? What was your role?

■ For each group place the source in the centre of a large piece of paper with the heading, 'What does this source tell me?' This piece of paper stands on three pieces of paper of increasing size so that they overlap each other with the headings: 'What guesses can I make about it?' 'What does the source not tell me?' 'What other questions do I need to ask?' The children write their ideas on the appropriate piece of paper around the source. Are there more responses to one of the questions? Do some sources inspire more responses? Why? From everyone or some children?

■ Site visits: Visiting a site is not mere information collecting. Children need a genuine historical puzzle within which to root their activity. The puzzle, or enquiry, must be historically worthwhile and personally motivating and negotiated with the children. Pupils need to work on their own line of questioning. They must be prepared before the visit, so that they arrive focused and ready to go and they need to know what they have learned about historical enquiry. How many of the pre-visit questions came from the children? How many were answered? How many of the follow-up activities were their ideas? How much of their learning were they aware of; was it process plus content? Why did they enjoy this project?

Recent research studies investigating children's work with artefacts

Making sense of the past through local sources

Pinto (2013) investigated her pupils' understanding of historical sources, in their local town of Guimaraes, in Portugal. Walking around the town they reflected on its old buildings, plaques and monuments. Pinto thought that this was important in constructing their identities, both as individuals and as members of the community and that such sources challenge children to make sense of the past by relating the sources to their own experiences, perspectives and questions They connect what they see, do and feel and already understand (Barton and Levstik 2004: 153) in constructivist ways. This enriches their appreciation of the cultural, social and economic contributions of diverse groups to their communities. She argues that knowing how to 'read' heritage sites helps children to perceive the linkage between local and international events and trends and to find out about differences and similarities in local and in more international and global events. They ask questions which are significant to them. Pupils were given tasks related to the development of history-learning skills to complete, at a series of points on a walk around the city of Guimarez.

When pupils' responses to the questions were analysed, categories emerged, for example 'making inferences from existing details'. In this category students regarded writing in these sources as direct information, without considering the implications of what the writing suggested. Pinto concluded that these children were thinking at a concrete Piagetian level. However in the category 'inferences from context and questioning', the pupils made personal inferences, questioning the context in terms of evidence and hypothesizing on several possibilities, in terms of the political, social and economic context. Pinto concluded that responses in this category reflected an incipient level of formal operations, in that these pupils were considering alternative various possibilities; either . . . or, if . . . then, both . . . and. Pinto, like Hodkinson (2004a), suggests that these responses to local evidence of this kind are rooted in children's cultural and educational backgrounds and that teachers should aim to enhance their ability to 'read' objects, sites and buildings.

Paintings as historical sources

Kang (2010) explored how 9-year-old children in Korea formed historical inferences using pictures of historical paintings and, if they could, how they made plausible inferences about the lives of the people depicted. The pictures were about a period of Korean history the children had not studied. This task required close observation and substantial knowledge. However, Kang found that most of the children demonstrated some general, or even detailed knowledge of the period. Pinto (2013) and Hodkinson (2004a) also found that children had knowledge about a period that was acquired from a variety of different sources; from a combination of sources and previous out-of-school knowledge from their own life experiences. Kang's study builds on previous work on children's ability to make reasonable, historical inferences about pictures (West 1981; Blyth 1994; Harnett 1993). This suggests that they already shared some common culture, again illustrating Piaget's Concrete Operational Stage. It seems, then, both that we underestimate what children know about the past from outside school sources, and also that this study endorses other findings that 9-year-old children can relate the inferences they make from images to their own experiences.

Documents, photographs and oral accounts

In their project entitled Recreating Histories, Schmidt and Garcia encouraged 8–9-year-old children in Campina Grande do Sul, a small community in Brazil, to collect documents, photographs and oral accounts of their family histories. They analysed them, with the help of their teachers. Then they wrote their own illustrated narratives about their families and their community. These were collated and published as a book (Schmidt and Garcia 2003), which was then used, along with additional activities, for teaching other children of the same age (Schmidt and Garcia 2008). Other children then used this book as a text book.

These authors analysed both the initial narratives and the narratives of the children who used the textbook. They found that both groups developed the following concepts in writing their narratives: causality, continuity, changes, incorporation of previous knowledge, use of temporal concepts and sequential narrative. In some instances they identified differences between received information and the information in their documents, thus revealing a real understanding of the processes of historical enquiry.

As a result of this project Schmidt and Garcia (2010) were critical of the existing history education in Brazil. They examined children's understanding of historical consciousness in terms of personal identity and concluded that the current pattern of history pedagogy in Brazil neither develops in pupils an understanding of their own identity through personally conducted national or world narratives, nor provides the conceptual tools that would enable them to do so themselves. It would be interesting to replicate this project with 9-year-old children in the UK, as a depth study within a local study, albeit on a smaller scale. Would they be able to write narratives involving the concepts used by the Brazilian children in their narratives?

In this chapter, we explored how historians find out about the past from sources, sometimes through making deductions, but usually through making inferences, and we considered the reasons why inferences may differ, although they may be equally valid. There was evidence that children can make deductions and inferences and that these become more complex and valid with increasing maturity and experience, if supported by a variety of supportive teaching strategies. Historians select and combine inferences about sources to construct accounts of the past. How does this influence the accounts they write? This and the implications for teaching and learning are considered in Chapter 3.

3

Interpretations and accounts

What are interpretations?

At Key Stage 1, children should 'identify some of the ways in which the past is represented'. At Key Stage 2, 'they are expected to understand how and why the past is represented in different ways'; 'how our knowledge of the past is constructed from a range of sources' and themselves construct accounts of the past based on sources, and 'to construct informed responses that involve thoughtful selection and organization of relevant historical information' (DfE 2013). Interpretations of the past are accounts of a period, an event or a person in the past, written in a later period. To try to make sense of the past, historians combine their inferences about sources to create accounts of the past. In Chapter 2, we considered the many reasons why sources may be interpreted differently. In this chapter, we shall consider how selecting sources, interpreting and combining them to create an account can create interpretations which may differ, but be equally valid. Questions may investigate whether the Iron Age was (or was not) a sophisticated civilization, that the Roman Empire significantly changed Iron Age Britain (or perhaps did not), that Greece was the 'father of European civilization' (or maybe not), that Britain in the 'Dark Ages' was very 'dark' (or quite enlightened), that King Alfred was a great king (or was not). Such questions can lead to different accounts and different but equally valid interpretations, which contests the idea that history is one Grand Narrative, reflecting unexamined cultural values.

Interpretations differ for many reasons

As explained in Chapter 2, sources may be incomplete but they are also numerous and wide-ranging. Historians therefore have to select the sources relevant to their accounts. Selection depends on the focus of their accounts for, as we have seen, there are many types of history, from political, social and economic to sports history, history of music or art, histories of groups or individuals and broad or in-depth histories.

Historians may focus on gender, ethnicity, politics or social class

Gender

Rowbotham (1973), Beddoe (1983), Boulding (1976, 1977, 1981) and Hill (1989, 1996, 2001) take a female perspective. Recent research (p. 17) offers a feminist perspective on the Stone Age. Herodotus, travelling in Egypt in the fifth century BCE, found that, while in his native Greece women only performed household duties, in Egypt they had far more freedom; they traded agricultural goods in the market place while the men wove at home, and there had been five women on the throne of Egypt. Egyptologists found accounts of women receiving the same pay for labour as men and of their legal rights.

Ethnicity

Fryer (1984, 1989) writes from the perspective of a black historian and Vishram (1988) from an Indian perspective. Hakim Adi, at the University of Chichester has written widely, including *The History of African and Caribbean Communities in Britain* (2014) and Olivette Otele writes on and researches the links between history and collective memory (www.bathspa.ac.uk/our-people/olivette-otele/).

Politics and class

C.V. Wedgwood's (1955) account of the English Civil War is different from that of the Marxist historian Christopher Hill (1980). Chinn (1995) takes a working-class and a female, though not necessarily feminist, perspective. Samuel's fascinating book *Theatres of Memory* (1994, repub. 2012) is not concerned with mainstream history but with cultural history telling the 'accumulated stories of past generations', stories of those actual men and women whose lives sometimes fit with academic accounts of the past and sometimes do not. Everything from the past should be included. *Theatres of Memory* allows a dialogue between the dead and the living to be rekindled. This was, and remains, a new approach to history.

Accounts reflect the times in which they are written

Accounts reflect the dominant values of the time in which they were written. The Victorians, for example, focused on finding aspects of British freedoms and rights embedded in Saxon laws. In the statue of Queen Victoria and Prince Albert, in the National Portrait Gallery, London, commemorating Albert's untimely death, they are wearing Saxon costume!

History is dynamic. Historians challenge previous interpretations. The raids of Bomber Command in the Second World War were seen as necessary and effective for a variety of reasons until Max Hastings (1979) questioned this, saying that the raids were both ineffective and disproportionate. (As a result red paint was thrown over the statue of 'Bomber Harris'.) Anthony Grayling (2006) demonstrated the bombing to be, according to the laws obtaining at the time and subsequently, an essentially immoral activity.

Wild Scots (Fry 2005) challenges the dominant account of the Scottish clearances by pointing out that many Highland landlords were benevolent Tory paternalists who went to great lengths to maintain the ties that bound the people to the land. Dee Brown's *Bury My Heart at Wounded Knee* (1991) challenges the traditional image of the 'Wild West'. Niall Ferguson's *Colossus* (2002) re-examines America's dominance and argues that America really is an empire, before going on to argue that this is something to celebrate. Churchill once said that he would ensure his place in history by writing it – but historians are still writing it.

Apparently Captain Bligh, immortalized in *Mutiny on the Bounty* as the cause of the crew's spontaneous revolt against a tyrannical captain and cast adrift by his second-in-command, Fletcher Christian, has now been found to have been a seafaring hero and a humane captain, victimized by Christian when he ran out of laudanum (Hellen 1998).

Interpretations change with place

A letter in *The Times* (30.12.1996) from Dr Olga Ashby illustrates what she describes as 'the cultural divide between the two sides of the Iron Curtain'. She lived in Moscow during the 1980s before moving to England. She recalls how she was taught that the battle described in Tennyson's poem, 'The Charge of the Light Brigade', which was lost as the result of the blunders of the British commanding officers, was represented in Russia as a triumph of Russian strategy. In Russia, the 'original nurse' of the Crimean War was not Florence Nightingale but Dasha Sevastopolskata.

Children can compare interpretations

Information books

Children can compare different written accounts at their own levels by comparing different information books on the same historical subject. As discussed above, how has the content been selected? Is the focus on everyday life, on rich or poor, on art and artefacts, on individuals or events, on the perspectives of an indigenous people or people of other ethnicities? Are there inferences about beliefs and values, thoughts and feelings, and how are these justified? Are statements supported by evidence of why this is thought? Is a book written from the perspectives and interests of children – from different backgrounds? Do the books represent and value men and women equally? Are they illustrated with artists' impressions, themselves interpretations, or with photographs of sources? What is not included? How do children's books published at different times in the past differ from those of today, in language, hidden messages, selected content?

Accounts written at different times

Hoodless (2004) analysed 10- and 11-year-old children's understanding of the changing attitudes and values revealed in historical stories written at different times in the twentieth century. She found that they were able to identify changing styles of presentation with a subtle understanding that adults' different attitudes are transmitted through historical accounts and stories written in different periods. After reading about Boudicca in Sarson and Paine (1930) and in Deary (1994), the children commented on the way each reflected the values of its time; the earlier text avoided dwelling on death and the embarrassment of suicide. The children thought that, in the romantic style of the earlier text, Boudicca was treated with the respect due to a queen and her husband was considered to have done 'the right thing'. They were conscious that the writer's style was intended for children who were regarded differently from children today, and also of its response to the time in which it was written:

> 'It seems to come out of that time. It reads like it was written just after the war, all proud about how we defend ourselves.'

Another child commented:

> 'You have an image of what other people thought of her, how she was very brave. The problem with that is that because of the time it was based in you don't know if that's what it was actually like . . . Stories change in the time they're told . . . It can completely change the image of someone.'

They recognized that the first version was told as a matter of fact while in the second they were invited to decide between various possibilities. Children commented on how they preferred making their own decisions because 'people's opinions, written up in stories, might be wrong'. Fictional stories about the past in historical settings are also reconstructions. Children can read these or write their own, identifying what is known and what is 'guessed at' to fill in the gaps.

Interpretations through re-enactments and reconstructions

Accounts of the past are not made only by historians. There is now an enormous variety of forms of interpretation of past times. They may be living reconstructions such as the Black Country Living Museum (www.bclm.co.uk) or Beamish Museum (www.beamish.org.uk) or re-enactments of events. Kentwell Hall in Long Melford in Suffolk is the setting for a Tudor recreation for schoolchildren for three weeks each year. The surroundings of the redbrick Elizabethan manor are peopled with 400 're-enactors' at any one time, for the children to interact with: dyers, woodsmen, weavers, chandlers, alchemists, cooks, pedlars, seamstresses, musicians and gentry. A long list of living history re-enactments is given on www.reenactor.net.

Reconstructions may be static museum reconstructions, for example the prehistory galleries in the Museum of London, or reconstructions such as the Iron Age Village at Butser in the Queen Elizabeth Park, Hampshire (www.butserancientfarm.co.uk). Such reconstructions are the product of informed historical enquiry or, as with Butser, of archaeological research (Reynolds 1979). Children can try to find out how such reconstructions were made (what is the evidence?) by asking questions on the site, comparing with other sources or information books, and consider why they were made and their validity.

Less academic accounts are made for different purposes and may have different levels of validity. Benjamin Britten's opera *Gloriana*, the BBC television serial *Blackadder II* and the BBC film *The Virgin Queen* give very different interpretations of Elizabeth I that are easy for young children to identify and explain (Cooper 2012: 136–137). The Iron Age farm at Butser is a scientific reconstruction (www.butserancientfarm.co.uk/). The statue of Boudicca on the Embankment in London represents a different interpretation of the period from that in *Asterix in Britain* (Goscinny 2004). New interactive media technologies are making new kinds of historical interpretation possible. It is possible to walk through virtual museums and virtual sites.

Children's accounts through re-enactments

If children can create their own interpretations through reconstructions this is not only fun but helps them to consider how interpretations are created and their validity. They may be reconstructions created through play. Play in historical contexts is discussed elsewhere (Cooper 2002; 2004; Harnett *et al.* 2014; Dodwell 2017). Older children may create considered historical drama (as seen on TV!) over a longer period, researching character, place, setting and examining a problem or an issue, considering what is based on research and what needs to be imagined based on what is known. In the English and Literacy objectives (DfE 2013), drama is seen as a 'chance to develop socially, emotionally culturally, intellectually, spiritually'. If it were made into a film this would also have ICT objectives and the cross-curricular approach would justify the time spent. Why not add design and technology – designing sets? This would also be a way of 'communicating results of an enquiry'. Or there may be two dramas made, an interpretation from a female and male perspective. (Getting carried away now!) There are companies that provide units of history work resulting in a musical production (www.educationalmusicals.com). They have titles such as, 'The Warrior Queen', 'The Saxon King' and 'The Lucky Viking'. Historical costumes for Key Stages 1 and 2 can be purchased from a number of companies. So can sewing patterns, but for early societies it is quite simple to improvise; even children can make their own. We once did a performance of the musical *Oliver!* and discussed it in relation to factual enquiries about the poor in Victorian London. I have the photograph on my wall still of me dressed as a chimney sweep – because it's fun for teachers to join in too!

Children's interpretations through paintings, displays and models

Interpretations created could be a series of paintings or murals, maybe as a background to a museum exhibition, depicting aspects of a period studied, based on what can be researched about different aspects of life or different key events; there are links to art here too. Any display is itself a reconstruction in which some things are selected and others neglected; models are reconstructions within a display reconstruction. Making models – Viking boats, Greek temples, Roman forts, Iron Age huts – is fine as long as, in the process, children find out what they can from sources – and become aware of the problems involved in reconstructing from sources.

Interpretations and 'double vision'

Interpretations do not only involve accounts from the same period, created for different reasons or from different perspectives. They may be a bit more complex; accounts written in one period, interpreted by a subsequent period, but not the present. This requires thinking about the period in which the later account was created and why, in order to consider how true it may be. Card (2004: 6–9) calls this 'double vision'. Double vision is necessary to evaluate some sources related to the period of the Saxon invasions (c. 460–600 CE).

For example, Gildas was a mid-sixth-century Welsh monk, who says Roman influence on Britain was still strong. His interpretation of the period is that the English were weak and wicked and Saxons bellicose. See *De Excidio Britannia*, Sections 18, 23–24, www.tertullian.org/fathers/gildas_02_ruin_of_britain.htm.

Bede (2008), *Ecclesiatical History of the English People* (Book 1, Ch. 15, p. 26), identifies the invading tribes and his focus is on the need to convert the invaders. See https://en.wikisource.org/wiki/Ecclesiastical_History_of_the_English_People/Book_1 p. 26.

Geoffrey of Monmouth, writing in the twelfth century, a period when myths flourished, *Historia Regum Brittaniae (History of the British Kings)* provides wondrous accounts of the fifth and sixth centuries full of wizards and magic. See www.caerleon.net/history/geoffrey/prophecy1.htm (Book 7, Ch 3, short extract from beginning Para 2).

Young children might discuss one of these interpretations of the Saxon invasions written in a later period and consider why the writer might interpret the arrival of the Saxons in this way. The process of doing this would be:

> List values/attitudes of second age, look at second source extract. Can you pick out what the writer of the second source thought/felt about earlier period and why? How does second source make *you* feel? Why?

Older children can cope with more than one source, and consider how and why they are different.

Historical fiction: writing interpretations

In one case study, Year 6 children learned the history of the local castle, agreed questions they would like to investigate during a visit and how they would record their findings (Cooper and West 2009). Emma and Jane planned to write a story set in the past. They took photographs and wrote notes. Their story was based on people known to have lived in the castle and an old legend, and illustrated by the photographs of the parts of the castle described as the story unfolds. Gaps we cannot know about are filled in ways which are valid: descriptions of the season, weather and common human feelings, as in this short extract.

> It was a lovely Spring day at Brougham Castle and Lord and Lady Clifford were enjoying a walk in the garden . . . So they went through the gatehouse and into the keep. The gatehouse was the most sturdy thing in the whole castle. It had metre thick walls made of sandstone and a huge portcullis which was fully open.

The soldiers were terrified as they ran through the chapel. The priests were sitting on the sedila, a big chair, and praying. The soldiers were shouting that they had seen something they never wanted to see again . . .

I shall leave you in suspense.

Children exploring interpretations of Alexander the Great

Brown and Wrenn (2004) worked with Year 5/6 children to investigate different interpretations of Alexander the Great, in order to decide whether Alexander was indeed great. When the children entered the room they were confronted by three contrasting pictures of Alexander the Great. They were divided into three groups, representing three people who had written about Alexander at different times and some information about them. Iskander the Hateful was a hostile Arab chronicler whose country was defeated by Alexander. A school textbook author had to be as balanced as possible. The Hollywood filmmaker wanted to make people love Alexander. Based on their information each group had to make a tableau of an event from Alexander's life.

Each group was given a few props and background images to project onto an interactive whiteboard. Then each group had to decide how Alexander would stand, the expression on his face, what he is doing, the event from his life they were portraying and what objects and people to put in the background. (The tableau inspired by the Arab chronicler, for example, was of Alexander killing his friend Clitus.) The tableaux were then photographed and put onto the whiteboard. Each group discussed what idea of Alexander was given in each tableau and discussed why historians and filmmakers say different things about him. After this introduction, the class investigated the first sub-question, 'Who was Alexander the Great?'

After watching the trailer to the film, *Alexander the Great*, children worked in teams to investigate a second sub-question, 'What does Oliver Stone's film say about Alexander? Each person in a team was given a different focus for analysing the trailer (commentary, sound, camera action, costume and lighting). Finally, they created a poster to advertise the film with images and text to persuade potential film-goers that Alexander was indeed GREAT!

The third sub-question was, what do historians say about Alexander the Great? After reading the contrasting views of several historians, two were selected for analysis. Children had the texts as an electronic file, so that they could analyse them, using bold and underline for positive and negative aspects, and colour codes for facts and opinions, in order to reach a conclusion about how balanced each text was.

The final enquiry was, 'So why do film makers and historians differ?' The room was turned into a press room with 'an historian' (tweed jacket and beard – no stereotypes here then . . .), the 'film producer' in shades and tee-shirt and the teacher as chair. The rest of the class interrogated the historian and the film producer about their purposes, audience and methodology. The debate was then written as a tabloid-style newspaper report.

This case study is described in detail because it is an excellent model for a unit of study. First, it is structured as an overarching question, with subsidiary questions, leading to a conclusion. Second, it was FUN. And most importantly, interpretation was integrated with both prior knowledge and the processes of historical enquiry. This structure could be replicated in a number of other contexts. There are plenty of films, DVDs, clips and historical sources available on Alfred the Great, the Roman Conquest of Britain, the Vikings, and YouTube clips of Stone Age, Bronze Age and Iron Age Britain, which could be used to analyse, evaluate and compare the reasons for different interpretations.

Why is it important to understand 'interpretations'?

Understanding how and why accounts of the past are made has been found to be a neglected aspect of historical enquiry in primary schools, yet children enjoy thinking seriously about accounts, which can nevertheless be lighthearted and funny. They enjoy accounts made using different kinds of information technology. Since the past, heritage, family and local history are now frequently regarded as popular leisure activities and as entertainment, it is increasingly important that children can evaluate them. There are also more serious reasons for learning why there is no single view of the past and that accounts of the past are dynamic and may vary and change over time. Children are learning to challenge validity and assess validity and to recognize different motives behind creating accounts. For history is the most politically powerful subject in the curriculum and earns constant attention from politicians.

Interpretations in international contexts

Northern Ireland

The importance of allowing pupils to discuss alternative interpretations of the past is made painfully clear in societies where history is contested, such as Northern Ireland or South Africa. Barton and McCully (2005) emphasize how history plays a contentious role in popular discussion and community conflict in Northern Ireland, and one purpose of the school curriculum is to provide alternatives to the sectarian, historical perspectives pupils encounter elsewhere. Their interviews with 253 secondary school pupils demonstrated the strong impact of community influences, especially family members, but they also revealed that pupils consciously and explicitly expected the school to provide alternatives to those interpretations.

The British Empire

Harnett (2005) analysed how the British Empire and Commonwealth Museum in Bristol attempts to construct the narrative of Empire and takes account of different interpretations and alternative viewpoints within its collection. The museum, reflecting the work of contemporary historians, revises the Victorian view of Empire, epitomized by Cecil Rhodes's remark that 'the British are the finest race in the world and the more of the world they inhabit, the better it will be for mankind' (Cannadine 2001) with contemporary interpretations that reflect current values of equality of opportunity and human rights. (The history of Britain in the nineteenth century and the first part of the twentieth century is central to the history of Empire, whether viewed from a peripheral or metropolitan perspective.) In Harnett's study, primary pupils investigated the lives of different individuals and social groups within the Empire, the challenges of the early settlers, the colonization of Australia and the experiences of a Caribbean immigrant.

South Africa

Hilary Claire gives many suggestions about how to help children to understand different perspectives (Claire 2005: 24–43). Gail Weldon (2004) explains how it is the explicit aim of the revised history curriculum in South Africa to identify and develop values of 'democracy, equality, human dignity and social justice'. She points out, however, that the teachers were conditioned, in varying degrees, to the attitudes and prejudices of apartheid society, and as a result projects have been set up to support teachers and learners in education for human rights and democracy through history, with Nazi Germany and apartheid South Africa as case studies.

Canada and Germany

In 2004, Jon Nichol and I set up the History Educators' International Research Network, through which researchers in history education could share their work. We have since had fourteen successful annual conferences in countries such as Brazil, Russia, Turkey, the United States and across Europe, with participants from every continent. The 2005 conference on museums was about identity and citizenship. A number of the papers focused on the extent to which pupils are encouraged to understand that there may be more than one interpretation or that interpretations can change. In Quebec, Jocelyn Letourneau (2005) tried to contest the French Canadians' interpretation of Canadian history as a golden age until the British arrived and took it over for their own benefit. The Quebeckers are depicted in textbooks as childlike, dominated by their seigneurs and priests until the British invaders imposed commerce and progress. In 1995, nearly half of Quebeckers voted to split from Canada. Letourneau tried to set up a museum exhibition challenging the partial view of Canadian history but the challenge was not responded to. Alternative interpretations were not accepted. Other examples can be found elsewhere. In Germany there is a different interpretation of the past taught in the former East Germany and West Germany; the former teaches only about the positive values of the GDR and the latter, only the negative. Pupils are not invited to compare and discuss these interpretations. In the United States of America, Rozensweig (2000) has suggested that pupils see themselves as conscripts or prisoners and teachers as drill sergeants or wardens.

Conclusion

History is about asking questions, is interpretive and controversial. As children have said, you 'get to argue', and 'There sure aren't many facts!'. Young children may not be debating the major issues through comparing interpretations, but they are learning that there is more than one version of the past, and beginning to understand why. In the previous two chapters, we considered how sources are investigated, and combined into accounts of past times. But central to history is time, comparing past times, the reasons for similarities and differences between them, what caused them to change and the effects of changes and the links between different societies. These central aspects of history are discussed in Chapter 4.

4

Chronology, time concepts and other key concepts

The process of historical enquiry, as discussed in the second chapter of this book, involves selecting sources, any traces from the past which remain (artefacts, images, plans, maps and documents) and making deductions and inferences about what they might tell us about the past. Deductions and inferences about sources are combined to create accounts of the past. Chapter 3 discussed the reasons why accounts may differ and change over time and therefore there are many valid interpretations of people, events and periods.

The first part of Chapter 4 is about the chronological frameworks of measured time, within which accounts are located and sequenced: days, weeks, months, years, decades, centuries and millennia. And it is about the concepts of time, that we use in order to discuss the passing of time, based on this chronological framework. *Duration* considers whether something continued for a long time or a short time; periods and societies are compared using concepts of *similarities and differences* and consideration of the *causes and effects* of change. These may appear self-evident concepts, but are not always easy to determine. The National Curriculum expects children at Key Stage 1 to talk about changes in national life within living memory, about events *beyond* living memory and to *compare* aspects of life in different periods. At Key Stage 2, they should develop a secure chronological *knowledge and understanding* of local, British and world history, regularly *addressing* and sometimes *devising questions* about *change, cause, similarity, difference and significance*.

The second part of Chapter 4 considers concepts historians have devised to describe periods of time (Victorian, Elizabethan), concepts used in history but no longer used or used very differently today (villa, bailey and common) and concepts central to history but not exclusively historical (agriculture, trade and defence).

Chronology

There is good evidence (Ofsted 2011; Historical Association Primary Survey 2015) that in the past children have had detailed knowledge of the periods they have studied, but they have not had the chronological framework, or frequently and regularly used the language of time, to enable them to discuss, compare, contrast and look for similarities and differences between societies, or for causes and effects of changes over long periods of time and space. They were not able to engage with 'The Big Picture' of history.

Chronological frameworks are important in trying to make sense of the world. We use multiple chronological frameworks that range from the micro – personal, familial and local – to the macro – tracing changes over thousands, or millions of years. Frameworks provide skeletons for structuring historical narratives, accounts, situations and events. Essentially, chronology is a scaffold that can be returned to, developed, reinforced and built upon. It requires a knowledge of 'facts', such as key dates of significant figures, of important events and of the periods into which historians have divided history, for example the Stone Ages, Roman Britain and the Saxons.

Measurement of time varies across cultures

Ancient civilizations recorded the passing of time in cycles, in relation to seasons or planets or significant dates in their culture. In Europe, time is represented as linear and based on the Gregorian calendar, calculating time as BC (Before Christ) and AD (After Christ), or to use non-religious terminology, BCE (Before Common Era) and CE (Common Era). The Islamic system is based on the Hijri Era, calculating time from 'H', the time when Mohammad and his followers migrated from Mecca to Medina (which is 622 AD/CE).

Chronology is not just remembering dates

Chronology is derived from the Greek meaning a study of time. It is not simply a matter of reciting the dates of the kings and queens, which in itself has little purpose. An illustrated chart of the Kings and Queens of England, distributed with *The Times* (2011), accompanied the cartoon-style portrait of each monarch with particularly useless information: Athelstan (924–939) 'liked to collect relics and hunt'; Edward 1 'made the first laws to punish burglars'; Ealdred (946) 'had a weakness of the feet and had to spit out food he couldn't swallow'. Knowledge and chronology are by no means synonymous with historical understanding.

What does a good timeline look like?

Of course there are many answers, depending on the purpose of any particular timeline. Bev Forest and Stuart Tiffany offered useful and thought-provoking suggestions in a presentation at the Historical Association Conference in 2016. They began by discussing the inadequacies of a timeline they had seen consisting of about ten coloured pictures of events from 'the age of dinosaurs' to the forthcoming 'World Cup'. Each event was the same size and had a single date on it and the pictures were evenly spread and next to each other. (And the problem is . . .?) A good timeline, they suggested, is accessible, is frequently used and provides opportunities for seeing where things overlap and for seeing the relationship between local, national and international contexts – and it must be memorable (Tiffany 2012).

Stuart Tiffany said that in his school there was a whole-school approach and teachers introduced and reported on the success of new ideas. A novel example for an Anglo-Saxon–Viking timeline was to divide the class into Anglo-Saxons and Vikings, invite them to find a partner from the other civilization, to find events on the timeline which linked them and to ask questions based on these events. Forest and Tiffany also presented an impressive example of how a child had used a timeline to describe concurrent civilizations: the Greek civilization in the Mediterranean, the Romans in Southern Europe and the Egyptian civilization in North Africa were all around at the same time.

Concepts of time

It was said by a primary school head teacher contributing to the Cambridge Review (Alexander 2010: 247), that children learning history do not need to know a lot of dates because they can look them up on the internet. The Review makes clear the difference between knowledge as facts or information and propositional knowledge, the ways in which we find out about the past: methods of enquiry, explanation and criteria for verification. Enquiries in history are essentially about time and change, the causes and consequences of changes in societies and between societies, the reasons for similarities and differences between different periods and the relationship between things that change slowly and events, for rapid and gradual changes in different aspects of a society. Chronology is a framework within which to explore these changes, and primary school children can engage in this process, at different levels, but they need guidance in how to do it. Such exploration is the ninth aim of the Cambridge Review. It involves 'enlivening the child's amazement, perplexity, curiosity, discovery, invention, speculation, fantasy, play and linguistic agility' (2014–2016: 257). The following section discusses methods we use to make meaning, connections and patterns from the passing of time.

Sequencing

Young children's knowledge of the passing of time is measured by personal experience, recorded as sequences of days of the week, months and seasons and birthdays. There has been much research into the ability of pupils from 2 to 6 years old to sequence days, months and seasons (e.g. Thornton and Vukelich 1988). Young children's understanding of the passing of time also derives from conversations with family about generations, family events and 'old things', using time vocabulary (old/new; then/now; for a long time; before/after). It can develop through stories, discussing what happened next and why, or discussing illustrations of nursery rhymes and stories about the past.

Sequencing using timelines

Children between 5 and 7 years old can create their own timelines and family trees. See Figure 11.7 showing Gemma's questionnaire for her parents and the timeline she constructed from it. The timeline was illustrated by a sequence of photographs of Gemma's clothes and toys, sequenced over this period. Her teacher then made a timeline, using the same scale for her 25 years, illustrated by her photographs and clothes, including her wedding dress. The head teacher, aged 50, displayed her family tree and related photographs and artefacts, in the school foyer, which gave rise to much interest, comparison and discussion, not least among the staff and parents. Children compared the timelines, using the same scale.

Older children can construct their own timelines of periods they have studied, based on information they have found out, either individually or as a class, perhaps each child writing on a card an explanatory note about a photocopied illustration and hanging these from the ceiling in chronological sequence. This process, both with children and working with a group of teachers, raised interesting questions: why some cards did not have precise dates: why some changes were rapid, but other developments occurred over a long and imprecise period; about causes and effects and who may or may not have been affected; about the benefits or problems of changes. Other groups have constructed parallel timelines, illustrating different aspects of change during the same period, using the same scale (for example events, technological inventions, children's lives, growth of towns and transport), which were displayed in parallel. This promoted discussion among a Year 6 class I was working with about the connections between the timelines. Timelines should become more complex and thought-provoking as children mature and use different scales. Bearing in mind recent criticism of children not having 'the big picture', it is important to relate timelines within periods to timelines across a continuous span of time, maybe around the school hall. It is important that such a timeline continues to the present and includes periods after 1066 so that children feel that they are involved and connected with this continuum.

Sequencing using time trails

Time trails are a recognized activity for helping children to develop a sense of chronology through contexts within their own experience. During a walk, children identify and photograph buildings or features of buildings, then in school they can sequence the photographs and find out where to place them on a timeline.

Sequencing narratives

Bage (1999) explored ways in which narrative interpretations of the past can be used to develop children's historical understanding, if they are encouraged to criticize rather than copy stories. He suggests, for example that the storyteller plans to suspend the story at points, in order to discuss motives and causes of decisions and to discuss moral issues. This makes the story motivating, forward looking and meaningful.

Explaining why things happened

The CHATA project (Concepts of History and Teaching Approaches at Key Stages 2 and 3), funded by the Economic and Social Research Council (www.esrc.ac.uk/myesrc/ Grants/L208252006/read), investigated the development of children's understanding of cause and effect in detail. For example Lee *et al.* (1991–1996) show how children's ideas about explanation in history depend on their understanding of the situation the person was in, on knowledge and on 'historical imagination'. All 320 children, aged between 7 and 14, were able to offer rational explanations of why the Roman Emperor Claudius invaded Britain. There was progression in their explanations from simply, 'because he wanted to get the gold and silver' at 8 years old, to recognition of his public role as emperor at 10 years old: 'He wanted more people to like him'; 'He wanted to take over other countries of the world'; 'to be better than Julius Caesar'. At 8 years old, nothing puzzled the children about Claudius' motives, whereas at 10 years old some children argued that he could, for example have 'stayed at home and had a better life'. By 12 years old, pupils were beginning to see that his motives were not confined to personal wants or on what to do as emperor; they also considered the situation he was in: 'He was at peace and had spare soldiers; not all British tribes were friendly with the Romans'.

Duration

Understanding duration, how long situations or periods lasted, helps children to have a sense of period and of time, and to see close and distant relations between events. It enables children to be aware of, for example, the enormous duration of hunter–gatherers in Britain, compared with the duration of the New Stone Age and with the duration of the Bronze Age in Britain. In relation to these periods they can see how relatively brief the Roman Occupation of Britain was and compare this with the Anglo-Saxon period. They can compare the 600-year Anglo-Saxon period with the 500-year period from the time of Elizabeth 1 until now. Such comparisons really do begin to give us some awe–inspiring awareness of the relative duration of periods of time. And comparing durations of time within periods, for example the life of King Alfred (871–899) within the Anglo-Saxon period, helps us to understand both significance, the short span and sometimes considerable action within one lifetime and how one lifetime is part of the flow of events; for example Alfred fought the Vikings, but they were invading Britain from 793 to 1066.

Contemporaneity, similarities and differences

Table 8.3 describes similarities and differences between the characteristic features of the four ancient societies of Sumer, the Indus Valley, Egypt and the Shang dynasty of China, which were – more or less – contemporaneous. The National Curriculum aims for children to understand and use abstract terms such as empire, civilization and peasantry and to understand similarities and differences between societies, making connections, drawing contrasts, analysing trends and framing historically valid questions. We can use the table to discuss what these civilizations had in common and the reasons for 'the expansion and dissolution of these empires' (DfE 2013) (see Chapter 8).

Flashback

Many books (for example Burningham 1992; Sendak 2007) and television programmes (for example *Dr Who*) involve 'playing with time', or time-travel, through flashbacks or parallel stories. These rely on a strong innate sense of chronology, which quite young children appear to have (Hoodless 1998).

Skills needed to develop chronological understanding

Sorting skills

The ability to apply chronology in asking and answering historical questions depends on number skills (Hodkinson 2004). Young children need to be able to sort photographs, pictures and artefacts into sets (old/new; now/then) and later to make Venn diagrams (old/new/could be either) in order to discuss increasingly complex questions about time and change, similarity and difference and to justify their reasons.

Number skills

Using increasingly large numbers, children need to be able to read, write and order numbers, to count on and back on a timeline, to add and subtract. Older children should understand positive and negative numbers and BCE and CE.

Displaying and interpreting statistics

Older children can transfer statistics, for example census data, to bar charts, spread sheets or line graphs that may illustrate slow and rapid and gradual changes, and look for and explain causes, effects and patterns. Correlation may be discovered between changes in occupations in a locality and population growth, or ages of death in different areas compared, all of which can be linked to maps, newspaper information and other sources to build up an understanding of causes and effects of changes over time. Other statistics concerning change include those referring to birth and death rates, immigration and emigration, enclosure, imports and exports, height and weight (of people or cattle!). Table 7.1 shows opportunities for applying the National Curriculum for number and statistics to chronology and time questions in history.

Case studies: teaching strategies investigating children's use of timelines and time concepts

Chronology at Key Stage 1

In solving problems about chronological sequence, children need to understand past tenses (it was), causal connectives (because, therefore), temporal connectives (when, while, during) and probability language (perhaps, I think, maybe). Hodkinson (2003) argues that since linguistic phrases such as 'a long time ago' are subjective and can be interpreted in many different ways, children should be helped to progress to more precise language (before x; after y; at the same time as z). Sometimes vocabulary needs to be specifically taught (duration, span, era, age, period, decade, century and millennium) if children are to be articulate about what they deduce and infer from timelines.

Children can also construct their own chronological narratives, as picture stories or chapters in a book, which recreate a real story about the past or life of a real individual, possibly even writing in flashbacks or writing contemporaneous stories. Narratives need to be based on evidence and might be reconstructed through drama.

Children constructing timelines and comparing periods

In this case study with Year 5/6 children (all four of them) in Langdale School, Cumbria, I was interested in how they could construct, rather than memorize historical sequences (Cooper 2011).

- Could the children sequence periods they had not learned about?

- Could they work out what had changed between periods, from the pictures/text?

- Had they any notion of the time span between periods?

- In each case I was interested in their discussion and the reasons they gave for their answers.

I chose *Horrible Histories* for this exploration of children's understanding of chronology because I thought it would be fun – and I approve of the *Horrible Histories*. They use sources, question sources, provide alternative interpretations and recognize what is not known and that historians are not always 'right'. They give information about key aspects of each period: daily life of different classes, beliefs, crime and punishment, causes and effects of changes. I selected two key themes, which run through the series: 'children' and 'law and order'. I chose four periods well spaced chronologically: the Celts, Medieval, Georgian and Victorian. I scanned and printed a single page illustrating each theme, in each period.

Sequencing

I asked the children, 'Can you put these pictures/text in sequence, starting with the earliest?'

- Where do you think they should be placed on this timeline (0 CE–2,000 CE; 2 inches represents 100 years)?

The key information on the pages selected was:

- *The Cut-Throat Celts* (Deary 1997). From 7 to 17 children lived with a neighbouring tribe. The boys were taught to fight by women warriors. Girls married between the ages of 12 and 14.

- *The Stormin' Normans* (Deary 2001: 65). Children had to collect wood for the family fire, acorns and nuts to feed the family pig, turn the grindstone for the men to sharpen their sickles and (p. 74) learn to be a knight.

- *The Gorgeous Georgians and the Vile Victorians* (Deary 1999: 171). Life of boy and girl chimney sweeps and (p. 54) abandoned babies and the Thomas Coram's Foundling Hospital 1741.

- *Villainous Victorians* (Deary 2004: 26). Child living rough found by policeman and sent to prison.

The children were able to sequence the pages correctly.

- We've done the Vikings. I think that if they had 'tribes' that was a long time before the Vikings.

- The Victorians are a lot later than the Vikings. That's what girls and boys had to do in Victorian times.

- The one about training to be knights is earlier than the Victorians. The knights were before Victoria. That was a very long time ago.

- The one with the Bobby in is Victorian too. Poor children had a bad time in Victorian times.

- And THAT one (Thomas Coram) has got a date on it. It says 1741. Victoria died in 1901. She lived in the 1800s. So that must be before Victoria but after the knights.

Identifying differences between periods

'In the first one [Celts], you were sent away from your family to learn that you belong to the whole tribe and to learn to fight for the tribe'. 'In this one [Normans], the children work with their families and help with farming. They help each other. The children help the adults.' Originally the children thought that the simple clothes looked Greek or Egyptian but after discussion decided that there was no other evidence to suggest this and that collecting wood and keeping pigs sounded more like England.

'The boys learning to be knights are rich; you'd have to pay to learn to be a knight. There are similarities [sic] between these three [Georgian and Victorian]; in the Victorian times children had to work themselves to death. In the other they die when they're babies.'

Implicitly the children are tracing communal life in the tribe, followed by working together on the land as a family, for the good of the family, then a stable (feudal) society. Finally, they describe the impact of industrialization, fragmenting family life and social stability (William Morris would be pleased; he looked back, with nostalgia, to the values of Medieval society in an age of industrialization!).

Making a distinction between periods

Given the 0–2000 timeline, the children placed the page about the Celts at the beginning, and the Georgians, followed by the Victorians, at the other end in the 1800s. Learning to be a knight was placed halfway along the timeline. They did this based on minimal information on the pages selected, little experience of timelines and having only studied Vikings, Tudors and Victorians. (They thought they would 'do the rest' at secondary school.)

This study showed clearly that these children could make inferences, based on what they had studied in school, although I suspect that they were also drawing implicitly, on what they knew from other sources. The concept of knights, for example, and highwaymen seemed not unfamiliar.

But really I was interested in the children's ability to reason in order to chronologically sequence the pages, hypothesize about time spans and about similarities and differences and the reasons for them. The children extrapolated from what they knew and applied it to a new context (Bruner 1963), through reasoning and discussion (Vygotsky 1962). They constructed their own knowledge. Charlotte Mason, the innovative nineteenth-century educationist, advocated children constructing and building on their own timelines based on sources, museum visits and local history. This, she says is a far better foundation for all historical training than 'cramming dates and names and facts' (Mason 1993, Vol. 1: 282).

Finding out what children know about time

Moore (2017) describes how Emma, a final year education student, questioned 5–7-year-old children about their ability to understand the passing of time. She wanted to find out what they actually knew. Emma showed the children a bag of Egyptian artefacts:

E. Who do you think used these objects?
R. Indians
E. Does anyone have any other ideas? L?
L. Are they from. Hang on a minute . . . I know what it is from but I just can't think it.
E. Well L, we will come back to you then. Who else thinks they know? S?
S. Dubai?
E. Nope they aren't from Dubai, in fact they are Egyptian.
L. Hey that's what I was going to say!
E. But do you know why they are Egyptian?
R. It's because they have pyramids.
E. Fantastic R. But did they live a long time ago or not so long ago?
R. A long time ago.
E. But how long is a long time ago?
R. 17 years ago.
E. Ohh R says 17 years. Thumbs up thumbs down. Who agrees? (Three children put their thumbs down.) L why are your thumbs down?

L.   I think it's a very long time ago because mummies don't exist anymore.

E.   Well done L, Who agrees with L? Thumbs up, thumbs down? All agree, apart from V. V's a bit unsure – why is that V?

V.   I think it's a very, very long time ago.

On another occasion the student was talking to Alex, an able 8-year-old, who was telling her about the Romans. She wondered whether he could use numbers to describe the passing of time, so asked him if he could tell her when the Romans were in Britain. His answer was 'about 66 BCE' (near enough to Caesar's 55 BC invasion). When asked how long ago that was he calculated in his head and said, 2,780 years. (If we transpose those digits we get 2,078 years – the exact answer.)

'Thinking Big' with timelines

Sossick (2011) describes an interesting activity he prepared for student teachers, to demonstrate the fascination of a timeline covering a long period. He uses a transportable timeline (a length of string with units stuck on with Velcro; 40 metres represents 100 years). He invited students to research a character from the past and to dress up as the character. Most, interestingly, were bunched up on the last 200 years of the timeline. He asked the 'Claudius' to position himself on the timeline where the Romans left. Then he asked Princess Diana to move the same distance along the timeline in the opposite direction. To people's surprise she found herself almost bumping into Queen Elizabeth. Next he produced some marker cards showing, for example key inventions and objects representing significant introductions (tobacco, a potato and a chocolate) and students were invited to treat the line as a time machine and walk through time to meet and talk to another character. John Lennon found himself agreeing passionately with Boudicca about the need to attack the Romans. The students found this a very useful experience.

Planning for teaching chronology and time concepts

Hodkinson and Smith (in press), drawing on empirical evidence, strongly suggest that young children are capable of grasping complex temporal concepts, specifically chronology, if teachers carefully plan for their development through targeted activities. Hodkinson's research (2003a, 2004b) found that, given appropriate teaching methods and learning environment, Year 4 and Year 5 children were able to understand chronology and temporal concepts. For this to take place, he says, the teacher must design, plan and deliver effective teaching programmes. Such programmes must enable children to become active, constructive processors of information. He says it requires highly focused short-term lesson plans that enable teachers to become pro- and re-active to learning needs. These short-term lessons, he continues, must employ a wide range of teaching strategies which aim to develop conceptual information. Each lesson should facilitate the application of newly acquired skills and concepts through discussion and problem-solving activities. The aim should be for children to be independent learners and to develop 'automatic sub-routines' (Hodkinson 2004a, 2004b). Throughout these lessons the teacher should be a facilitator, extending children's learning and reintroducing concepts that have been poorly understood. The chronological content running through such lessons must be taught, reinforced and extended. The onus is on the teacher to actively promote learning of such concepts. Oral work is a powerful learning method. Hodkinson and Smith (forthcoming), contend that the usage of a fast paced introductory, as well as a plenary session, which are specifically designed to develop chronological skills are advantageous to the development of temporal cognition. These sessions should also try to teach the multi-faceted nature of temporal concepts and application to differing contextual settings. Unless the multifaceted nature of concepts is specifically taught in this way, they say, children will have great difficulty in transferring their knowledge of chronology to different learning situations. Therefore teachers should focus on careful use of language, taking time to introduce and discuss specialized vocabulary and encourage a range of language use. Hodkinson and Smith conclude that the onset of the development of dating concepts is much earlier than previously thought and it is manifest that teaching can make it possible for children to master dating conventions very much earlier than previously thought. The research also found that children who learned to use dating conventions remembered significantly more historical knowledge because it provided 'hooks' on which to hang new knowledge. However, they stress that the importance of knowing dates is that it provides a structure for organizing the past. The learning of dates should not dominate lessons.

I am not sure that short quick lessons are always the best way to encourage children to work independently, to discuss and reflect. But there is much useful guidance here about the importance of chronology and time concepts running throughout history lessons, in different ways.

Progression through assessment using timelines

Formative assessment

Counsell (2014) describes her use of timelines with Year 7 which could be modified for younger pupils. At intervals, she gave the children what were ironically known as 'fun tests'. 'Let's amaze ourselves with what has stayed in our heads! . . . Let's amaze ourselves where, when, how . . .' Pupils then drew timelines of different kinds on different occasions, reflecting all they remembered of the topic. Counsell says that the retrieval of old knowledge, through the timeline created from memory, triggered by the test, assisted in the assimilation of a new topic and was also a way to get a sense of the maps and stories in pupils' heads, and the gaps, which might be remedied in a few minutes or require some tweaking in planning. It also gave pupils a satisfying sense of the quality of their own mental maps.

Summative assessment

Counsell also gave a different kind of timeline test which the students prepared for, was analytic and related to the puzzle at the centre of the enquiry question, in preparation for a final debate about it. This required them to consider and memorize both the facts and their arguments, in response to the enquiry question. She took notes on students' performances and constructed a mark scheme for this activity. In the same article Elizabeth Carr describes how she uses timelines, again with Year 7 to secure knowledge within and across Key Stages. At the start of Year 7, to diagnose chronological knowledge and sense of period, pupils were asked to assign a period label to images of period-typical people and buildings taken from a text book and to list these time periods in chronological order. At the end of the term they were asked to draw a timeline showing the periods of history they had learned about this term, then focus on the Anglo-Saxon period and write about what they have learned about it. However, it became clear that there was no evidence of how children were retaining and linking knowledge from earlier topics, to link causal knowledge between events. So students were encouraged to draw their own timelines, focusing their attention on recalling sequence, timing and spacing of events, and selecting and justifying the events they included. These were assessed to identify whose knowledge was secure, and to see concurrent events and relationships between events and between topics, British and non-British, in a diagrammatic form. These timelines were used to inform interventions and future planning. There seems no reason why primary school children could not construct similar timelines to both reinforce, and think more deeply about, both their historical knowledge and their knowledge of duration and change, causes and effects, similarities and differences between and across the units they have studied. (See Chapter 11 on formative and summative assessment.)

The language of history

Language describing periods in the past

In order to compare and contrast societies, children need to understand what is meant by the names historians use to describe particular periods: the Stone Age, Anglo-Saxon, Medieval, Tudor, Elizabethan and Victorian. They need to understand key characteristics of these periods, in order to define and compare them.

Concepts used in history but no longer used

Children love to be introduced to and use 'strange words': a Roman *villa*, a Saxon *burg*, a Saxon *fyrd*, a Roman *legion*, a Sumerian *ziggurat*, an Egyptian *pyramid*, *undeciphered* Indus Valley writing, Egyptian *hieroglyphics*, Shang dynasty *oracle bones*. And such vocabulary is often useful in comparing similarities and differences between societies.

Key concepts central to all societies

Children also love learning and using 'hard words'. And abstract concepts provide a framework for comparing the similarities and differences between societies. Eight-year-old children can relish discussing 'hard words' such as 'agriculture', 'beliefs', 'artefacts' and 'trade'. Vygotsky (1962) found that if such concepts are explicitly taught, by discussing what they mean, children can learn to apply them in different contexts. Subsequent researches (e.g. Doise *et al.* 1975; Doise and Mugny 1979; Ausubel 2000) have endorsed Vygotsky's findings. Abstract 'umbrella' concepts are learned through explicit explanation of their meaning, by linking them to their subordinate concrete concepts (things that can be visualized) and through images and repeated discussion.

Learning key concepts

When my class of 8-year-old children was learning about the late Stone Age, we talked about forest clearance, root and cereal crops, the domestication of animals and looked at pictures of these activities in information books during Neolithic times. Children were then introduced to the concept of 'agriculture'. I explained that this means farming. The children told me that farming is about growing crops and keeping animals for food. We listed all the different jobs this involves and agreed that they are all part of 'agriculture'. The children learned to spell agriculture and I used the word constantly. Children became keen to use it, and to write it themselves. The word was one of a number of abstract key concepts similarly taught and used throughout the year, during the following topics on the Bronze Age, the Iron Age and Roman Britain.

In studying the Bronze Age, we talked about some people returning to hunter gathering (Table 8.2). In Iron Age Britain, we discussed subsistence farming, holes in the chalk to make wells, fields fertilized with mast from the oak trees, a simple iron plough (Table 8.4). When studying Roman Britain, we talked of increased trade but little change in farming methods (Table 8.5) and when studying the Anglo-Saxons, we concluded that they farmed in similar ways to the Vikings, but more successfully (Table 8.6). At the end of the year, all the children demonstrated that they could spontaneously use and write these abstract concepts and could make comparisons and draw contrasts between the periods taught (Cooper 1991).

In Part I, we have considered each of the strands of historical enquiry which historians – and children – use to find out about the past. It is very important, however, to remember that all of these strands are interdependent: interpreting sources, explaining similarities and differences between societies, explaining rapid and slow changes and considering causes and effects of changes are all integrated in investigating a historical enquiry and in writing an account, or interpretation, of the findings of that enquiry. In Part II, we shall consider other connections we make, in finding out about the past. Chapter 5 considers how children like to engage with the past, to feel connected with people in the past, and how teachers can help them to do this.

PART

II

Connecting with the past

5

What makes history enjoyable?

It seems that what makes history enjoyable, especially for teachers and children, is the feeling that it connects us to the past, the past in which people very like us lived their lives, in some ways very differently from us, but in other very similar ways, because we share our common humanity. We are part of the continuum of past, present and future. We begin by analysing the ways in which John Fines challenged children to connect with the past.

What the children say

When John Fines (2011) asked children, 'What makes history enjoyable?' their answers fell into two categories. First, they appreciated the way he invited and respected their views.

'He's not strict and bossy. He treats us as if we're adults.'

'He doesn't treat us like children who are meant to be learning.'

'He respects out contributions.' 'He values our opinions.' 'They're all treated as valid.'

'He treats you like a historian; we can argue with him.'

'We're given open choice about what to say; he involves us all and he's on our wave length'. 'He knows what we'll find interesting.'

'He makes us want to take part; he doesn't force things into our head – he encourages us.'

They also demonstrated metacognition. They understood the enquiry processes he was teaching them.

'I think he is making us like historians, because the way he puts it he makes our minds think historically.'

'He helped us think in a different way; how to use our evidence and how to develop.'

'He makes you do historical thinking, improves your thinking – makes it fun.'

'He always argues his opinions. If you say something to him, he makes you argue your point – it's more fun, and you learn from the arguments because he tells you something real in the arguments.'

'He wants you to have your own opinions; he has his own opinions, but he wants to hear yours.'

'A good piece of history work looks at different arguments, brings in other people's views, shows understanding, decides what's most likely, gives an opinion, sticks with an idea, supports answers with evidence . . .'

What an accolade! A lot for us all to aspire to there. How does he do it?

How John does it?

John Fines (2011) shows us four key ways in which he engages children so deeply in the subject.

He challenges children

He challenges them throughout, facing them with problems to solve.

'He only tells you what happened after you've argued – first asks you your opinion. It's a better way to learn the facts.'

'If you have one strong piece of evidence it's like a hill and there are lots of small bits all round it. It's like proof. If there's strong evidence you can't just say: "This didn't happen".'

He asks questions which drive historical learning

'John Fines asks us *why*.'

'In Year 5, we didn't have to find out anything for ourselves – they just told us, but now, with John Fines, we have to find out things for ourselves by looking at the documents.'

In-depth study

John said that study in depth and detail is the only way to achieve understanding that enables pupils to explain upon what their accounts – their histories – are based, that is their evidential provenance, know-how, knowledge.

'I like reading extra before a debate so that I can present a better argument, get more evidence.'

'Books don't go into depth – they give you the basics, but he goes into it – he tells you what it was like.'

'With Dr Fines we learn far more history in a shorter time than people would using normal methods; with him we learn more, and more deeply. With him we get more background.'

'He takes us inside the past, we are there; he makes the past seem real and modern; he draws you in; he doesn't just read – he acts the stories and tells them as if it's happening now – it's like fiction, but he uses real evidence; he gives us real history – keeps the same words.'

Authenticity

John urges us, where possible, to use authentic sources. Replica artefacts do not connect us with touching things that people made, and others touched, just as we do. And children can learn to work with small carefully selected passages from documents. The children tell us why they like authentic sources, and how they use them.

'Looking at evidence helps you to develop the skill of looking. John Fines gives us documents to read.'

'We prefer documents to books because documents go into more detail.'

'Documents help you with role play because you get more information.'

Case studies reflecting John Fines' philosophy

Each of the following case studies is a depth study related to a broader study unit. Each study involves hands-on experience, challenge, questioning and authenticity.

The Stone Age

There are 300 long barrows and prehistoric burial chambers in the UK. In this study, Taylor (2016) uses an historical site, White Horse Hill on Dartmoor, to develop historical knowledge and enthusiasm about the Stone Age with a Year 5/6 class.

Challenge

The children were shown extracts from a BBC news programme on the discovery of the tomb. They were shown images of the discoveries. In role as archaeologists, training to study Neolithic burials, they were asked to report on the discoveries, using the headings, 'I think it was . . .', 'It was buried with them because . . .', 'It suggests to me that the person . . .'. Then an experienced archaeologist gave his interpretation and this was compared with the interpretations of the 'trainees' and the differences discussed.

Questions

The children were given a talk by an expert, who involved them in a discussion of why was the barrow built here, who might have built it and why.

Authenticity

As 'trainee archaeologists' children visited the tomb. They were divided into three groups. Each group, in turn, crawled into the damp barrow and, using maps from Victorian excavations, made notes on their interpretation of the use of the two antechambers, discussed the reasons for the dip in the roof, considered how the outer layer of Cotswold stone had been formed and made an artist's impression of the barrow 5,000 years ago. They recorded key facts, from their observations and the information they had been given in a collage of combined information, fact files, blogs, written reports or recounts.

The Iron Age

In this case study (Glenard *et al.* 2016), students from the University of Chichester, supported by Linda Cooper, worked with Chidham Parochial Primary School. All sixty children in the school were involved.

Authenticity

First the children visited Butser Ancient Farm in Hampshire, to learn about context, see the reconstructions and learn some building techniques, for example wattling.

Questions

The children then discussed the building materials available to Iron Age people, the problems they foresaw in building a roundhouse, what life might have been like in an Iron Age house and how people had managed to survive. To answer these questions more fully they went online to find out what tools and materials would have been available. They visited to Museum of London to see how the materials would have been put together. To increase their contextual knowledge they made a timeline, showing developments between the potters' lathe and quern in the Stone Age and in the Iron Age and researched other sources: pottery, ploughs, boats, coins, aerial photographs of hill forts and burial mounds. They related these to lifestyle and beliefs and were introduced to relevant vocabulary.

Challenge

They wrote plans of how the roundhouse might be built and listed the problems they anticipated. Then, with the help of the students, the children constructed the base, inserting pea-rods to outline the roundhouse base, wattled between the posts, made clunch for the walls. Then after a week, when the clunch was dry, they constructed a means of supporting the roof from inside. Finally, they attached reed matting to the roof . . .

Parents and guardians were invited to come to an official opening of the Iron Age house. The children demonstrated how clay pottery was made, designed and made traditional Iron Age jewellery and prepared an Iron Age meal. An 'Iron Age' person, dressed in Iron Age clothes, (a volunteer from Butser) joined them. I never managed anything quite so ambitious as a teacher, but I should love to have had the opportunity to work with students and children on such a project.

Anglo-Saxon women

Authenticity

The following suggestions are derived from an article (Doull 2016) on Anglo-Saxon women in the home, the church and the court. Doull writes of textile bequests which are listed in the will of Wynflaed, a fairly wealthy woman in c. 950, which included head dress, hood, headband, nun's habit, underwear, tunics, coats, linen dress, tapestry curtain, chests of linen bedding and, interestingly, a seamstress and a female weaver, who she leaves to her granddaughter. Cloth-making was exclusively a female occupation in all households.

Challenges

- Can you spin wool as the Anglo-Saxons did?

  https://regia.org/research/life/textiles.html

  http://anglosaxondiscovery.ashmolean.org/Life/clothes/spinning.html

  http://tinofbeans001.blogspot.co.uk/2011/10/spinning-and-wool-preparation.html

  www.youtube.com/watch?v=7gXTWgMeMgI

- Can you make a piece of Anglo-Saxon embroidery or a small garment?

  Messent (2010) is a wonderful book.

- Can you make Anglo-Saxon clothes?

  Three simple lessons are given at http://anglosaxondiscovery.ashmolean.org/teachers _resources/resources-lessons.html

Women in the Church: St Hilda, d. 684 CE – challenge

- Read Bede's account of St Hilda (Doull 2016: 24). Find out more about her www.bbc.co.uk/programmes/p0144xrk.

- Look at some images of St Hilda (Google search images St Hilda).

- Design a modern wall-hanging to commemorate St Hilda. Will you show her as a nun, a princess? How will you show what kind of a person she was, based on the evidence in Bede?

Women in court: Aethelflaed, wife of King Alfred, sister of King Edward

- Read about Aethelflaed (in Table 10.4) and do further research.

- Make a banner about her to take to a rally of modern feminists.

How did a professor's enjoyment of history begin?

Justin Champion is Professor of the History of Early Modern Ideas, at Royal Holloway College, London University – where I read history, as it happens. Champion (2017) identifies five things that 'ignited his passion for history', at a very young age. First, visiting castles, on holidays in the Welsh Borders. 'The idea of being in places of antiquity, where battles were fought, and men and women from distant times had lived and died, literally kept me awake at night. I wondered always what might have happened on the exact spot I was sleeping on.' Second, living in a city with historic buildings – Cambridge. Third, he enjoyed his local museum (which, in his case, was the Fitzwilliam). Fourth, he loved historical fiction; he mentions *Eagle of the Ninth* (Sutcliffe 2004) and *Viking Sunset* (Treece 1985). And fifth, he loved historical films. In 1970 he saw the film *Cromwell*, starring Richard Harris and Alec Guiness. 'The image of Archbishop Laud nibbling at William Prynne's ear was a visceral and enduring image for a 9-year-old.' So Professor Champion was excited, as a young boy, by castles and Medieval buildings, by ancient artefacts, ceramics and gold objects in a museum. Emulate Professor Champion and excite and inspire young children, as he was inspired.

What do teachers enjoy about history?

The *Cambridge Review* (Alexander 2010) found that teachers and children enjoy history because it involves activities and 'hands-on' experiences, so the next section presents more examples of hands-on activities.

Connecting with the past through hands-on activities

An Egyptian day

I visited this class on the very last day of these children's time in primary school, and the culmination of a project on Ancient Egypt (Capita *et al*. 2000). The children and teacher were elaborately dressed in costumes they had made at home, by copying wall paintings or artists' illustrations in books. The girls had spent much time on exotic eye make-up; one explained how the cone on her head was designed to drop perfume throughout the day! Anubis had to remove his dog's head to speak, and a rich merchant proudly displayed his replica jewellery and his slaves. They were working in rotating groups to investigate a variety of questions about Ancient Egypt. It was multidimensional, and involved 'playing with ideas' in mathematics, language, art, science and technology. James was using 3D shapes to try to find out how pyramids were constructed; Shelley and John were making puppets of an Egyptian prince and princess in order to re-enact a story written by an Egyptian scribe 3,000 years ago, in which the son of an Egyptian king wooed and won the daughter of the King of Naharin by leaping high enough to reach her in her tall tower.

Paul and friends were playing senet. Andrea, Jack and James were designing mummy cases, looking in books to get ideas for the sort of patterns to use. Levi made a model shaduf and Jason was sitting in the sunshine grinding seeds using a quern. Laura and her friends were writing a diary account of a farming family over ten years, suggesting how their lives might have been affected each year by different levels of flooding of the Nile, which were determined by a dice game.

Another activity involved a group of girls using sources, found in wall paintings, books, video and on the internet, to construct an account of an Egyptian banquet, which was audio-taped for a 'radio programme' – 'Ancient Egypt'. When I met them they were discussing the myth of Isis and Osiris and, in particular, with 11-year-old knowingness, how Isis became pregnant:

'After all Osiris had died – AND he was away a lot; we shall never find out.'

'There are different versions. In one version she turned into a kite and flew over his body. We didn't believe that one!'

I was visiting the school with Dr Laura Capita, a Romanian colleague, who was fascinated. Reflecting on the lesson (Capita *et al.* 2000) she wrote that the English teacher's approach to teaching Ancient Egypt is quite different from classroom practice in Romania, mainly because the students are involved in the activities. The use of drama stimulates much more discussion than debate and the use of primary sources as a basis for drama re-enactment is interesting and is able to satisfy scholars' demands. Students team up and develop a holistic approach to history. The student-centred perspective allows them to develop their own perspective on a topic. Pupils use information which is relevant to their interests and the 'abstract' character of history is avoided. The development of communication skills should, in my opinion, underpin activities.

King of the Nile

This is based on the ideas of teachers in the previous edition of *History 5–11* (Cooper 2012: 57). One teacher's class explored gender in contemporary and ancient societies, as well as spirituality. Their teacher took them to see a play about Hatshepsut, an Egyptian woman who became a Pharoah. Another teacher, whose class also saw the play became so inspired that they wrote and performed a play, complete with painted backcloths, about Hatshepsut. The play this class saw is no longer running but there are several videos telling Hatshepsut's story, which raise interesting questions with no clear answers and have brilliant footage of Egypt and of the remains of her palaces, which could be equally inspiring. https://discoveringegypt.com/ancient–egyptian–kings–queens/hatshepsut/e

There is also an interesting book on Hatchepsut: Tyldesley J. (1998) *Hatchepsut*; *The Female Pharoah*, London: Penguin.

Connecting with the past through constructing a tableau

Children research the background to an event shown in a painting or photograph. I have done this as a workshop for student teachers, which was quite different from the ways in which they were used to learning history. They participated brilliantly and thoroughly enjoyed the experience. The first group was in Curitiba, in Brazil the second in Yaroslavl, in Russia.

Brazil

In Curitiba, I borrowed an idea from Sue Temple (Temple 2017: 58) and used a painting, which shows a variety of 'down-and outs' from different backgrounds, waiting for a bed for the night in a workhouse, in nineteenth-century London (*Applications for Admission to the Casual Ward* by Luke Fildes 1874; www.workhouses.org.uk/lit/Fildes)

This seemed to have been similar to the situation in Curitiba at the time. Each character represents a typical person: an 'adventurer' asking directions from a policeman, a mother with a black cloak, perhaps a widow or unmarried mother, a burglar, a workman with his sick wife and family, a drunken 'aristocrat' who has probably gambled on his way home and a family who have lost their lodgings. Students each chose one of the characters and made up their background narrative about why they were waiting at the workhouse. Participants in each tableau were questioned, in turn, about why they found themselves in this situation. This required imagination, based on the facts and knowledge of the urban poor in the nineteenth century.

Russia

In Yaroslavl, I projected a painting by Kustodiev, celebrating Shrovetide in a Russian provincial town. www.jigidi.com/jigsaw-puzzle/18FYBM4H/Boris-Kustodiev-Shrove-Tide-1919. First we decoded the painting.

(i)   Starting to engage with the picture

What is the painting about?
Principle features?
What people can you see? Who do you think they are?
Where are they? Why?
What are they doing? Why?
What do their gestures suggest?
Are there any letters, numbers? What do they tell us?

(ii) Details

What can we deduce about . . . ?
What are they wearing? Therefore . . .
What buildings can you see?
Shops – therefore . . .
Church – therefore . . .
Fair – therefore . . .
Transport – therefore . . .

(iii) What can we infer about people's thoughts, feelings? What might they be talking about? What sounds might you hear?

(iv) What would you like to know?

(v)   Historical imagination

At this point the students formed groups, representing the groups of people in the painting: people in the foreground talking, those on the sleigh, those outside the shop, waiting to go into the theatre or returning from church. Each person developed their character then their group interpreted the conversations these diverse people may have been having. The group conversations were enacted in turn for the rest of the class. They displayed a good interpretation of provincial Russian society in the nineteenth century, the weather, the celebration and likely local gossip. It was hilarious. I pointed out that they were interpreting an historical source and making deductions and inferences from it, which is what historians do.

Later we discussed time concepts: compared the painting with contemporary images of Maslenitsa (Shrove Tuesday), the similarities/differences now and then, continuity and changes, causes and effects. Finally, we considered the painting, the source, as an interpretation. Who painted it? When? Why was it painted? How valid is it as an historical source? Are there contradictory images? This was a very informed and open discussion – and a total novelty to these students, who participated enthusiastically. Later I was asked to comment on a masterclass on Stalin. The teaching approach was somewhat different.

Connecting with the past through drama

How, you may ask, will this, a painting of Pancake day in Russia, help me teach pre-history and early British history? Well I had one class of 8-year-old children who had projected slides of cave paintings onto the wall, then painted the projected images with oxides from the pottery area (paint and charcoal would be fine). We had also been reading *The Changeling* (Sutcliff 1974) about the abduction of a baby from a tribe in Ancient Britain.

Inspired by the cave painting as a background and by the story, a group of children developed a detailed story which involved, I remember, the hunting of a deer, a near death and a recovery involving health-giving herbs, mixed in clay pots which the children had made and fired in the school kiln. The recovery was aided by a ritual dance of supplication to the gods, accompanied by 'Stone Age' instruments. The children decided to present this for an assembly, held in the drama studio, in a dramatically dark 'cave'. They had created this without adult intervention, mostly during their lunch hours.

The Stone Ages in Britain and in Japan: Making connections

I was working recently with a Japanese friend who is researching the aims and methods of history education in England and comparing it with history taught in Japan. She was investigating whether primary school children in Japan, who learn selected historical facts in a very didactic way, would be able to make deductions and inferences from historical sources. We devised a PowerPoint® lesson using sides of artefacts from Sannai Maruyama, a Stone Age site on the Northern end of Honshu Island, in Japan, where, 6,000–4,300 years ago, people lived by hunting and gathering.

We taught the lesson to a Year 6 class in Cumbria, and Japanese teachers, working with my friend Hideyo, taught it to several classes of 11-year-old children in Southern

Japan. The Japanese children used a timeline (1 metre represents 500 years) to put the period into the context of their history. All the classes discussed images of (reconstructed) sources: a pit dwelling, made by covering a hole in the ground with bark and branches, another pit dwelling which was a large communal building, the contents of a rubbish tip, a decorated pot and a structure reconstructed from post-holes, the meaning of which is not known.

The children were asked the same questions about each source. What do you know *for certain*? What can *you guess*? What would you *like to know*? (Familiar? See Chapter 12.) There was a whole-class discussion of the first slide, followed by group notes recording small group discussions of the second slide, paired discussions of the third slide, and finally individual completion of an 'Archaeologist's Record Sheet'. Although this approach was totally novel to the Japanese teachers and children, they all said they enjoyed it very much. (The English teacher was so kind as to say it would be regarded by Ofsted – who had just inspected the school – as 'an outstanding lesson'. Well, I was once invited to be an Ofsted inspector – but declined . . .). The data were analysed and it revealed that the Japanese children had just as many valid and imaginative deductions and inferences as the English class. The only part of the lesson they were not so good at was the final activity; in four groups, silently, to mime people living in a pit dwelling house, in a communal meeting house, making the pot and collecting rubbish for the tip. The Japanese children had no experience of such a plenary activity, which was intended to see what they had understood. A Japanese professor who was observing asked, 'Whatever are they doing this for?' The English children knew exactly what was expected and provided some brilliant ideas; for example two children created the tiny doorway of a pit dwelling and the third demonstrated how it must have been entered, and another group made and fired a pot, then it was dropped and broke, so it was taken to the tip.

Creating accounts

Connecting with the past by creating accounts through pictures

Charlotte Mason, writing at the beginning of the twentieth century (Mason 1993, vol. 1: 294), showed that if children draw pictures as accounts

> The drawings of the children in question are psychologically interesting, showing what various and sometimes obscure points appeal to the mind of a child and also that children have the same intellectual pleasure as persons of cultivated mind in working out new hints and suggestions.

Connecting with the past through model-making

Models based on evidence are themselves interpretations, particularly if they are informed reconstructions of ruined buildings. We may have the ground plan of a Roman villa or the post-hole plan of an Iron Age hut for example. Researching what the building may have looked like and making a model can involve all the processes of historical enquiry to produce a valid interpretation.

Connecting with the past through drama

Challenging enquiries may be presented as role play, drama or video/audio-recorded for a radio or television programme. The enquiry may be researched to create a biography of an individual (for example, King Canute), to investigate a newspaper account (perhaps of a recently reported archaeological dig), or an excerpt from a document. Michael Wood's videos, King Alfred and the Anglo-Saxons, based on film combined with readings from the Anglo-Saxon Chronicle, are an inspiration (see Chapter 4, p. 194) The Great British Story, a Peoples History, (Episode 1, from the end of the Roman Empire to the coming of the Saxons and Episode 2, which, through the eyes of ordinary people, explores how the English, Scots and Irish nations emerged due to the impact of the Vikings) are equally brilliant models. (They are all very reasonably priced from the BBC Store; www.store.bbc.com.) They may inspire a documentary programme discussing an artefact, a place, a Saxon house or church if there is one in the locality or a visual source. Perhaps a statue of Boudicca on Victoria Embankment would stimulate preparation for a television discussion: who was she, did she represent the British tribes, did she win against great odds, who made the statue, what did she look like, how realistic is it, why did Prince Albert have the statue made, why would a rebel against the Roman Empire glorify the British Empire?

Finding the past in your locality

In *Bringing History Alive through Local People and Places*, Dixon and Hales (2014) draw on conversations with children, which reveal the impact of local and community history on a child's personal identity. *Children, Their World, Their Education* (Alexander 2010: 262–263) argues that primary schools should respect and build on children's non-school learning, experience and capability, that the local component encourages this and that communities have massive potential in this regard. It fosters relations between children who may come from different backgrounds. It takes account of their interests and is well-stocked with stimulating material. The Rose Report (Department for Children Schools and Families (DCSF) 2009) said that every subject should begin with 30 per cent local content. A depth study linked to one of the British areas of study is an obvious way of working with the community. Local studies are discussed further in Chapter 8.

Local archaeology

First there are many local organizations you can consult about local archaeological sites. The Association of Local Government Archaeological Officers (ALGEO) represents archaeologists working for local authorities and national parks. Members embrace all aspects of the historic environment including archaeology, the built environment and historic landscapes. Collectively members provide a range of outreach and community activities to increase understanding of the historic environment, including education resources (www.algao.org.uk/localgov/community). Contact addresses for your local archaeological officer can be found at: www.algao.org.uk/membership. The Council for British Archaeology aim to promote participation and archaeology for all: http://new.archaeologyuk.org/join-a-cba-group and contact addresses for local group can be found at http://new.archaeologyuk.org/join-a-cba-group. The Council for British Archaeology (CBA) is an educational charity working throughout the UK, which aims to involve people in archaeology and the historic environment: http://new.archaeologyuk.org/discover/

Ancient local words

Many Anglo-Saxon, Viking and Celtic words are still in use today in localities where they settled. Children like to trace how their areas are directly linked to the immigrant groups from c. 500 to 1066 CE. Words used today seem to put us in touch with our Anglo-Saxon, Viking and Celtic roots. Predominance of certain words in particular areas links us to specific aspects of the settlement of Britain, but more widespread usage shows how these languages became integrated across Britain. Melvyn Bragg (2003) has traced the origins of the buried words that he is proud to claim as his Cumbrian dialect: 'Aah's gaan yem'. *Gaan* was an Anglo-Saxon word, to go, and was known to the Vikings; *yem* means home in Scandinavia, *heim* in Old Norse. As for 'laik in t beck'; *leik* is Old Norse for play and *bekkr* for stream, still beck in Cumbria. Bragg, as a child, used Anglo-Saxon and Celtic words, crag, tor, pen and some Romany from the annual gypsy fair, which harks back to an Indian dialect of Sanskrit, *gadji* for man and *parnee* for rain. One Cumbrian school started looking for Viking words in their own speech, then went on to a place-name study as the beginning of a unit on the Vikings. Words still used, which have Viking roots, are given at www.babbel.com/en/magazine/139-norse-words and at www.ibiblio.org/lineback/words/letter_a.htm. The Anglo-Saxons never reached Kernow (Cornwall) of course and the original Celtic inhabitants spoke their own language until Tudor times.

In Norfolk, Joe Mason writes, 'spink, the Norfolk word for finch, was unique to our dialect, but in fact the word occurs in dialects as far north as Scotland. It is an Anglo-Saxon word, that survived in the Norfolk speech far longer than elsewhere'. He continues, saying that many of the words we regard as Norfolk's own dialect are in fact Anglo-Saxon; many others like *staithe* (a landing-place), *flag* (yellow iris, preserved in the Flegg district of South-East Norfolk) and *group* (a shallow trench) are Danish, reflecting the ninth-century occupation of East Anglia by the Vikings (https://joemasons page.wordpress.com/2015/02/07/norfolk-dialect).

Many words with Anglo-Saxon origins can be found at www.collinsdictionary.com/word-lovers-blog/word-origins/anglo-saxon-words,7,HCB.html. Word meanings, second names and place-name origins can be found on the internet.

An aspect of a significant site from beyond 1066

In addition to archaeology there are many heritage organizations, related to, for example industrial heritage and landscapes (including historic houses, ancient monuments): http://heritagehelp.org.uk/organisations/category/architecture. English Heritage has a strong educational focus and has 400 sites and excellent videos and other resources (www.english-heritage.org.uk/learn/school-visits/). Local archives and libraries are another essential resource to support local studies. Themes and aspects of history extending chronological knowledge beyond 1066 may well have local sources relevant to the theme or to a turning point in British history, in which case the locality would be a good starting point.

Local heritage site and family history

Pat Lewis, a teacher in Blaenavon in South Wales, makes clear to her pupils that their town has the same historical status as the pyramids or the Great Wall of China (Saunders 2004). A similar study could be undertaken in any of Britain's industrial areas as a *very* significant turning point in British history or as a study of an aspect of history dating from beyond 1066 or as part of a longer project on changes in aspects of social history, from a largely agricultural society through an industrial society to a post industrial society.

Blaenavon is a World Heritage site recognized for the dynamic part it played in the world's first Industrial Revolution, the powerhouse of the British Empire. It had coal, iron ore, quarries, furnaces and a primitive railway system. 'It's the part they and their families have played and are playing that makes it so special,' she said. The children have family histories, stories, photographs and artefacts. Following a cross-curricular project that included history and science (exploring types of forces and energy), art (working with an artist to produce costumes, flats for the school play and paintings of the locality), music (taking part in the Eisteddfod), citizenship (exploring regeneration plans) and language of different genres, children took part in a *son et lumière* held through the town, playing the parts of nineteenth-century children. To prepare for the event children invited historians and archaeologists into the school to help them research the history of iron and its impact on the Industrial Revolution. Useful resources about the Blaenavon iron and coal industries can be found online (www.newportsouthwales.net/revolution).

Working with parents, families and the local community

Working with parents

I always invited parents into school before beginning a topic to explain to them the topic we would be studying, why and how. This encouraged their interest, led them to discuss it with their children and to support it in different ways; joining us on visits, working on it in school in different ways that needed extra support such as pottery, model-making, book-making. Often they became personally involved and learned with their children, planned their own visits, watched relevant television programmes and discussed them. Some parents had valuable local knowledge to contribute.

I told the children and their parents what the study unit on the school's long-term plan would be and discussed possibilities of what we could focus on, teaching approaches we could use, what might be particularly interesting to the children and what parents and their community contacts might be able to offer. From this it was possible to frame a group of key questions and possible ways of investigating them. This would feed into an overarching enquiry, a medium-term plan within which smaller studies by individuals and groups could contribute in different ways, concluding with some form of account, display, presentation or drama for parents and others involved. Everyone would understand and monitor the learning objectives of the medium-term plan and how these were broken down into learning objectives for the smaller studies. If the unit was taught over a number of weeks the children and adults could review and modify the medium-term plan weekly. Even if the unit was taught as a block, perhaps preparing for and following up a visit, there were constant instances of children deciding to do things differently. When they continue it at home, as previously said, you know they ARE enjoying it!

I remember one 8-year-old child who had to get herself off to school because her parents were at work, telling me that she had read her 'Beowulf Poem' to the milkman (hem); another child had given her grandparents an impressive guided tour of Norwich Cathedral, modelled on a class visit to Canterbury; and one boy, when told by his mother about a television programme on Maiden Castle that she had watched the previous evening, said, 'But Mum, what was the *evidence* for that?'

Involving families

> To forget one's ancestors is to be a brook without a source, a tree without a root.
> (Old Chinese proverb)

Given the internet resources now available, researching family history has become very popular among adults and might become a way into a history topic for all the family. A useful website for young people is www.ffhs.org.uk/general/youngpeople.htm.

Working with the school community

Other members of the school community enjoyed being included. In groups, throughout a topic, children made a lunch using recipe from the historical period studied, with the help of a parent. The Iron Age lunch, based on the evidence that they had wild root vegetables and Soay sheep, was a mutton stew. Guests were invited to share lunch by each group: the school nurse, the local policeman, a librarian, a school governor. This required social skills, language skills and responsibility – especially when it came to washing up.

Working with older people in the locality

A Darby and Joan club could maybe teach children old dances and games as well as be willing interviewees, in which case you may spend a lot of time on changes in living memory. You may have children whose families are of other cultural heritages who could help select and find out about 'significant men and women' or past events from the wider world. You may be flexible enough to see where and for how long the children and their resources take the enquiry. You may discuss your options with parents, or the local history or photographic society or, for example, the Cumbrian wrestlers club.

Cross-cultural links throughout history

The struggle to succeed has faced each generation of immigrants: Ancient Britons from Central Europe (40,000 BC), Celts (7000 BC), Romans (AD 43), the Norsemen, the Normans, the 2,000 black people living and working in Elizabethan London, seventeenth-century Huguenots, nineteenth-century Irish, Russians and Jews. In the twenty-first century, Britain is the home of people with many different ethnic backgrounds. A combination of British history integrated, as it is, with international and global history may, perhaps make the process of assimilation easier. Chapter 8 illustrates ways in which Britain was connected, from the earliest times with global movements, interactions and patterns. In selecting people and events at Key Stage 1 and in developing a Local Study, a Theme of British History, an ancient civilization and a non-European Study, whatever your locality, it is important to take 'The Big Picture' into consideration.

Making contemporary cross-cultural links

Sensitive issues need to be dealt with in an atmosphere of trust by sensitive teachers. A democratic model needs to be set up where everyone is free to speak, subject to an understood code of conduct. Draw out similarities and differences slowly, as you go, and make sure that the lessons are structured and grounded in the curriculum. Evaluate the effectiveness of the cultural diversity aspect by asking children to reflect on changes in their thinking.

Pupils should be taught about the social, cultural, religious and ethnic diversity of societies studied. Pupils should learn about change in their own area and in other parts of the world. Hilary Claire points out that the Race Relations Amendment Act of 2000 means that 'teachers must pro-actively strive in the curriculum towards inclusion of minority cultures, take responsibility and work to reduce racial tension and prejudice, paying more than lip service to a wider inclusive curriculum which challenges racism and Euro-centrism' (Claire 2002, 2003, 2005).

This means giving every child, and particularly children in mono-cultural environments, a sense of their own identity and worth, tolerance of diversity and understanding of local, national and global connections. Children need to learn about their own, and other children's, heritage, about life in the places their families lived before, and why families move around.

Insider/outsider?

The Parekh Report (2000) on the future of multicultural Britain has suggested that the position of the Irish in Britain as 'insider/outsiders' is uniquely relevant to the nature of Britain's multicultural society; the experience of 8 million citizens of Irish stock has been neglected owing to the myth of homogeneity of white Britain. This can be a particularly useful introduction to cultural diversity where there is not much cultural mix in schools. Year 3 children can easily relate to the plight of a woman (in role) as an Irish mother during the famine and this understanding can be extrapolated to other areas of famine.

At Wilberforce School, in London, Year 2 children worked with Hilary Claire and their teachers, using role play, to discuss three significant black people: the black aviator Bessie Coleman, Ruby Bridges, who went to an integrated school during the American civil rights movement, and Frederick Douglass, a slave who escaped to become an important figure in the abolition movement. The older children tackled issues such as racism, with help from visitors who talked about their own childhoods. One arrived in Britain from the Caribbean in the 1950s and the other was a refugee from Nazi Germany.

Artefacts from ancient civilizations in the British Museum

Teaching these ancient civilizations as part of 'The Big Picture' of history is developed in Chapter 8.

Ancient Sumer

The Sumerian treasures in the British Museum are fantastic: the Ancient Sumer excavation of the city of Ur in the 1920s by C. Leonard Woolley, the discovery of the tombs and their contents, offer revealing insights into daily life in Ur. As a challenge pupils play a game found by Woolley in a tomb at Ur (www.mesopotamia.co.uk/tombs/home_set.html), and they can address questions about the tombs. Other sources include https://traveltoeat.com/sumerian-treasures-of-urbritish-museum-london/, www.zipang.org.uk/teachers/SumerIntro.pdf and www.twinkl.co.uk/resources/ks2-history-ancient-sumer.

The Indus Valley

It is possible to explore the Indus Valley Civilization and an archaeologist's notebook showing images of what was found there and fascinating notes, *raising questions* about the artefacts, a fictional story about a bead-maker's son, and a *challenge*, to identify pots you find as an archaeologist. Publications for active learning about the Indus Valley at Key Stage 2 and replica artefacts can be found online (www.harappa.com/teach). Resources include cross-curricular activities such as making and testing terracotta wheeled toy carts, board games and a DVD made when Mohenjo-Daro became a World Heritage Site. Ilona Aronovsky (2014) also gives suggestions for teaching the Indus Valley unit.

Ancient Egypt

The British Museum offers a huge range of resources and courses for teachers and practical sessions for Key Stage 2 about a variety of aspects of life in Ancient Egypt. The sessions explore *questions*. For example how did the book of the dead help people on their journey to the afterlife? How can a painting spark enquiries into many aspects of life in Ancient Egypt? Online PowerPoints® pose *challenges*, about paintings available on line (www.britishmuseum.org/learning/schools_and_teachers/resources/cultures/ancient_egypt.aspx).

The Shang Civilization of Ancient China

The British Museum provides a good information resource for teachers, but this needs to be mediated for use with children. However, good suggestions can be found at www.britishmuseum.org/PDF/Teachers_resource_pack_30_8a.pdf.

Good resources for the Shang Dynasty include http://teachinghistory100.org/objects/about_the_object/shang_bowlw.britishmuseum.org/PDF/Teachers_resource_pack_30_8a.pdf.

Early Islamic Civilizations

The British Museum offers a PowerPoint® study of early Islamic societies, linked to its Islamic Gallery. A new Islamic Gallery (2018) will give visitors 'a new understanding of the diverse and wide-ranging cultures of the Islamic world', to encourage engagement with Islamic art and culture.

Starting with the children's interests

Children need to have a sense of ownership of their environment. This depends on planning a rich variety of themes, play settings and experiences.

Working back from contemporary tastes: music and clothes

Since history involves every aspect of life in the past, we can find out a lot about a particular period from a chosen theme. Individuals or groups of children can select their own theme to research the same questions – for example, how did this change over the period? What were the causes and effects of the changes? – then combine their enquiries to draw overarching conclusions. Tracing changes in popular music and songs as a theme of British history beyond 1066 will involve finding out about changes in technology and in society, finding out where new styles (e.g. jazz) came from and why, and making inferences about changing values and ways of life. Similarly, an interest in clothes might lead to an interest in changes in dress. Here Joanne and her friend in Year 3 are discussing a wedding photograph taken during the Second World War:

> They didn't have much money in the war. They couldn't have new dresses. She's wearing a normal dress like you'd wear to a party. She's got a small bunch of flowers and no veil. They had short dresses so they could run down [to] the shelters.

Let children do things 'their way'

Here is an exemplary tale, which illustrates how children, given the flexibility, will turn a teacher's plans into something that actually interests them – and still meet the teacher's objectives. I was an advisory teacher doing a local study with a Year 6 class based on four buildings in the locality, one of which was the church. 'What do we have to do this for?' two recalcitrant boys dragging along at the end of the line asked, as we trudged through the rain. 'I thought you might like to make a model,' I replied brightly. 'Nah.' Yet a few weeks later they had created a wonderful model of the church, with an indicator board that lit up and explained different parts of the church and its history, 'stained glass' windows that could be illuminated from inside, accompanied by a tape recording explaining the images and church music that played. What makes such activities part of a historical enquiry is the questions we ask – what do they tell us about the people who made and used them? – and seeking other evidence, perhaps from books, which may extend or verify our inferences.

Children and teacher plan a unit of study

Southbank International School in Hampstead uses the International Baccalaureate Organization's Primary Years Programme. This is based on a pupil profile setting out characteristics schools wish to develop and make children aware of in themselves: enquirers, thinkers, communicators, risk-takers who are knowledgeable, principled, caring, well-balanced and reflective. Pupils from three to twelve play a big role in determining what and how they learn. 'You find out what they know and what they want to learn, then you can shape your unit; it's a big leap of faith sometimes', the programme co-ordinator said. For a Year 5 unit on the Saxons, for example, children's questions are posted on a bulletin board. What animals did they have? How did they go to the toilet? If they were wounded what did they do? Did the children go to school? From this starting point the teacher spends some time reflecting with the class on how to answer these questions, using mainly primary sources, and what further questions may arise.

Breadth and depth studies

The Historical Association (2015) (Primary Survey 2016) found that many schools construct breadth studies which include parts of their favourite topics from the previous curriculum. For this reasons, I include the following case studies from the previous edition of this book. The Quarry Bank visit could be used as an inspiration for planning an investigation of the Industrial Revolution as part of a local study or a breadth study after 1066 of the Industrial Revolution. The Southwell Workhouse theme (also see Temple 2017), could be developed as a local study in many areas or as part of a theme of a breadth study of, for example, caring for the poor from Medieval to modern times.

Quarry Bank mill

See www.nationaltrust.org.uk/quarry-bank/features/learning-opportunities-at-quarry-bank.

This visit might be linked to a study of an aspect of 'a turning point in British history', the Industrial Revolution, or developed in school in any pre-industrial city. At Quarry Bank cotton mill in Cheshire the National Trust staff, in role as mill owner or worker, talk about how their lives have been changed by the Industrial Revolution. Then the pupils are divided into groups: handloom weavers and spinners, mill workers and mill owners. They explore issues such as the mill owner whose profits are falling following a slump in business. Does he lower wages or sack workers? What do the weavers and spinners do, threatened by the new water technology? Do they sell up and go to the workhouse, apply for a job at the new mill or protest and break up the machinery? If they do the latter, what will happen? With no police force the army will come in as at Peterloo and they may be killed. The discussion involves questions of social responsibility, political, spiritual, moral and cultural values, empathy, debate and conflict resolution.

The Southwell Union Workhouse

See www.nationaltrust.org.uk/the-workhouse-southwell

This might be part of a theme in British history that extends pupils' chronological knowledge beyond 1066. The theme might be, for example, 'Who cares for the poor' with focuses on Medieval monastic care, Tudor sturdy beggars, almshouses bequested by benefactors, the Victorian workhouse and the Welfare State. In the Workhouse, Southwell, social change, human rights and responsibilities, employer and employee rights, conflict resolution and moral and social dilemmas are debated by the children in role as workhouse inmates. In prioritizing wants and needs they need to consider where to place freedom of expression or freedom to practise their own religion. They debate issues such as child labour, adopting the role of mill owners, pauper children and social reformers. The exercise is illustrated with case studies, statistics and contemporary photographs. (Planning is discussed in Chapters 9 and 10.)

Part 1 of this book, on the processes of historical enquiry, followed by examples in this chapter of how enjoyable enquiries connect us to past times, leads well into Chapter 6, which shows how historical enquiry is inevitably creative – and who does not enjoy creativity?

6

Connections between historical enquiry and creativity

Creativity involves making connections between things that may appear unconnected: collaborative enquiries and activities generate new ideas through team-work and discussion; historical imagination creates hypotheses; risk-taking suggests probabilities that have to be defended.

This chapter recognizes the tensions created by a perceived emphasis on English and mathematics but argues that teaching history must inevitably be creative, and that this requires time for problem-solving, hypothetical thinking based on knowledge, discussion and reflection. It analyses what is meant by creativity, and the ways in which creativity is intrinsically meshed with the processes of historical enquiry, supported by examples from practice. Next it considers the teachers' dispositions and the school ethos necessary to implement creativity. Then it discusses case studies, in which aspects of historical enquiry are integrated with creativity and illustrated in practice. It concludes with medium–term plans, which illustrate planning for the various aspects of creativity.

Tensions in teaching creatively

One head teacher said recently that history should be kept simple, following the basics of the programme of study, because she did not see history as a priority when the school's literacy results were mediocre and staff were already exhausted with the focus on the core subjects. The Cambridge Review (Alexander 2010) recognizes these tensions. It states that 'creativity, the arts and the humanities continue to cling by their fingertips, in the primary phase, especially in Years 5 and 6' (p. 44). Teachers have warned that, forced by the constraints of the curriculum, their creativity, imagination, expertise and confidences are being undermined (p. 499). The Review regrets that in these severely utilitarian times it has become necessary to argue the case for creativity and the imagination, on grounds of their contribution to the economy alone (p. 199).

The case for the creative teaching of history

However, the Cambridge Review (2014–2016) emphasizes the intrinsic value of exciting children's imagination, saying that to experience the delights and pains of imagining and of entering into the imaginative worlds of others is to become a more rounded person. Many submissions to the Cambridge Review put creativity 'at the heart of the curriculum' (p. 138), because it is linked with empowering children, through shared experiences and collaboration (pp. 64–67) and 'a vital aspect of cognitive and social functioning' (p. 99). Creativity, it is argued, is a cognitively demanding process, which supports perseverance and problem-solving and enhances children's moral and social development (p. 191). It claims that it is important to excite children's imagination in order for them to advance beyond their present understanding, extend the boundaries of their lives, comprehend worlds possible as well as actual, understand cause and consequence (p. 199) and 'develop understanding through enquiry' (p. 296).

Creativity and historical enquiry are interdependent

This section argues that good history teaching is intrinsically creative. It examines the criteria which define creativity, based on extensive literature, then shows how these are reflected in the processes of historical enquiry. It considers the classroom ethos and organization necessary and gives illustrative examples from case studies with which to foster creativity.

Creativity involves generating ideas. Craft *et al.* (2001: 45–61; Craft and Jeffrey 2008) make a distinction between the 'high creativity' of, for example Einstein or Tolstoy, at one end of a continuum and creativity with a small 'c', which may be simply ideas new to a person's thinking, which anyone can learn to generate. The key criteria for creativity are

- curiosity, identifying problems and asking questions, being-open-minded, possibility thinking (see creativity literature below);

- generating new ideas (or creative behaviour, without necessarily producing a product (Scruton 1974);

- imagination (Elliott 1971; Passmore 1980; Kenny 1989), risk-taking (a can-do approach);

- acting both individually (Leach 2001) and collaboratively (Craft 2005);

- knowledge of the enquiry processes of a subject (knowing how) and knowledge of subject content (knowing that) (Ryle 1979). Children's knowledge of both kinds depends on age and ability (Dewey 1933; Montessori 1949; Kant 1989);

- connectivity, making connections between what may appear unconnected (Nichol 2017a).

Each of these criteria will be considered in turn, with examples of its application to practice.

Curiosity, identifying problems and asking questions, being-open-minded and possibility thinking

Being curious requires taking *time to reflect*. Kounios and Beeman (2006), using neuro-science technology, found that this reflection involves first an intense mental search, which may seem negative, but is followed by a mental shift to explore new insights which have arisen, *identifying problems*. Through this process of reflection (which in fact involves intense mental activity), we generate questions to investigate *problems*. These may give rise to *new questions* (Gardner 1999; Craft 2002). Asking problematic questions requires being *open-minded* to new information (Langer 1997), the tenacity to pursue, and being prepared to accept that there may not be a right answer. Open-mindedness involves thinking about probabilities and possibilities and alternative interpretations, which must have a perceived goal. Generating ideas may lead to creative behaviour and creative action, experimentation and innovation (Levin and Nolan 2004). Langer (1997) calls possibility thinking 'mindful learning', which, he says, is a state of mind. Reflecting on subject matter while processing information sees it from different perspectives, which means that learning is absorbed and can be used in a new context, so that learners are empowered to make learning their own (Bruner 1963, 1966 endorsed here). Cremin *et al.* (2006) see this as the crux of creative thinking.

In history, Collingwood (1939) defines the process of asking questions. He saw this as beginning with a sequence of ordered, specific questions about sources: who made them, why, what did they mean to the people who made and used them? This leads to new questions or to hypotheses about the society that created them. The third stage is 'what else would we like to know?' Each of these stages involves probability thinking, the ability to consider alternatives, to think 'what if' or 'what might have happened'. In the National Curriculum (DfE 2013: 3) this is referred to as the ability 'to address and sometimes devise historically valid questions . . . and construct informed responses through thoughtful selection and organization of historical information . . . from a range of sources'.

Curiosity, identifying problems, asking questions and open-mindedness in practice; generating new ideas

The medium-term plans in Tables 10.1–10.3 involve each of these criteria. Alternatively, they could be turned around so that the enquiries test a hypothesis: that there was little change during the Stone Age, that Roman Britain was a wild and barbaric place, or that Alfred was a great king; children set out to test the hypothesis, which may cause them to change their thinking. A Welsh case study illustrates ways in which children did research which challenged their thinking and resulted in weighing the evidence and reaching different conclusions. It could be transferred to other conflict situations in a longitudinal, local study after 1066 (Harnett *et al.* 2014: 121–127). Children

(9–11-years-old) investigate who they think was responsible for the riots of coal miners in Tonypandy in 1911. After investigating coal-mining history through a visit to the local museum and watching a television programme to stimulate their curiosity, they collected data from a variety of sources, discussed and critically evaluated it. This led them to generate their own thoughtful conclusions, weighing the relative responsibilities of the miners, the mine owners and the police.

Acting collaboratively to generate new ideas

The following examples illustrate the collaborative process in generating new ideas.

Examples of children's discussions

Figure 11.8 illustrates how children can generate new ideas through discussion. It gives an extract from a discussion in which a group of 8-year-olds discuss what they know and, following on from that, what they can infer, from images of Stone Age tools.

Enquiries explored through collaborative activities

Enquiries are not limited to discussion or research followed by discussion. They may be carried out through activities, which may be what is generally thought of as 'creative', through drama, making models or replica artefacts, drawing and painting. But such activities can rightly be regarded as an enjoyable indulgence if their purpose is not to investigate an historical question. However, Moore (2017: 80–84) describes an activity making a Roman shield. It begins with asking questions 'What did shields look like? How were they used? How big were they? How were they decorated? When were they used?' Moore refers to websites which quote sources where this information can be researched.

- http://artgallery.yale.edu/collections/objects/5959

- http://trajans-column.org

- https://the-qrcode-generator.com

- www.britishmuseum.org/research/collection_online/collection_object_details.aspx?assetld=600632001&object=1363156&partld=1

Making several shields would make it possible to replicate the testudo formation, the Roman tortoise (http://primaryhomeworkhelp.co.uk/romans/formation.html).

Dodwell (2017: 136–144) shows how children can research what a place was like in a particular period and share their ideas, in order to construct a drama. Sources for a drama set in Roman or Anglo-Saxon Britain are given in Temple (2017: 99–101). Nichol (2017: 65–67) shows how children can discuss the question 'Why did the Vikings leave home and settle abroad?' through a carefully planned re-enactment. The plans can be found www.history.org.uk/primary/categories/765/module/3694/romans-anglo-saxons-and-vikings/3701/the-thing-and-viking-migration.

Creativity involves historical imagination

Imagination involves the ability to imagine a variety of possibilities and so, is essential to creativity (Craft 2002). This is a thought process that establishes a new idea, seeing other possibilities. Imagination produces outcomes that are original and valuable. The National Advisory Committee on Creative and Cultural Education (DfEE 1999) and Passmore (1980) differentiate between imagining as some form of mental image (imagining as supposing that something is the case, hypothesizing and imagining another's perspective) and being imaginative (creating a novel outcome). It has been claimed that imagination is superior to intellect because it makes it possible to build up new worlds. 'The objects of imagination are created, not discovered; it is disciplined not fanciful' (Kenny 1989: 114). Being imaginative means going beyond the obvious and seeing more than is initially apparent, or interpreting something in a way that is unusual; to proceed imaginatively is to be creative (Elliott 1971). If enquiry is concerned with people imagination will include empathy, the capacity to imagine, based on what is known, how someone else may behave, think and feel in a given situation.

In history, imagination is also 'disciplined'. It must be based on evidence, conform with what is known about the relevant period and be a possibility: is it possible/likely? Evidence is often incomplete and sometimes the symbolism of objects has been forgotten. Is a Saxon sword symbolic, and if so what does it symbolize? We probably have no evidence of the thoughts and feelings of people who lived in the past. Elton (1970) saw historical imagination as 'a tool for filling in the gaps when facts are not available'. In history, Passmore's (1980) definition of imagining as hypothesizing can be applied to probability thinking about sources, how they were made and used and what they meant to the people who made and used them, or to hypothesize about a sequence of events, causes and consequences of actions, or the behaviour of an individual or a group and their possible feelings and thoughts, based on what we know of their behaviour and the society they lived in. Passmore's definition of 'being imaginitive' in history reflects combining sources to produce a novel outcome, creating an account or interpretation.

Examples of imagination in history

Eight-year-olds discuss a replica of a Saxon sceptre in the British Museum (Cooper 1991). They interpret it within the framework of their knowledge of animals in Anglo-Saxon art, the uncertainty of Anglo-Saxon life, the need for loyalty and tales of boastful leaders (Beowulf) and what they had learned of kingship, power, law and succession.

P. The golden deer may be saying save our lives or where we live.
C. Maybe the deer is a symbol of something to do with animals.
D. Or the stag may be a symbol of good luck; they wanted good luck because they were always fighting.

A. It may be a symbol of loyalty; they had kings, so they had to be obedient. So maybe it was a symbol of power. It was hard to make, and precious; it must be unique.

R. Was it to make people think he had power to rule? Would the people think it ruled their minds? I expect he was friends with other Saxon kings. I expect his father and grandfather were crowned with it to show they were kings.

K. I guess it could have been a gift from his government; if so he had a good government, he was a good king and hard worker.

E. Was it a symbol because they were finding different religions?

Risk-taking

Considering possibilities which are open to different interpretations, requires children to listen to the views of others, to consider ideas which are not predictable and to have their thinking candidly challenged. They may need to make choices from conflicting suggestions. Possibility thinking requires confidence and tolerance but is essential to social and emotional development.

This excerpt from a group of 8-year-olds discussing Strabo's (Geography, Vol. 2, Bk 4, Ch. 5) description of Roman Britain shows how children took risks, in making suggestions and how others in the group gently corrected them if they were factually incorrect.

F. They couldn't write in the Iron Age.

G. Well Strabo could.

T. Where did he come from?

M. France? Germany?

G. No, he came from Rome I imagine.

G. They got the gold and silver out of the rock.

J. So they could disintegrate things.

T. No they could *smelt* things . . .

Acting both individually and collaboratively

There has been analysis of the ways in which discussion and working collaboratively can foster creativity through communication. It starts with a problem (this is important) and may result in a novel product, for example a drama, model or work of art. Collaboration works through developing a shared understanding; only thoughts which are spoken are important and everyone must contribute verbally. Leach (2001) sees creative learning as a social process expressed in team work. Bredo (1994), Lave and Wenger (1991) and Rogoff (1999) researched this process of learning as situated social practice, arguing that it depends on interaction with others and with materials. Craft (2005), however, also recognizes the importance of individual creativity.

Examples of collaboration in history

It is important that the reason for collaboration is to investigate, although not necessarily solve, a historical problem. Research has been done to analyse this process through collaboration in history, although not, I think in drama or creating an artwork or a model. Yet such activities are common in practice. The Key Stage 1 investigation, 'What was Kendal Castle like in the days of Katherine Parr?' (Figures 11.2–11.5) involved children in defining their own enquiry questions, working in groups on a site visit to investigate them, then in school researching Medieval banquets, in order to create a reconstruction. Their work at the beginning and end of the topic certainly provided evidence of considerable new knowledge learned through children collaborating to plan and carry out investigations in relaxed and highly enjoyable ways.

Many other examples spring to mind, often child-initiated: deciding to undertake and record an archaeological dig in the school grounds (previously allotments) at lunch time, which showed that they understood measuring the site, recording positions of finds (e.g. half a pottery beer mug, toy car and old shoe), attempting to sequence them chronologically and writing interpretive labels, then continuing their researches after school by interviewing a local resident and visiting the library to find out more about the previous use of the site.

Or the decision of a group of children to investigate why the farm we had visited, dating back to Elizabethan times, had remained very small. They created 'road surfaces' of clay soil, gravel, stone and grass in cardboard boxes, then tied a toy tractor to a force meter, which pulled it over the edge of a table and measured the force needed on different surfaces. The farm was on clay soil in a valley. Conclusion: they could not get the crops up the hill, through the heavy clay soil, to market.

Knowledge-based creativity

Our knowledge of the past consists of interpreting a range of sources. Consequently there is no single correct history, but many histories, which vary and are constantly changing, depending on the aspect of the past an historian is writing about, the evidence available and the time in which it is written. If we are asking children, who are immature and have limited knowledge, to construct their own interpretations of the past, how far should they draw on the authority of others in doing so? The philosopher A.C. Grayling argues that the key condition for knowing something is your justification for knowing it (www.theoryofknowledge.net/knowledge-and-knowers/what-is-knowledge/). On this basis it seems reasonable that children should have an understanding of chronology, at whatever level they are capable of, and knowledge of, when important things happened, about which there is generally consensus. And they need knowledge of aspects of geography which are appropriate for their enquiries. These are generally not contested. Secondary sources, contemporary history information books, provide reliably established information and information about sites, for example factual information. It is also helpful for teachers to be aware of significant new research findings, which are published in newspapers and other media (for example pp. 17–19) This is the factual framework for historical enquiry, which enables children to think creatively in history, in the ways discussed above.

Connectivity

Craft *et al.* (2001) make a distinction between creativity (teaching creatively, using imaginative approaches, making learning interesting and effective) and teaching *for* creativity (developing creativity in the learner). Nichol (2017: 151) defines teacher connectivity as transforming academic historical subject knowledge into pedagogic knowledge – teaching and learning. In describing a pupil simulation in which they explore the reasons why a group of Vikings decide to leave their village, he explains how 'teacher connectivity' translated a short passage from an academic account by Foote and Wilson (1970) into a teaching and learning activity casting pupils in role as Viking villagers. For the learner, creativity in history might mean making emotional connections between personal life experiences, for example of pleasure, fear and anger, which make it possible to make connections with people who lived in other times. Collingwood (1939) says that, although we can never understand the feelings and motivations of people in the past, except through their actions, it is possible to make connections, because there are some overlaps which can connect past and present on the basis of shared humanity. Connectivity in making connections between different societies and places in the past, a cornerstone of the 2013 curriculum, also requires imagination, based on knowledge and reasoning. Connectivity is creative in allowing us to engage, imaginatively, emotionally and cognitively with the past and in allowing us to develop a coherent 'Big Picture' of the past.

Creativity flourishes in a creative environment

Jones and Wyse (2004: 5–6) say that in creative lessons there is a different kind of relationship in the classroom, in which the teacher is not an authoritative figure who holds all the answers, resources and power; there is mutual respect, trust and above all enquiry and curiosity. Children ask questions and together the children and teacher provide the answers. Bage (2000) says that a creative classroom emphasizes the social, emotional and personal aspects of learning and Cropley (2001: 73) identifies these as 'curiosity, determination, fascination, excitement, satisfaction, pride, anticipation and elation'. The characteristics of a pedagogical creative environment is a balance between freedom and structure, risk-taking and playfulness, which helps children to exercise control over their learning and ownership of their activities (Davies *et al.* 2013). Collaboration is frequently seen as generating creativity, but there also needs to be time for reflection. Wood and Jeffrey's research (1996) working with Years 1–6 in forty-eight schools, found that teachers and children creating and sharing knowledge together was effective in developing children's awareness of the learning process and enabled them to articulate their perspectives about it.

Conclusion

This chapter has examined the connections between research defining the concept of creativity and the processes of historical enquiry. Both involve a disposition to be curious, to identify problems, ask questions, be open-minded, take risks, develop historical imagination and probability thinking and to understand the processes of historical enquiry. There were examples of each aspect of creativity applied to the processes of children's historical enquiry, although of course there are many combinations of these interactions in practice. Chapter 8 explores connections between history and other disciplines and the ways in which such cross-curricular links can enhance and enrich both history and other subjects – and manage time effectively.

7

Connections between history and other subjects

Introduction

This chapter explores ways in which history investigations can also involve thinking in literacy, mathematics, geography, information and communication technologies and art, and so allow time for thought, talk and problem-solving across these areas. The Historical Association Primary Survey (2016) found that 44 per cent of respondents said that history was most frequently linked with English and literacy, 91 per cent with geography and 55 per cent with art. Links with each of the other subjects were all under 5 per cent. This chapter focuses on how links may be made with English, geography, art and information and communication technologies.

The National Curriculum for English requires that English is taught across every subject, and it should also encompass the particular thinking skills of each discipline. This increases time for both subjects. Links with geography can also be made in ways beneficial to each subject, as is made clear in Chapter 10; links across time and place lie at the centre of the curriculum. Art and history are closely linked. All art provides many valuable historical sources for understanding a society. Art, like history is also extremely politically powerful, and both reflect the difference between open and closed societies. This chapter also focuses on links with mathematics because there is enormous potential for linking questions about chronology and time concepts on a regular basis, particularly in Years 4–6 as children's knowledge and understanding of number and calculations increases. And there is a section on using information technologies, as these are now an important dimension of historical enquiry. Indeed, since history is an 'umbrella subject' any subject could become the focus of a study of changes in British history since 1066. If a history enquiry is linked to another subject, it is important to state in what ways, in the medium-term plan for both subjects, with references showing how it relates to the Programme of Study and contributes to assessment in that subject, if time is to be managed effectively.

Language and Literacy

The National Curriculum Programme of Study (PoS) for Language and Literacy (DfE 2013: 13), states that 'English reflects the importance of spoken language across the whole curriculum cognitively, socially and linguistically. Spoken language underpins the development of reading and writing'. It also states (6.1) that teachers should develop pupils' spoken language, reading, writing and vocabulary across the whole curriculum. It is particularly important, the PoS says, that children should learn the language appropriate to each subject in its own right.

Spoken language, reading and writing in history

Oracy (listening, hearing, exposition, questioning, dialogue, discussion, argument, debate and presentation) permeates every aspect of history from the beginning of a historical enquiry, through questions and questioning, to the composition and presentation of pupils' extended reflective writing. Reading is crucial to writing because it provides information and evidence, which informs the content of children's writing. It also provides models of different styles, voices and genres to draw upon in writing in history. Reflective writing can draw upon many genres, for example writing fiction or poetry. Discursive writing requires a reflective and balanced imagination of an historical question, teasing out evidence, arguments and interpretations, in the form of, for example, narrative accounts and explanations. Both reflective and discursive writing can consider alternative interpretations and arguments in reaching a conclusion. Or writing may be persuasive and intentionally mono-perspectival, an account from a particular point of view.

English and the discipline of historical enquiry

The National Curriculum for English specifically relates to aspects of language which can be interpreted in terms of the discipline of historical enquiry.

Speaking and listening in history

In Section 6.2 the curriculum states, in speaking and listening, that pupils should

- 'speak clearly and convey ideas confidently'; there are many opportunities for whole class, group and paired discussion in history;

- 'justify ideas with reasons'; deductions and inferences about sources require statements based on I think . . . because . . . (e.g. Figure 12.1);

- 'ask questions'; finding out about the past requires asking and trying to answer questions: who, why, what, when and how?

- 'negotiate, evaluate and build on ideas'; there are examples of children discussing ideas, suggesting alternatives and building on each other's thinking (Figure 11.2);

- 'give well-structured descriptions and explanations';

- 'develop understanding by speculating, exploring and hypothesizing ideas'.

Links between the National Curriculum for speaking and listening and history are explored in the Historical Association online Continuing Professional Development unit on Storytelling (www.history.org.uk/primary/module/1348/storytelling).

Reading and writing in history

The curriculum (6.3) states that teachers should

- 'promote wide reading, in fiction and non fiction'

- 'teach them to compare similarities and differences' . . . and evaluate . . .

- 'expand children's range of writing' . . .

- write summaries . . .

Vocabulary in history

Teachers should develop vocabulary actively, building on pupils' current knowledge. The way in which teachers can develop children's vocabulary in history is described in Chapter 4, p. 53–54. It is suggested that learning abstract key concepts is important in making connections between societies and so an aspect of planning and assessment in history.

Presentations, debate and drama in history

In Section 3 of the English Programme of Study, formal presentations, debate and drama are seen as a 'chance to develop socially, emotionally culturally, intellectually and spiritually' (e.g. Chapter 3, pp. 35–36). The Curriculum for English states that pupils should 'adopt create and sustain a range of roles, responding appropriately to others in role' and have opportunities to improvise, devise and script drama for one another and a range of audiences (e.g. Chapter 3, p. 36). Role play and drama were said in the Historical Association Primary Survey (2016) to be genres of historical enquiry which teachers and children particularly enjoyed.

Examples of the English Curriculum applied to historical enquiry

Reading and writing in different genres

Historians write in many genres. So can children. There are many exciting genres in which to write history. They may be accounts, explanation, interpretation, explaining an enquiry, persuasive writing, reports, fiction, poetry or a recreation of what a scene may have been like, based on evidence. Reflective and discursive writing can include articles, biographies, accounts, newspaper and magazine articles, television and radio programmes, plays, commentaries and animation. Writing may be multi-media as well as textual.

The writing process in history

Nichol (2014: 17–23) suggests that there are three phases to writing in history:

- First, there is a preparatory phase, in which children build up a reservoir of information, evidence and related arguments, ideas, hypotheses and interpretations. This information may draw on discussion of visual sources, artefacts and private or shared reading, followed by example modelling a particular genre through shared writing.

- In the second, 'expressive phase' children draft writing in a free and spontaneous way.

- In the third phase, they write in one of the genres modelled in shared writing (for example as an archaeologist, a journalist, a newspaper reporter a play script, a television programme maker). They write in a voice appropriate for a particular audience and the content they are communicating.

Finally they present their writing in whatever form the genre requires. Here are some examples of genres used by historians and children.

Writing about objects

McGregor (2010) describes objects representing a span of 2 million years and many civilizations. The text is based on scripts for 15-minute-long radio broadcasts. He says that *A History of the World in 100 Objects* (2010) is only one history of the world and he hopes that readers will enjoy making their own connections and constructing their own history of the world'. Children would enjoy making their own history of the civilizations they study, perhaps each child carefully drawing an object, describing it and making inferences about how it was made and used and its impact on the people who made and used it. Each text could be combined into a book or a radio presentation, with the class discussing the connections and similarities and differences between the objects. Or they might write the stories of the object based on factual knowledge and inferences. Or, as part of a breadth study, they might write about changes in a relevant artefact and its influences on peoples lives, perhaps on an object involved in changing technology such as cloth-making, or in the management of water supply.

Writing about an archaeological site

This might be a paper with plans, diagrams and photographs, written in an academic style, with labelled figures, captions, an abstract, headings and subheadings. This would be good experience for later describing and explaining key information in a logical, structured way.

Diaries, letters and oral accounts

As part of a local study children might collect personal accounts, from oral and archive information, of a particular time or event and investigate to what extent people in the locality were influenced by national and perhaps global events. This might make an interesting programme of radio interviews – or a drama.

Reviews

Children who enjoy historical fiction, by for example Rosemary Sutcliffe, may like to model review writing.

Narratives

Creating individual timelines from memory, at the end of a unit of study, then writing a brief history of the period would be a good indication of what children had remembered. Writing a Brief History of the British Isles would reveal much about what children do and do not know, what received information they have gleaned from different places and perspectives. Writing an account of the Battle of Hastings based on images from the Bayeux Tapestry from either a Saxon or a Norman perspective, might be a good opportunity to differentiate between knowing, guessing and not knowing and using the language of probability to create different interpretations.

Case studies showing how reading, oracy and writing interact in an enquiry

Key Stage 2

This case study outline is taken from Nichol (2014: 156–170). It is related to 'The Roman invasion and its impact on Britain'. The children work as spies for Caractacus, a British tribal leader, who fears a Roman invasion.

- Reading

  The class first investigated what a Celtic village might have been like, using a contemporary Roman account, secondary sources, a map, a timeline, an artist's impression.

- Oral

  They discussed where they would like to go on holiday and why. Then they worked through and discussed the genre elements of a travel brochure: its authors, purpose, audience, content, form/design and what it said about the role and nature of holidays in modern, British society. Next, with the teacher, they created a storyboard for a visit to a Celtic village modelled on the brochure.

- Writing

  The children then produced individual brochures for a visit to a Celtic village.

- Reading

  The children are sent by Caractacus, the British tribal chief, to find out about the Roman army fighting in Gaul. In groups of four, children listed questions to find out about the Roman army (e.g. how many soldiers, types of weapons, where they will attack from, type of armour, strategy, location of camp).

- Oral

  They then watched the battle scene from *Gladiator*. Next they discussed information about the Roman Army and decided on the most useful information for Caractacus.

- Writing

  The selected information was listed, in groups, on 'spy sheets'. Then the children listened to how to structure their writing in the genre of a report. It covered three elements: setting the scene, details of what the report would contain, based on the spy sheet and advice to Caractacus. They understood that they must be aware of the purpose of the report; they were writing it as spies, in order to give Caractacus information about the enemy's army. They were given a 'Spy report genre frame', to guide them. This included key 'trigger words' to put in the report. Analysis of the report showed comprehensive knowledge of the topic, which drew on their reflective and discursive teaching and their understanding of the report genre.

Key Stage 1

The aim of this three-day project was to find out more about Medieval castles, with a focus on the local (ruined) castle in which Katherine Parr, one of the wives of Henry VIII had lived, in order to plan a banquet which might have happened in the days of Katherine Parr (Cooper 2012: 150–153). Italics indicate the interaction of talking, reading and writing this involved.

The class *talked* about what they knew about castles, mostly about castles in fairy tales. They drew and *labelled* their images of castles (Figure 11.2). Then they were told that they were going to visit a castle in the afternoon. The whole group *discussed* a list of *questions* they wanted to find out about the castle, which were collated into four key *questions*:

- Now and then: What can you see from the castle mound now and what would you have seen a long time ago – certainly; possibly?

- Attacking the castle: Why was it built here; how could you attack; where?

- Daily life: Where did they cook; wash; get water; have banquets?

- Survey of the site: Measure curtain wall, windows, doorways; note materials; where did they come from?

During the visit they worked in four groups, each supported by a student. They *recorded evidence* in response to their questions as *drawings, words* or *notes organized under headings*, depending on their abilities.

The following day they researched their questions further by *reading the text*, (or *labels and captions*) *in reference books* about castles, looking particularly for information about Medieval banquets, ladies and knights. They took turns in making a rubbing of replica brasses of a Medieval knight and lady to find out more about their clothes. Having *read* about Medieval banquets, children *wrote invitations*, modelled on their own past invitations, *wrote stories*, modelled on fairy stories, to be read during dinner, *wrote menus* based on their research. They made replica food and each child made a small 'Medieval' artefact based on the *information books*, to wear to the banquet. Jesters wrote 'Medieval' jokes. Some children chose to *write* a children's *information board*, based on the one designed for adults at the castle and on what they had found out, and everyone danced to Medieval music.

History and mathematics

I have made connections between history and geometry, making model buildings which required constructing and measuring nets of cuboids and triangular prisms, which could relate to any period, and drawing golden rectangles when finding out about 'the legacy of Ancient Greece'. We have done calculations based on Tudor problems and solved them using an Elizabethan method, a Gelosia algorithm (http://ed.ted.com/on/pYi5 GRBC). We have worked out time and distance problems for stage coaches and voyages of discovery, and when 'doing' the Victorians, calculated using a Victorian abacus. When this fits with the current National Curriculum for mathematics, this is fine.

In the current curriculum, making nets and building 3D shapes applies to the Year 6 curriculum, the golden rectangle, perhaps to Year 5/6, the Gelosia algorithm to Year 4 and the Victorian abacus to Years 1–4. Graphs calculating distance and speed apply to Years 4–6. However, number systems from other societies can be used to calculate at any level and are both historically and numerically interesting. Pre-historical, Sumerian, Babylonian and Egyptian accounting systems and Ancient Greek, Roman, Mayan, Chinese and Islamic mathematics is interestingly explained at www.storyofmathematics. com/egyptian.html.

But the area in which the current history curriculum, with its emphasis on the measurement of time and arithmetic, is integrally linked, is in chronology; timelines and time concepts. Discussion of time concepts is also integral with the curriculum's emphasis on spoken language in relation to mathematics in order for pupils to clarify their thinking to themselves and others. So regular discussion of time-related questions, at the appropriate level is beneficial for both disciplines. Statistics are relevant when studying, for example local history archives, such as census data. Table 7.1 shows how the National Curriculum for number can be applied to timeline calculations from Years 1 to 6 and requirements for statistics from Years 4 to 6.

TABLE 7.1 Opportunities for applying the National Curriculum for number and statistics to chronology and time questions in history

Year	National Curriculum: Number	National Curriculum History: Examples of time calculations and statistical representations and calculations
1	Count across 100, forwards and backwards. Read and write numbers 1–100 Add and subtract one-digit and two-digit numbers to 20 Sequence in chronological order Recognize language relating to days, weeks, months, years	Events/people beyond living memory up to 100 years ago. How long ago? Personal timelines, siblings' and pets' time lines. Older than, younger than . . . Put events/people, in families, significant individuals in chronological order Apply to events, lives of people in the past
2	Identify, represent, estimate numbers on number line Read and write numbers 1–100 Compare and order numbers from 0–100. Use < and > = signs Solve problems with addition and subtraction, derive and use related facts up to 100 Add and subtract 2-digit numbers Compare and sequence intervals of time	Order events/people/objects on a 100 number line Which person/event was earlier, later, at the same time? How long did an event last/a person live?
3	Recognize place value in a 3-digit number Add and subtract 3-digit numbers. Solve number problems using addition and subtraction Estimate the answer to a calculation Read and write numbers to 1,000	Relevant to understanding; sequence; perhaps calculating (comparative) duration of Roman Iron/Bronze/Iron Ages, Anglo-Saxon/Viking periods
4	Negative numbers Recognize place value of th.h.t.u. Order and compare numbers beyond 1,000 Estimate Solve practical problems with the above with increasingly large numbers (comparative, sum and difference problems). Check with calculator Pupils begin to relate graphical representations of data to recording change over time and to use a greater range of scales in their representations (non-statutory guidance p. 125)	Understand calculations involving BCE and CE Calculations involving thousands, e.g. ancient civilizations, prehistorical periods Sequences, overlaps, duration Record changes over time variety of scales Record statisics (e.g. archive data in local study such as census returns or time and distance calculations for sea, carriage, foot travel)

TABLE 7.1 Continued

Year	National Curriculum: Number	National Curriculum History: Examples of time calculations and statistical representations and calculations
5	Read write and compare numbers to 1,000,000 Interpret negative numbers in context Solve number and practical problems involving the above Pupils should be taught to solve comparison, sum and distance problems using information presented in a line graph; complete and read information tables	More confident and complex use in calculations involving ancient societies, prehistory durations and BCE/CE calculations This may relate, for example, to local archive data Time and distance calculations
6	Read, write, order and compare numbers up to 10,000,000 Use negative numbers in context and calculate intervals across zero Pupils should be taught to interpret and construct pie charts and line graphs and use these to solve problems	By Year 6, pupils should be confident in making time calculations within and between all the periods studied in order to discuss reasons for similarities, differences, comparisons and overlap of durations, continuity and change For example, in presenting data from local archives; time and distance calculations

History and geography

I have become increasingly aware that history and geography, people and places, are intrinsically linked over time.

Key Stage 1

In learning about changes within living memory and about significant events, people and places in the locality, children have the advantage of developing locational awareness, through first-hand observation of the physical and built environment of the place in which they live. Learning about 'significant national and global events and people' will develop their knowledge of the United Kingdom and of different countries and continents. Where relevant, they will encounter geographical vocabulary, the names of other countries and continents, and the geographical features of places. If the curriculum and their learning are to be coherent, it is well worth finding the places they are learning about on globes and maps, using compass directions, tracing routes and looking at photographs of the places in which people's stories were set.

Key Stage 2

There are opportunities, at Key Stage 2, to build on local geographical knowledge in the local study unit; finding out about a significant event in the locality at a different period, or about evidence of prehistory or Roman, Saxon or Viking settlement or over a longer period. As at Key Stage 1 it is important to build on children's ability to use maps, globes and photographs to locate and ask questions about places. Comparing an old map and a recent map is fascinating. For example, a modern map can reveal Celtic, Saxon and Viking place-names which are evidence of the importance of the geographical features of original settlements. In Celtic *afon/avon* means a river, *bre/don* a hill. In Anglo-Saxon, *bourne* is a stream, *dun*, a hill. In Viking, *bar* is a stream, *barrow*, a hill (Dixon and Hales 2014: 31).

Children can extend their geographical understanding of Europe and the Mediterranean when studying Ancient Egypt, Greece and Rome, and of other continents when learning about the Maya and Benin and the Ancient Middle Eastern, Asian and Chinese civilizations they study. Children can consider how people decided on what is essential for a settlement in any place and period, why locations for settlements changed in different periods, what features the earliest empires had in common which enabled them to grow. (See Chapter 8 for local, national and global links.)

History and information and communication technologies

The National Curriculum Programmes of Study for computing aims for pupils to be 'responsible, competent, confident and creative users of information and communication technology'.

Key Stage 1

At Key Stage 1, children should use technology purposefully to create, organize, store, manipulate and retrieve digital content. They might use information (text, images and sound), related to the significant people and events they are learning about from CDs, DVDs, television and the internet. This investigative process may be developed at Key Stage 1 by planning and writing short accounts, picture stories or storyboards and exploring situations through simulations, considering where they fit within a chronological framework, identifying similarities and differences between ways of life in different periods and places and discussing different interpretations.

Key Stage 2

At Key Stage 2, children should understand the opportunities that computers, the internet and the world wide web offer for communication and collaboration and they should be discerning in evaluating digital content. They will use the internet in specified ways, with emphasis on selecting suitable sources, and working with others to interpret, analyse and check relevance. The wealth of opportunities to use ICT to develop children's historical understanding is daunting, and clear decisions need to be made about how this is planned and organized.

Interactive whiteboards

Interactive whiteboards make possible the interaction between resources such as CD Roms, website pages, Word documents and PowerPoint® slides. They can be used to model how to complete tasks, to gather the views of a class, and to shuffle up and move around text and pictures by dragging and dropping. Pupils can play with ideas using frameworks such as circles to create interactive Venn diagrams, hierarchical ordering schemes and thinking organizers; this helps them to memorize concepts and ideas, which might not otherwise stick in their minds. For example, working with Year 3, I used the whiteboard to collect what they told me they knew about Roman Britain and collated this into categories with headings, in order to discuss what they thought was most significant and why. Children selected different categories, supporting their argument with reasons. The categories were then printed out on separate sheets, which they used to individually write to the local museum officer, arguing for a special display on what they thought was most significant. Their letters were scanned and sent as emails. So was the reply from the museum discussing their various choices.

Modelling

Alternatively the teacher could model for the whole class how to sort a variety of images of a given period using one set of criteria, for example, Celtic and Roman, Sumer, Indus Valley, Egyptian and Shang dynasty writing, Roman and Saxon artefacts, and discuss similarities, differences and reasons for these. Children could then work in groups on their laptops or desktop computers sorting the images according to other criteria across or within periods: for example men/women/adults/children in Saxon times or Stone Age and Sumer religious buildings or whatever criteria they may devise. If the whole class could collect examples under the same headings they could share the work of all the groups and work out what they could deduce and infer about the period. If they are identifying characteristics of different periods or civilizations they can decide on criteria for collecting examples other than those modelled by the teacher, for example religious buildings, transport, homes, images of goods traded and tools or weapons.

Children could also develop their understanding of key concepts by collecting images of concrete concepts, for example, Stone Age artefacts, then sorting them into categories of their choice (e.g. different shapes, sizes, materials), then sort them into predetermined categories (tools and weapons) and discuss what each category has in common and what is different. What are tools for? What are weapons for? Or they could start with an abstract key concept, (e.g. beliefs, trade, agriculture, technology and writing) and collect labelled concrete examples as they study each new period. These could be saved on disks and added to as a new period is studied. This would provide language and images for subordinate (concrete) concepts and the name for the overarching abstract concept and be used to discuss similarities and differences between periods and cultures (see Chapter 4, pp. 53–54 and Chapter 10, pp. 115–122).

Sequencing

Electronic timelines can be useful for discussing sequencing activities, because objects can be moved around. Ideally children will collect the images themselves giving themselves ownership of their timelines (see Chapter 4, p. 44).

Place-name analysis

The teacher, with the whole class, might identify and list place names on a map, which are related to Romans (e.g. castra/caster Lancaster – a Roman camp), the Saxons (e.g. bury, a fortified place, Banbury), or the Vikings (e.g. by, town, Wetherby). See www.bsswebsite.me.uk/A%20Short%20History%20of/placenames.html.

In groups, the children could collect other Viking place-name endings, or Roman or Saxon ones and look for them on maps, possibly using maps of differentiated scales. The information could be combined to find out the sorts of places in which Vikings (or Saxons) settled and discuss what the place names tell us about the kinds of places they chose to settle in and why they chose those places (see Chapter 5, p. 68).

Document analysis

An except from a document can be shared on an interactive whiteboard and analysed. (Nichol 2014: 23–24) shows how this connects a challenging document with the world of the pupil and can be used by the pupil. Moore (2017: 71–86) showed images of a Roman coin and Roman documents on a whiteboard then modelled how to decode them.

Using a data projector to discuss artefacts, paintings and photographs

This is particularly useful for discussing small artefacts as a class. A small coin, for example, could be put on a table and projected onto the screen. Or the detail on a larger artefact could be zoomed in on, in order to discuss what we know, what we can guess, what we should like to know.

The teacher could show the class how to explore a painting or photograph by moving around the image with a mouse or graphic pen pointer and magnifying small details. This could be radio-connected and passed around the class.

Or two different interpretations could be compared, contrasted, explained, as could two images that illustrate changes over time. A whiteboard with a graphics tablet could be used in the same way and would be a cheaper option.

Labelling, clueing and information-gathering using PowerPoint®

This activity could be used in preparation for, or as follow-up to, a visit. If it follows a visit the children could take it in turns to collect their own images using a digital camera. This would teach them that there are decisions to be made about what to include and what to leave out in creating accounts, interpretations and documentaries.

A hyperlink in PowerPoint® can be created by clicking and dragging a shape over the portion of the picture you want to be linked to another file. Click on the 'slide show' and on the menu click on 'action settings'. In the dialogue box that appears, highlight the 'hyperlink' option. By pressing on the scroll down arrow you are presented with the option of linking to another PowerPoint® slide or any file, page or sound. Choose where you want the link to take you to review the slide show. Once thoroughly tested, use 'line' and 'fill' colour option from the drawing tool bar to hide the link; select 'no fill' and 'no line' to make the shape completely transparent. (Hint: use very specific windows.) The shape needs to have no fill-in colour and no line. This means it is a hidden link.

This could be used for labelling and adding information. For example, make a square over the portcullis so that when a child clicks on it a label saying 'portcullis' appears. Or it could reveal a clue, pose a question, or link to another page of information. By moving the mouse over the image at random the child may accidentally find other information.

You could create a virtual tour of the building in this way, prior to a visit, opening different doors inside a building, to familiarize children with the place or to help them to plan an investigation in advance of a visit.

Creating a sound recording in a PowerPoint® document

Another possibility would be to insert sound into an image. In a Key Stage 1 study of a significant person, or for a local history study at Key Stage 2, an image of a person could be accompanied by a reading of something they said, for example, or an image of a job or craft that no longer exists could be explained by a former practitioner. If possible clips from an archive of speeches could be linked to images of the speakers. Images of people from the distant past are more problematic because there are so many, none based on reality.

Plug a microphone into the computer. From the menu select 'movies and sounds'. Click on 'record sound'. A dialogue box appears that allows you to record your own voice. When finished, click on 'OK' and the speaker icon will appear in your file. To run as a slide show, click on the icon for playback.

Using a desktop to compare interpretations

You could put visual information into a photo-editing programme (Windows/digital/ photoedit/paint), in order to show why there are different interpretations of what a derelict place or ruined building may have been like in the past; for example a Roman villa, a ruined castle, a disused Second World War airfield. Children could look at a picture of the ruin, draw their own interpretations of what different parts may have been like, print these out and compare and evaluate them. (Why did you think it was like this? Which seems most likely? Why?) Then they could see artists' interpretations and compare them with their own. This is a way of scaffolding children's historical imagination.

Making reconstructions using technology

Moore (2004) helped Key Stage 1 children to manipulate digital photographic images to convey what they thought their own area looked like in the distant past. They took a digital photograph of an area where they could see houses and a road but also plenty of trees and green. Then he used a photo-editing programme (Photoshop) to cut and paste trees, green, marsh and so on all over the houses and roads. (Do not re-size or crop.) The children then used PowerPoint® to 'dissolve' or 'fade' transitions to make all the buildings and roads seem to disappear from the original photograph. This was done by matching up the before and after images on consecutive slides in PowerPoint®, the modern photograph first. When children viewed the show and clicked on the mouse button to bring on the next slide, the houses and roads seemed to disappear but the areas of the photograph not worked on remained. This would work well for any local study.

At Key Stage 2, children can make their own digital videos (http://windows-movie-maker.org/). A video-recorded role play could be used for assessment, self-assessment and peer assessment. For example, children could make a video that is the culmination of a long-term role-play project, with settings, characters and events gradually built up through research. Pupils may take on roles as directors, editors, artists, musicians, camerapersons, researchers and scriptwriters as well as actors. On a site visit, which pupils record, they can use their cameras (or iPads) to record key aspects of the day and furiously scribble down accompanying notes. On their return they can edit their film and so reflect upon the day more than they would otherwise.

Then and now

Young children can, for example, identify images that are old or new in a photograph and add a text box to explain why, as a basis for discussion and also for assessing progression in chronological understanding. Older children could, for example, sort abstract concepts into examples from different periods; for example sort images of artefacts, of attack and defence, images related to beliefs, settlements, or technology into categories of Stone, Iron and Bronze Age, as suggested in Chapter 8.

Examining artefacts online

Artefact databases give us access to information and stimulate children to ask genuine questions like historians and to discuss interpretations, by annotating the images on an interactive whiteboard. For instance, www.britishmuseum.co.uk contains 3,000 artefacts. As an example, children's inferences about the Sutton Hoo purse can be collated under headings, such as evidence of wealth, imagination and technical skill, extensive trade links, use of a range of materials; they could speculate about the possible symbolism of the decorations. Such activity models the process of asking questions and making inferences about sources which, with time, children become able to do independently. The ability to download the British Museum into your classroom stimulates both teachers and children.

Podcasting and parents

Of course, parents can be involved in all of the above activities, but with podcasting they can also go on visits, share parts of lessons and become involved in work at home. For example, you could make a movie of the local area that you are studying, or of a lesson or visit, with suggestions for how to follow it up and podcast it. It will then be permanently available on your server for anyone given access to it to download when they are able to.

The golden rule for using ICT

The golden rule is only to use ICT if this is the best way to achieve your learning objectives. Is it allowing you to access sources that are better than is otherwise possible? Looking at a real object or painting in a museum conveys the feel, the texture, the size and weight of an artefact better than an image on screen. Is this the best way to develop children's historical thinking in a particular context? Sometimes scribbled diagrams on a whiteboard are a more immediate response to a question than a beautifully crafted PowerPoint® presentation. Sometimes drawing on a site or in a museum forces you to observe and reflect much more carefully and to remember better than a more wide-ranging video recording. Does the interactive whiteboard or a video recording stimulate more discussion than would otherwise occur or does it encourage passive viewing?

Useful resources

The National Archives

www.nationalarchives.gov.uk/education/sessions-and-resources/?key-stage=ks1. This only has sources from the early nineteenth century.

The British Museum collections database

See www.britishmuseum.org/research/collection_online/search.aspx

Census material

This can be used in all sorts of ways to research and present information about, for example, occupations in a locality, life expectancy, family size, movement into the area, employment, but of course only since 1941: www.ukcensusonline.com/census/1841.php

Support for teachers

The Historical Association (www.history.org.uk) offers excellent support for the teaching of history 5–11.

English Heritage

www.english-heritage.org.uk/education

English Heritage helps teachers to use the environment as a resource, supported by a huge resource catalogue of books, videos and photo packs.

Museum of London

www.museumoflondon.org

This site has a rich variety of sources, videos and pocket histories online.

History and art

The National Curriculum for art and design says that 'as pupils progress they should be able to think critically and develop a more rigorous understanding of art and design. They should know how art and design shape and reflect our history and contribute to the creativity, culture and wealth of the nation'. It aims for pupils to *produce* creative work in a variety of media, *evaluate and analyse* creative works and know about *great artists, craft-makers and designers* and understand the *historical and cultural developments of their* art forms. The National Curriculum for history states that pupils should, '*gain historical perspective by placing their growing knowledge into contexts . . . understanding connections between . . . national and international history, between cultural . . . religious and social history . . .*' It is therefore important to study art as an important dimension of British history and in the history of other civilizations.

Art as an historical source

Visual images, paintings, sculpture and photographs from past times are important historical sources. They are embedded in the narrative of history. Simon Schama's television series *Power of Art*, demonstrates the combined educational power of art and history. Arnheim (2004) says that every visual pattern, whether a painting, building, ornament or chair, makes some statement about the nature of human existence. This may be a brief statement but it is worth reflecting on what he means by this.

In the context of history this means analysing art (architecture, images, fabrics and artefacts) as historical sources (why was it made, by whom and what was its impact on the people who made and used it?). It also means tracing changes over time in British art (an interesting possibility for a breadth study of British history which offers insights into 'cultural, military, political, religious and social history'). Art and architecture are central in 'the legacy of Greek and Roman culture on later periods of British History'. Artists, craft-makers and designers provide the main sources of information for finding out about and comparing the Indus Valley, Sumer, Ancient Egypt and Shang dynasties and their impact on each other. It is central to finding out about the Early Islamic, Mayan and Benin cultures and about Stone Age, Bronze Age and Iron Age Britain.

The early Anglo-Saxons produced stone crosses and wonderful, sophisticated metal work `and later Saxon embroideries and illuminated manuscripts are superb (see p. 60). Anglo-Saxon art reflects a wide range of cross-cultural influences and also the changes in spiritual life from Pagan to Christian.

Using sources to develop designs in a variety of media

Second, the criteria for art in the National Curriculum can also be addressed by the ways in which children carefully observe, discuss and record history in different media (see pp. 103–105).

Key Stage 2

At Key Stage 2, children 'should have increasing control, and increasing awareness of different kinds of art, craft and design. They should use sketch books to record their observations, improve their mastery of drawing painting and sculpture, using a range of materials and be taught about great artists, architects and designers in history'.

Interpreting images as sources

Power relationships

Gombrich (1982) discusses how strong feelings can be displayed by images. For example, *The Kneeling Captive* (Bibliothèque Nationale, Paris) demonstrates through posture the stark contrast in statues of imperial Rome between figures of authority and submission. Can you think of other power relationships shown visually?

Questioning images

Innumerable images of saints, donors and worthies in churches, with their folded hands, evoke piety. (See Samantha's comments on the image of a praying knight in a brass-rubbing and her vivid drawing of him on the battlefield pp. 206–207). What were they really like? Why the difference?

Well-known stories – personal emotions or symbols?

Greek vases illustrate familiar narratives (These provide scope for studying both everyday life and myths and legends here. I remember one large painting of 'The hoplite race' taken from a Greek vase, with a caption asking, 'What would you like to know about them?' One response was, 'Were they married?' An interesting question). What is the symbolism conveyed by of images of Christ, saints or parables in stained glass windows in churches and of gargoyles on the drainpipes outside? (Good clay work possibilities here!)

Connecting with thoughts and feelings in the past

Philosophers in Ancient Greece highlighted the importance of the visual image. Plato expressed this poetically, saying that the gentle fire that warms the human soul flows out through the eyes in a stream of light and establishes a bridge between the observer and the observed object over which light rays travel through the eyes to the soul.

Collingwood (1924, 1938) was a philosopher who wrote extensively about both art and history; he was an archaeologist and a historian. The connection between art and history was clear to him. Art is a personally constructed interpretation and so reflects the culture that led to its creation. It is not possible to understand the thoughts of people in the past by describing their actions. But, Collingwood claims, through looking at a piece of art, the artist and the spectator come to share certain mental states with the artist.

Dewey (1958) similarly said that through an expressive object the artist and the active observer encounter each other, their material and mental environments and their culture at large. This demonstrates the connection between art and everyday experience. Dewey says that to emphasize what is aesthetic is to emphasize a manifestation of a record, a manifestation of a civilization and of the quality of that civilization.

Face value or values?

Interpreting a visual source can help us to move from the concrete to the abstract. Arnheim (2004) points out that a picture combines sensory appearance and reasoning. A portrait may be of a particular individual, portrayed as having particular physical characteristics and personality but is also a symbol displaying more. He explains how paintings and sculptures that portray figures, objects, actions in a more or less realistic style make no sense of what life was like in the past until the viewer can read what each symbolizes. This requires thought, language and discussion. Which of two images of a nineteenth-century harvest tells us more about what life was like for those portrayed: a ragged and hungry labourer taking a break and munching bread, or a painting of a rejoicing, rosy-cheeked group sitting among the harvested corn? This is not is a simple question.

A realistic portrait of Winston Churchill, for example, may portray him as a stout, thoughtful, elderly statesman but it may also be a symbol of more abstract qualities of the period: of oppression and resistance, determination and inner containment.

Visual images promote learning in history

Bruner (1963) stressed the importance of using imagery (iconic representation) in such a way that the pervading powerful ideas and attitudes in a discipline are given a central role. He emphasized (1966) the need to understand the questions to ask about an image in order to do this and said that this enabled children to transfer their thinking independently to new similar material and so avoid dependence on facts and memory. Once you know how to read a portrait or landscape you can both remember the painting and transfer the skill to understanding other paintings.

Charlotte Mason (1842–1923) in *The Original Home Schooling Series* (Mason 1993 4: 38) explains that 'Great artists, builders and musicians have the power of showing us their visions and we, by a similar power of imagination, may share their visions'.

Klausmeier (1979) discusses the role of images in concept formation. He says that images are stored. Shared characteristics can be abstracted, new information added and generalizations made. (See Chapter 4, p. 54; Chapter 8, p. 115.) The more Saxon churches we see the more we understand about the characteristics of Saxon architecture. He says that by collecting images of kinds of qualities, kinds of objects and kinds of events the mind grasps what they have in common and so organizes concepts. What are the common factors in images of a battle or of a religious building? By reflecting on our 'image banks' we are able to make connections between people and events across generations and cultures.

Art, history and personal development

Learning through visual images prompts individual responses, which enrich and enhance a pupil's development. Egan (1992) emphasized the importance of forming and articulating vivid images in teaching and learning. Bruner (1963), Dewey (1933) and Collingwood (1938) provide a firm foundation for bridging art and history, since they understand the centrality of history in the curriculum which aims to educate the whole child.

Gardner (1993), having introduced his theory of multiple intelligences, concluded that the most promising way of integrating the various forms of learning is to 'situate them'. When pupils see adults moving between various forms of knowing, combined in natural situations, they too are participating in a rich, engaging project. Here are some examples of adults working with children and moving between art and history.

Understanding history through making art

Developing understanding and skills in art and design

Children develop skills and understanding in art and design through first-hand observation, experiences, imagination and exploring ideas. They investigate a range of materials and processes used in art, craft and design, for example print-making, drawing, painting, textiles and sculpture. They should try out different tools and techniques, in order to represent observations, ideas and feelings, through designing and making images and artefacts. They should learn about colour, pattern and texture, line and tone, shape form and space. They should learn through investigating different aspects of art, craft and design during visits to museums galleries and sites and the locality.

Examples of children recording and making deductions and inferences about sources through art

This section allows me to take a trip down memory lane and remember some of the art and history combinations I have worked on with children over the years. By engaging in the processes of art and design, children can also develop their historical thinking. Interpreting sources requires close and detailed observation. Drawing artefacts and buildings, and especially drawing details and decoration engages children. It helps them to focus and concentrate on an object for a long period. This both raises questions and generates ideas and also records the object for discussion and further research at a later time.

Key Stage 1

At Key Stage 1, the art curriculum requires children to use a range of materials creatively to design and make products, in drawing painting and sculpture, using colour, pattern, texture, line, shape, form, space and to know about the work of artists, craft makers and designers. In studying changes within living memory, children may enjoy the pop art of Andy Warhol and the iconic designs of 1960s fashion, ceramics, pottery and fabrics, all of which can be researched on the internet. I have found that they love the bright colours, discussing key features, differences from present styles and attempting designs with similar features themselves. A 1960s focus raises questions about continuity and change; 'my gran never saw pop art' and 'my granddad never wore velvet bell-bottoms'.

I have also found that young children enjoy learning about and 'reinterpreting' the art Andy Goldsworthy makes with natural objects (www.ipadartroom.com/andy-goldsworthy-inspired-lesson/). I suppose, born in 1956, he could be compared with Andy Warhol (born 1928) to illustrate that changes within living memory are not always developmental . . .

Model making

I recall two doll's houses made by Key Stage 1 children in cardboard boxes. One was 'an old doll's house' based on a picture of a Victorian doll's house seen in the Museum of Childhood. The other was 'my house', which featured electric lights run from a battery. These models were made to demonstrate time and change, similarities and differences, now and then – including the lighting circuit installed in the contemporary model, as part of the work on electricity.

Drawing

I have many photographs of children with clipboards sitting on museum floors in front of showcases, drawing with immense concentration.

Silk screen printing

I was responsible for art in one of my schools, so had fun buying new equipment and experimenting with different techniques. One of these was screen printing. This technique involves a wooden frame with fine gauze stretched and pinned across it. The gauze is blocked out by painting a glue onto it or sticking brown paper onto it. Then a squeegee (I love the name!) is used to spread the dye, which penetrates the unblocked areas.

Spinning, weaving and dyeing

Having found out, from a visit to Butser Iron Age village reconstruction, that the Iron Age people spun wool from their Soay sheep and wove it into checked patterns, we had a go at spinning with spindles. The wool was provided by a local farmer. First it had to be carded so that the threads all lay in the same direction. Then a thread was twisted and attached to the spindle. This was drawn out as the spindle spun like a top on the floor and the hooks on each thread joined together. That's the theory anyhow. We did not produce a large quantity of wool. But we had enough to weave on two small hand-made looms (based on the design seen at Butser) and to dye one piece of cloth with onions and one with blackberries. The plaid pattern was beyond us.

Pottery

We had a kiln so had lots of opportunities to make replica Iron Age food vessels, with designs as recorded in the British Museum. One minor pottery success was a replica Roman board game, which involved clay balls, glazed in different colours. Carefully observed replicas of pottery from any early culture are interesting to make (small scale), particularly pots from Ancient Sumer, the Indus Valley which have simple decorations. The terracotta animals, toys and carts from Ancient Sumer are great fun for children to recreate.

Embroidery

While working on the Elizabethan project some of the girls found designs for Elizabethan embroideries. They enlarged parts of the design and drew them on white cotton. It was interesting to overhear them one day discussing exactly which of the many shades of green thread was the best match for a particular leaf. There are some wonderful books on Anglo-Saxon embroidery (see p. 61) which could inspire similar designs. Or alternatively, motifs from a Viking cross or sculpture in a Saxon church or from the Sutton Hoo grave or Staffordshire Hoard, for example, could be the basis for a creative design.

Pen and ink

We have all seen church windows recreated in black paper and coloured tissue, hardly reflecting the magnificent detail in Saxon glass. Silver scraperboard might do more justice to the stone tracery, but drawing with a very fine black pen, a medium I used a lot with children, also works well. I think it would be perfect for replicating a small detail, perhaps magnified, from Saxon illuminated scripts, such as the Lindisfarne Gospels or the Book of Kells.

Lino cuts

This technique lends itself particularly well to copying or imitating magnified simple details from a pattern in stone or wood.

Leather artefacts

I particularly remember, having been given a bag of soft leather off-cuts, the 'Iron Age shoes' and 'Iron Age bags', which were part of the Iron Age display. Children decided to make these. It was not my idea!

Combining sources

The artwork based on studying sources can contribute to a summative display of work related to a topic, beside the source, with deductions and inferences about the source and how the art was made.

Examples of children creating interpretations through art

Historical interpretations, constructed through art, may be paintings or drawings of an event or artefact based on evidence. Or they may be models, possibly based on incomplete evidence, part of the floor of a Roman villa, post-holes of an Iron Age hut, or a reconstruction of a room.

Art supporting problem solving

More recently Yapici Dilek (2010) has investigated students' ability to combine visual and historical thinking skills. She found that drawings were an effective way to access pupils' historical thinking and that artwork which visualizes the past supports historical problem-solving. For example, having studied written and visual sources, pupils were able to convey their understanding of chronological changes in the position of women in Turkey, and their feelings during different periods, through succinct drawings with captions showing changes in body language, facial expressions and dress. In a series of drawings a boy drew a couple under the Ottoman monarchy, in which the man is showing the woman the door. She wears the veil and chador. This illustrates that women were second-class citizens with no divorce rights. A drawing of the early twentieth century shows a woman campaigning for women's rights, wearing a chador but no veil. In a third drawing of the Republican era the boy illustrates women's acquisition of political rights showing a picture of a woman deciding who to vote for and of another woman electioneering. Or an interpretation of events may be recorded as a picture story; for example, I remember a picture story retelling the first part of the story of the siege of Troy, enthusiastically drawn by an 8-year-old who found writing difficult.

Reconstructions

A Greek temple was constructed in the corner of the room, using drama blocks as steps and huge corrugated card tubes painted white, wound around with ivy for the pillars. The portico was decorated with a genuine design enlarged on the photocopier then printed in sequence. This temple housed research on Greek gods and myths.

Another reconstruction was a Stone Age cave. A slide of a cave painting was magnified onto a large wall using a projector. Then the animals were painted using oxides from the pottery area. The cave entrance was decorated with branches and leaf rubbings. This prompted various dramas and story scripts over a long period.

Practical details

You may be wondering how so much time could be justified on such work. It was interesting that most of the ideas came from groups of children themselves. Since it was their initiative, most of the construction was done at playtimes and lunchtimes or done at home. Not all the children would be involved and participants drifted in and out of a project. But such pupil-initiated ideas both stemmed from and generated an enormous amount of dialogue, presentations, explanations, questions, planned research and story writing.

Book-making

Finally, it was the tradition of the school for each child to collate all their work on a project in a handmade book (excellent for assessment). The cover design would reflect the contents. (Parents were delighted with these. One parent told me recently that she still had them, all in her attic.) Today of course, books can be word-processed, but designing covers, whether paper or board, related to a history topic involves understanding of history and art, and writing contents pages, indexes and back blurb contributes to the English and literacy curriculum.

A refreshing example

Let us end with breaking news from a local paper, *Cumbria Crack* (08.06.2017).

Jane Lightfoot, 23, a 3rd year student teacher, it tells us, is bringing Viking history to life, with Year 3–6 pupils using several curriculum subject areas; painting wooden shields while researching the symbolism of colours used, and a Viking day, where children learned about Viking religion and customs, through drama and role play. They also designed and made a Viking boat, took measurements, calculated the costs of the project ordered materials, considered transport options, helped by their parents and the construction company, Northern Construction, who supplied the materials. The longship is divided into several sections and measures 3.5 metres long – large enough to seat all the eighteen pupils who designed it. Well done Shankhill Primary School!

The next chapter, Chapter 8 could be considered central to this book. It considers how children can build up 'The Big Picture' of the past, over different times and places, in a systematic, coherent and increasingly complex way.

CHAPTER

8

Local, national and global connections over time

The National Curriculum for England (DfE 2013) requires that pupils at Key Stage 1 should have some understanding of *local, national, international and global* dimensions of people and events in the past. They should be taught about significant historical people, events and places *in their own locality*, about changes within living memory related to aspects of changes in *national* life, about significant people who have contributed to *national and international* achievements and about events beyond living memory which are of *national and global* significance.

At Key Stage 2, they should continue to develop a chronologically secure knowledge of *local, national and world history*, establishing clear narratives within and across periods of study, *note connections, trends and contrasts* over time using appropriate historical terms and regularly address and sometimes devise historically valid questions about *change, cause, similarity and difference and significance*.

It is argued in this chapter that existing frameworks for identifying connections, trends and contrasts over time, in local, national and world history do not adequately support children in doing this. It presents a conceptual framework, which aims to support primary school children in making micro and macro connections, over time and between places, in increasingly complex ways. This is based on making conceptual connections which are central to all societies (see Chapter 4, pp. 53–54 and Chapter 7, p. 95). Suggestions are made about how this framework can be used to ask and answer questions related to concepts of time and to link it to planning. The framework is based on earlier research into concept development.

As a sixth former I was fascinated by Arnold Toynbee's *A Study of History* (1987). He analysed the rise and fall of twenty-six civilizations. His study began when he saw Bulgarian peasants wearing fox-skin caps like those described by Herodotus as the headgear of Xerxes' troops in the fifth century BCE. It reflects his sense of the vast continuity of history and his eye for pattern – 'the Big Story'. I was hooked. (My young brother's name for me was 'study pig' . . . No, you need not read Toynbee).

However, as a history student I rarely bothered to check where places were in an atlas. I thought that history was entirely about 'ideas'. I was good on Church and State in the 1640s. But how very wrong I was about maps and ideas. You cannot properly understand the ideas without an atlas as well as a timeline. An historical atlas is essential at Key Stage 2. I suggest, *What Happened in the World*: *history as you've never seen it before* (Dorling Kindersley 2015) and *The Kingfisher Atlas of the Ancient World* (Adams and Baxter 2006).

The first section of this chapter begins by considering rationales for teaching about connections between societies over time, explaining why these connections must be investigated and evaluated from different perspectives. The second section, 'Key Stage 1: time and place: local, national and global connections', considers opportunities for making connections between people and events in different countries and periods, then how links can be made between Key Stages 1 and 2. The third section, 'Key Stage 2: developing "The Big Picture"', suggests how similarities and differences between societies studied in the National Curriculum can be made in increasingly sophisticated ways, using key concepts. It provides frameworks for making global connections between Britain and other societies in the Stone, Bronze and Iron Ages, the Roman, Saxon and Viking periods. The fourth section of the chapter considers the locality and possible national and global connections. Sections 3 and 4 are supported by interesting new research. The chapter concludes with some case study examples and considers how making connections between different places and times might develop a sense of identity which is inclusive and meaningful to all children.

Rationales for making connections between societies over time

Historical consciousness

Many of us find the past fascinating, in its own right. But others see little point in simply knowing about past times. As one student said to me, 'I'm interested in the future, Hilary, not the past'. In many European countries, the rationale for studying history is 'historical consciousness' (Megill 1994). One central element of historical consciousness is the connection of the past with the present and future, and seeing ourselves connected to the past; the ability to relate history and judgments about the past to one's own life in the present, which should inform our future actions. Therefore, it is important to explore patterns of development over the whole of history up to the present. The questions raised throughout history are perennial, the universal features of the human condition and they relate to us.

The Cambridge Review

The aims of the Cambridge Review (Alexander 2010) proposed a balance of national and local content and also celebration of global culture and community, which, it says, should be local in orientation and rooted in knowledge and understanding (p. 256). It is explained that this is because a sense of community does not begin with abstract ideas of Britishness but with how people relate to each other locally (p. 259). On page 198, the Review quotes Bruner (1966), saying that, in promoting interdependence, advancing children's understanding of diversity and celebrating culture and community, education is an embodiment of a culture's way of life, not just a preparation for it. And the Review agrees that the global dimension in twenty-first-century education is essential (p. 193). Indeed two Year 6 boys made a joint submission claiming that they especially wanted to learn global history (p. 149). Submissions specifically on the place and teaching of history criticized the growing marginalization, at the Primary Stage, of a perspective on the world, which witnesses believed was of central importance in both education and life (p. 229).

The Association for Primary Education

The Association for Primary Education's submission to the review claimed that primary education aims for pupils to eventually become full members of society with an understanding of values, which can only be taught by the non-core Foundation Subjects, because historical and social thinking are not the same as thinking in other subjects. It is recognized (p. 194) that debate is needed on exactly what, in the context of primary education, the 'global dimension' should mean. Ofsted (2011) found that history teaching in primary schools was generally 'good or better' but that teachers found it difficult to establish a clear mental map of the past for pupils. This was essentially because 'the National Curriculum in 2011 treated topics in a disconnected way'.

How should we connect with the past: the danger of over-simplification

For children to learn patterns of thinking which will enable them to achieve this 'Big Picture' could be challenging. Before the current curriculum was finalized there was a fear, based on politicians' statements and the draft curriculum, that it would be a narrative history, based solely on memorizing facts and dates; in the words of Sir Richard Evans (2013), Regius Professor of History at Cambridge University, that it would be 'rote-learning of the patriotic stocking fillers so beloved of traditionalists'. So we must find ways of avoiding the shortcomings of previous ways of teaching history, illustrated at the beginning of this book. The emphasis on both breadth studies and depth studies in the history curriculum is an attempt to avoid over-simplification. But how can we teach children to make broad and meaningful connections over thousands of years, which still involve discussion and enquiry and create coherence?

The current history curriculum

The current curriculum (DfE 2013: 1–12) emphasizes 'a coherent knowledge and under-standing of Britain's past and that of the wider world', the role of history in helping pupils to understand 'the diversity of societies . . . as well as their own identity . . . how people's lives have shaped this nation and how Britain has influenced and been influenced by the wider world'. Pupils, it states, should 'know and understand significant aspects of the history of the wider world: the nature of ancient civilizations; the expansion and dissolution of empires; characteristic features of past non-European societies'. They should 'gain historical perspective by placing their growing knowledge into different contexts, understanding the connections between local, regional, national and international history, cultural, economic, military, political, religious and social history and between short- and long-term time scales.'

Key Stage 1: time and place – local, national and global connections

The following examples also involve the National Curriculum criteria for geography: knowledge about the world, the United Kingdom and the locality, locational and place knowledge, human and physical geography and geographical skills.

Changes within living memory: different times and places

Tracing changes may begin with oral histories, perhaps supported by written sources, artefacts and photographs. They may focus, for example, on changes in the locality, in schools, in homes, in occupations, shops, clothes, leisure activities and gender roles. If several people who come from different parts of the country or from another country are selected to talk to the children this will provide comparisons at a local, national and international or global level. In one case study (Cooper 1995a: 198) a parent from Ghana, brought in a traditional Ghanaian cooking pot and told the children how it was used for cooking and the types of food cooked in it. She told them about her childhood in Ghana, about her large house and swimming pool and her mother who was a head teacher. She also told how others lived, and still do, in entirely different circumstances. Another parent told them about her childhood in Shanghai, shared her family photographs and helped them cook a Chinese meal. A third parent had been brought up in rural Scotland and another parent had been to the same school as the children. So the four visitors had local, national and global connections to reflect upon – and the similarities and differences between them.

Events beyond living memory

These are required to have national or global significance. For example, if you selected 'the first aeroplane flight' as an event with international and global significance this could be both a depth and a breadth study, putting the first aeroplane flight into a context. Children might find out what Millville Indiana was like in 1867 when Wilbur Wright was born there. There are photographs and a lot of information about this small community in those days. It would not be difficult to extract key information to give children some idea of this small community and the lives of the brothers and so to discuss their remarkable achievement and how it led to the society we live in today (www.indgensoc.org/membersonly/county/henry/millville_history_1854_1954.pdf). A photograph of Millville today can be found at www.vpike.com/?e=39.9247688,-85.25191:0:Millville,%20Indiana.

Children could then find out if the Wright brothers really were the first to fly. Don't believe everything you read!

Significant individuals in the past who have contributed to national and international achievements

Children might learn about Elizabeth I and Queen Victoria, Christopher Columbus and Neil Armstrong, William Caxton and Tim Berners-Lee. In each case, (and in many others), they could focus on an in-depth study with local, national and global breadth dimensions. One Year 1 class studied famous explorers on every continent, neatly combining history and geography: Scott – Antarctica; Marco Polo – China; Cooke – Australia; Columbus – Central America; Livingston – Africa; Van Humbolt – South America; Hudson – Canada.

Significant historical events, people and places in their own locality

Local people and events could also be selected which have local, national and global connections. After children discuss the meaning of 'significant' they will see that most significant local events or people are more widely important. The connection may be a local visit from a significant person, perhaps a member of the royal family, on a significant occasion. It is most likely that a local person, commemorated in a plaque or statue, will also have national and perhaps international significance.

Connections between Key Stage 1 and Key Stage 2

Abstract concepts introduced in Key Stage 1, perhaps in folk tales and fairy stories, will be used again through Key Stage 2. Folk tales about people and places often include stories about farming (agriculture), about tools, making things and inventions (technology), about markets, buying and selling (trade), about conflict (attack/defence) or about beliefs and values. The meaning of these concepts can be explicitly discussed (see pp. 53–54).

It may be useful, in building on previous and familiar knowledge and making 'The Big Picture' coherent, to select people and events which children encounter at Key Stage 1 and again at Key Stage 2. They might be traditional heroes, such as King Alfred the Great or Boudicca or mythical figures such as King Arthur. If so, their perceptions may later be challenged and re-evaluated at Key Stage 2 (Moore 2017: 77–80; Andrews et al. 2017: 58–70). Children may be introduced to figures such as Queen Elizabeth 1, or Queen Victoria, if they are planned to be part of a breadth study at Key Stage 2. You may choose to select a significant person because of their gender. Mary Anning for example, who made a significant – and until recently unrecognized – contribution to discovering the importance of fossils. Children may come across fossils later in the Stone Age, or Mary Anning may later be part of a breadth study on women achievers or famous scientists. You may select Rab'ia al-Adawiyya, who lived in Iraq (717–801 CE) an eighth-century Sufi saint, who was born into a poor family, orphaned at a young age and was eventually sold into slavery, yet set forth the doctrine of 'Divine Love' (http://sufimaster.org/adawiyya.htm). Children will be finding out about Sumer, now Iraq, at Key Stage 2. Rab'ia al-Adawiyya might be contrasted with a contemporary American Muslim woman astronaut, Anousheh Ansari who, in 2006, became the first Muslim woman in space (http://anoushehansari.com; www.huffingtonpost.com/fazeela-siddiqui/10-muslim-women-you-should-know_b_1348903.html). When asked about what she hoped to achieve on her spaceflight, she said that she hoped to inspire everyone – especially young people, women and young girls all over the world and in Middle Eastern countries – not to give up their dreams but to pursue them, although it may seem impossible to them at times. Or children might learn about someone who will enable them to make simple connections between early societies, which they will find out more about later. For example, Ibn Battuta (1303–1368) travelled across North Africa, Egypt, the Swahili coast towards Mecca, through Syria, Turkey and Persia to Afghanistan, through India to Sri Lanka and across the Eastern coast of China, before returning to Morocco! (Harnett 2014).

Key Stage 2: developing 'The Big Picture'

Making connections

Lomas (2017) considered how to plan a 'well organised and purposefully designed curriculum' in which children see 'links, connections and inter relationships': following the sequence of the National Curriculum, following a chronological sequence, using timelines, adopting a thematic approach based on themes such as technology, art, communication, linking the local dimension to a non-European study or a British unit, linking a local study unit to a British study unit and reviewing connections between study units at the end of a year. But he recognizes that each of these approaches has disadvantages. In the final section, he mentions 'ensuring coherence in concepts'; his example being the concept of 'great' as in Alfred the Great. Having spent the last year thinking about the concept of coherence myself, and how it might be planned for, I developed the idea of a 'conceptual framework', which is explained below. I was fascinated to find this conceptual framework incorporates each all of Lomas' suggestions. It may seem a little complicated to start with, but I think it has convincing, exciting – and 'elegant' possibilities.

Reason for the study units selected

I show how the conceptual framework can be applied to selected National Curriculum study units. These are changes in Britain from the Stone Age to the Iron Age, the Roman Empire and its impact on Britain, Britain's settlement by the Anglo-Saxons and Scots, the Viking and Anglo-Saxon struggle for the United Kingdom and the earliest civilizations. Ancient Greece was included in the previous curriculum and the Historical Association Primary Survey (2015) showed that teachers are also drawing on periods with which they were already familiar to construct new local and thematic study units.

Conceptual framework for comparing and contrasting societies

The 'Big Picture' is bigger than a 'breadth study'. It is a 'Large Scale Study', which we can slowly build up, consistently from Years 1 to 6. Figure 8.1 shows the stages through which the conceptual framework can be implemented in order to make coherent structured connections between societies at different times and in different places.

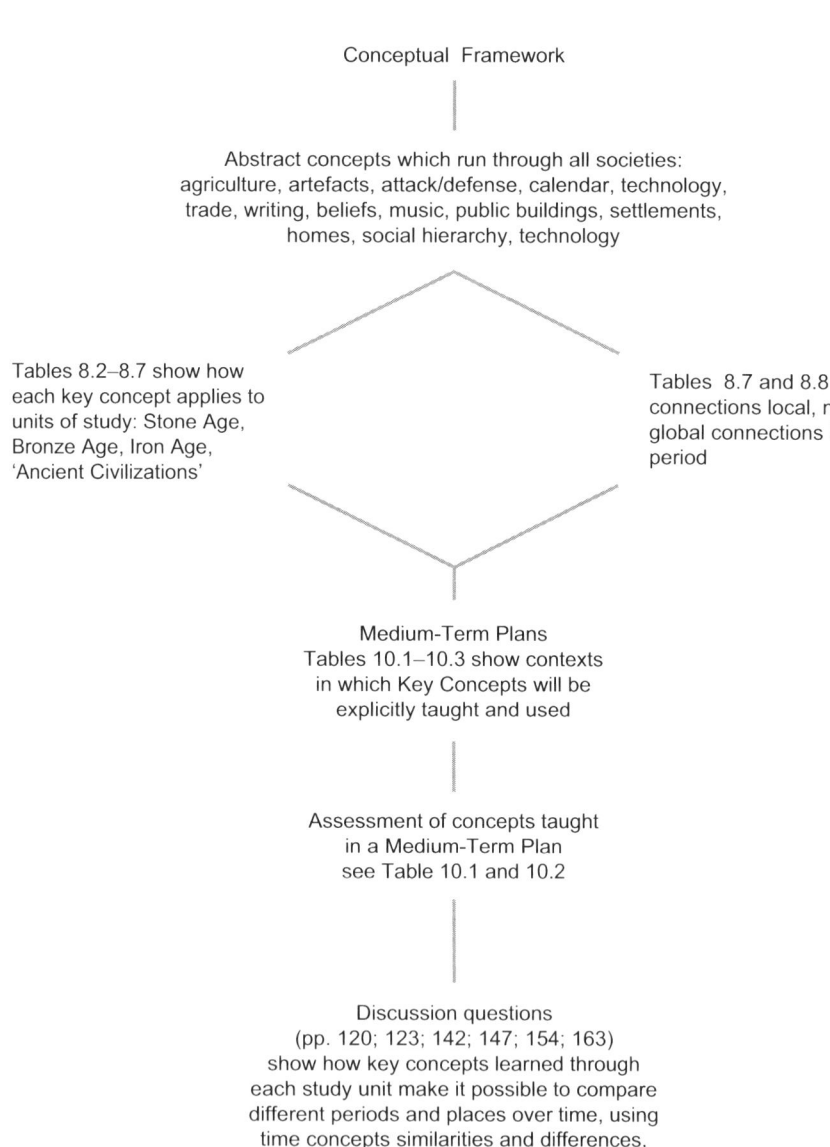

Conceptual Framework

Abstract concepts which run through all societies:
agriculture, artefacts, attack/defense, calendar, technology,
trade, writing, beliefs, music, public buildings, settlements,
homes, social hierarchy, technology

Tables 8.2–8.7 show how
each key concept applies to
units of study: Stone Age,
Bronze Age, Iron Age,
'Ancient Civilizations'

Tables 8.7 and 8.8 show
connections local, national,
global connections in each
period

Medium-Term Plans
Tables 10.1–10.3 show contexts
in which Key Concepts will be
explicitly taught and used

Assessment of concepts taught
in a Medium-Term Plan
see Table 10.1 and 10.2

Discussion questions
(pp. 120; 123; 142; 147; 154; 163)
show how key concepts learned through
each study unit make it possible to compare
different periods and places over time, using
time concepts similarities and differences,
causes and effects, continuity and change,
duration, trends and patterns

FIGURE 8.1 Implementation stages of the Conceptual Framework.

Tables 8.2–8.7 list the key concepts, which run through all societies, with notes on how they apply in the context of each period. Teachers can build these concepts into their planning. The notes are indicative not comprehensive. The tables are certainly not intended to be used to teach dates and facts by rote, but to suggest activities which will give children the knowledge to make links between, and ask and answer questions comparing any civilizations they study, at levels appropriate to their age, and so to build consistently on their knowledge and discussions through Key Stage 2. Apart from planning activities to explore the concepts further, the tables can be a basis for children researching the concepts themselves, perhaps individuals or groups researching different concepts.

The tables listing key concepts (8.1–8.6) aim to:

- give the teacher a broad, and it is to be hoped, inspirational picture, which may encourage their further research and relate to activities they plan for children. I prefer this approach to the stereotypical information I find on websites for children and in information books. My approach has always been to present material for children in forms they can engage with but never to infantilize them;

- inform the kinds of questions to discuss with children about changes between different periods and places;

- suggest memorable, visual examples representing each concept in a particular period;

- enable successive teachers to build coherently on what pupils know, by returning to concepts as they relate to previous study units and adding new information and more complex ideas;

- allow older children, perhaps organized in groups, to research these concepts themselves;

- raise awareness of the need to plan for key concepts which underpin changes, as well as events.

I found a British Museum website which might contribute to a conceptual framework. It develops six concepts: buildings, writing, cities, religion, technology and trade, and allows you to find out about and compare similarities and differences between ancient civilizations in relation to each concept (www.ancientcivilizations.co.uk/home_set.html). The civilizations it investigates include: Ancient China, Anglo-Saxon Britain, Benin, Egypt, Imperial China, the Indus Valley Maya, Mesopotamia and Roman Britain. The questions it investigates are:

- What types of monumental building did people build in the past?

- Why do people write things down?

- What features make a city?

- Is it possible to understand the religious beliefs of ancient civilization?

- What technologies were used by people in the past?

- What did people trade in the past?

TABLE 8.1 Changes during the Stone Ages in Britain, linked to key concepts

	Old Stone Age c. 800,000 BCE	Middle Stone Age c. 9,600–5,500 BCE (end of last ice age)	New Stone Age c. 6,000–2,500 BCE
	Intermittent occupation by hunter gatherers between Ice Ages c. 6,000–5,000 BCE cut off from Europe		
Agriculture			Begins with the introduction of farming, from c. 9,000 BCE in the Middle East, c. 7,000 BCE in Southeast Europe, c. 4,000 BCE in Northern Europe This is the time when cereal cultivation and animal domestication was introduced Agriculture gave rise to forest clearance, root crops, cereal crops which could be stored
Artefacts	40,000 BCE personal ornaments, small-scale moveable art	Middle Stone Age continues to produce more sophisticated artefacts, tools, weapons	Smooth stone tools, development of decorated pottery, usually geometric and simple and sculpted pottery
Attack/Defence		continues	continues

Calendar	5,000 years before the invention of the calendar in the middle east, a calendar was invented in Aberdeenshire which was in use 8,000–4,000 BCE. This is believed to be the world's oldest calendar. A complex of pits was designed to represent the months of the year and phases of the moon. Each lunar month was divided into 10-day 'weeks', representing the cycle of the moon. This enabled hunter-gatherers to calculate when herds would migrate and salmon run. It was probably controlled by shamans to encourage the belief that they could control the seasons www.independent.co.uk/news/science/archaeology/news/found-after-10000-years-the-world-s-first-calendar-8708322.html	Agricultural communities created property – crops and cattle. Therefore many communities were fortified. Causes of war might be bad harvests. Weapons increased. A class of fighting men who defended the farmers seems gradually to have emerged, with the village chief as commander See http://culture-of-peace.info/books/history/prehistory-war.html Previously thought to be peaceful period but recent research focuses on head wounds and wounds from projectiles This is the most discussed archaeo-astronomic period apart from the Mayans For example Stonehenge (3,000 BCE), grew over the centuries. It lines up with solstices and probably reflects rising and setting of moon during the seasons Similarly Great Tomb at new Grange, Ireland only lets light into its centre during the Winter solstice See www.arch.ox.ac.uk/IVNE.html
Beliefs		Stone circles and henges, 3,000–2,000 BCE. Was this a type of calendar? For rituals? Trade? Commemoration of the dead (1,000 in Britain) Barrows – burial chambers, passage graves
Homes/Shelters	Caves or tents of wood, which could be easily moved After 5,000,000 years discovered fire	Seem to have been built on an earth bank and shaped like a wigwam; made of pliant saplings, with mud and skins to cover them See replica homes at Stonehenge www.english-heritage.org.uk/visit/places/stonehenge/things-to-see-and-do/neolithic-houses/

continued

TABLE 8.1 continued

		Rectangular, made from tree trunks for posts, clay and stone foundations, roof timber and thatch. Middle/ Neolithic – brick fire on stone hearth. See video www.bbc.co.uk/programmes/p02mbf3m. 3,200–2,200 BCE Sjara Brae stone village www.orkneyjar.com/history/skarabrae/
Music	Probably began with first stone artefacts. Singing, clapping. See stone age music teaching pack www.dancenotes.co.uk/lessons/preview/The%20Stone%20Age.pdf. See video of Mezolithic instruments www.youtube.com/watch?v=RLxp9l5cvpc. Earliest instruments see www.crystalinks.com/prehistoric-music.html	Little evidence in Britain but probably similar to Stone Age instruments in other countries. https://ambpnetwork.wordpress.com/introductions-to-the-field/instruments-of-prehistory/
Public buildings		Stone circles and henges
Settlement		More food available, more people, more villages, finally towns/cities
Social hierarchy		More complex social and political organization
Technology	Harpoons, spears, adzes	Ploughs, irrigation systems. Towards end of period, copper metallurgy. In Near East ovens to bake bread. Control of heat in enclosed space to make pottery – led to smelting metals

		Recent new approaches to studying exchange routes and organization involved and roles of production and consumption. Study of stone axe trade in Britain and small networks of regional productions. Part played in long-distance exchange. Maps show distribution of stone access all over Britain (Bradley and Edmonds. 2008)
Trade	Possibly trade across land bridge between Britain 8,000 years ago. Wheat DNA found yet not grown for another 2,000 years in Britain, France and the Netherlands	International trade routes increase across thousands of miles. (Stone axes from Cumbria and SW Wales found in Ireland)
	Professor Vince Gaffney, one of the world's most respected theorists on archaeological evidence, believes hunter-gatherers had 'extensive social networks through which to exchange exotic foodstuffs across Europe'	Trade in surplus food New farming tools
Writing	See Von Petzinger 2016 for evidence of written language	

Synopsis

What changed between the Old Stone Age and the Middle stone Age in Britain?

1. Early example of a lunar calendar but only very gradual developments over 2,500,000 years.
2. Agriculture introduced. This created property (e.g. cattle, crops, permanent homes). This led to more warfare between groups. (e.g. when harvests bad).
3. Agriculture created people who did not need to work on the land, therefore able to co-operate on huge public buildings; stone circles. Therefore large meetings places for groups/tribes.
4. Therefore trade, national and international and trade in stone tools and weapons.
5. Therefore production and consumption; industrial flint mines, trade routes, new types of tools and weapons, pottery due to introduction of ovens.

My conceptual framework is less technologically based but, I think, more developed and flexible, so read on!

The Stone Age in Britain

Table 8.1 shows how changes during the Stone Age in Britain can be categorized using key concepts. This makes it easy to show the ways in which life in Britain changed during the Stone Age and the periods of slowest and most rapid change.

Questions to ask to compare periods and civilizations

Chronology and theories of concept development are discussed in Chapter 4 and time questions in Chapter 7. This chapter builds on both chapters. Exploring connections between places and across time depends, first, on asking *chronological* questions:

- When? Where? How long did these periods last?

- *Time concept* questions to discuss include:
    - How were they similar and how were they different?
    - How did each period begin and why?
    - How did it end and why?
    - Did different civilizations overlap?
    - What similarities are there between these societies?
    - What impact did they have on each other?

- Are there any patterns and trends we can trace in the ways in which societies change?

The Bronze Age in Britain

Table 8.2 Shows characteristics of Bronze Age Britain categorized by key concepts.

Comparing Tables 8.1 and 8.2 makes it easy to compare and discuss changes from the early Stone Age to the Bronze Age, causes and effects, similarities and differences and duration.

Four early Bronze Age civilizations

Table 8.3 makes it possible to compare similarities and differences between four other Bronze Age civilizations, and to consider what patterns you can see between them, their growth and decline, and why Bronze Age Britain did not develop in the same way.

The Bronze Age began with the Ancient Sumer c. 3,000 BCE, the Indus Valley civilization c. 3,300 BCE, Ancient Egypt c. 3,100 BCE and the Shang dynasty of China c. 1,600 BCE. It is clear that there was trade in luxury goods such as spices, textiles and precious metals between the Indus Valley civilization, Sumer and Egypt. This is the first evidence in history of an intermingling of cultures. Trade by water was along the main trade routes of the Nile, the Tigris and the Euphrates, and big cities developed along their banks. Later camel caravans linked the Indus Valley with the Mediterranean.

TABLE 8.2 Characteristics of the Bronze Age in Britain, categorized using key concepts

Key concepts	Bronze Age Britain
Agriculture	Crops and animals (But it is thought that population fell, due to climate change and some returned to hunter gathering life)
Artefacts	Grave goods: golden buckles, pottery jars bronze daggers, cups, necklaces. Sceptres in various stones Images at: www.bbc.co.uk/guides/z874kqt
Attack/Defence	Evidence of an enormous battle, involving 4,000 men across northern Europe; some may have been from 100s of km. away. Causes? Niall Ferguson identifies several preconditions that make war more likely but not inevitable: transition from nomadic to stationary life, high population densities, storage of food, domestication of livestock, long-distance trade that may be monopolized, major ecological events that reduce production of food, and political or social hierarchies and ranking. Even so, people in some places and times had all these factors present and apparently did not make war. See www.ancient-origins.net/news-history-archaeology/scant-evidence-early-prehistoric-people-warlike-020251
Calendar	Probably megalithic
Beliefs	The dead were cremated, and buried in small cemeteries behind each settlement. The large burial sites of the early Bronze Age were a thing of the past, as the land was now needed for agriculture. Round barrows in groups suggest family cemeteries, sometimes close to Neolithic henges. Buried men facing east, women west. Uffington White Horse For Bronze Age sites in Britain see www.aenigmatis.com/prehistoric-sites/england/england-4.htm
Homes/Shelters	The standard farming household consisted of two houses, a main living house and an out-house for cooking and textile production. See: www.ancientcraft.co.uk/services/school-bronzeage.html www.bbc.co.uk/news/uk-england-cambridgeshire-35280290 www.bbc.co.uk/news/uk-england-cambridgeshire-36778820 www.cam.ac.uk/research/news/bronze-age-stilt-houses-unearthed-in-east-anglian-fens
Music	Complex Bronze Age and Iron Age horns have been found throughout Europe, especially in Scandinavia. They were often buried with their owner but without the mouthpiece. The **dord** is a bronze horn native to Ireland, with excavated examples dating back as far as 1000 BC, during the Bronze Age. 104 original dords are known to exist. For Bronze Age pipes in Ireland see http://irisharchaeology.ie/2014/03/five-ancient-musical-instruments-from-ireland/
Public buildings	Major period of stone circle building; improved Stonehenge

continued

TABLE 8.2 Continued

Key concepts	Bronze Age Britain
Settlements	Settled agricultural communities
Social hierarchy	Bronze weapons led to importance of great warriors. In Britain, Ireland, Scotland important graves all contain bronze sword of warrior
	Gradually, from about 3,500 BCE, their way of life spread across Europe, eventually reaching Britain, Ireland and Spain, superimposing a new world order ruled by a more aggressive, male-dominated society built on controlling horses and making metal weapons. See www.independent.co.uk/news/world/world-history/a-military-revolution-how-bronze-age-innovations-ushered-in-an-age-of-violence-and-inequality-1608029.html
Technology	Textile production: womens' woollen skirts and short tunics, men knee-length woollen kilts, tunics, cloaks, round woollen hats
	The late Bronze Age also featured advanced pottery-making techniques, and more sophisticated weapon-making
	Beaker people arrived in Britain; rich grave goods: stone battle axes, metal daggers, with elaborately decorated hilts
	Copper mined in Wales
	Nomads transported precious bronze-making raw materials such as tin and copper from places as far-flung as Cornwall and Wales in the west to the Caucasus mountains in Asia Minor and beyond into the Middle East and India
Trade	Precious ornaments of gold and amber and golden cups similar to those of Mycenae, in graves, lead to speculation of trade with Greece
	There is plenty of evidence for Bronze Age communication between Briton and Europe, 3,000 years ago, when Stonehenge was still in use, and long before Tutenkhamun. In the Early Bronze Age swords and daggers from the Hallstatt culture (Switzerland) were a significant import
	Available evidence, though very limited, points to Cornwall as the sole early source of tin in Central and Northern Europe
Writing	In Sumer, Indus Valley, Egypt, Shang Bronze Age civilisations but not in Britain

Children are required to have an overview of these ancient civilizations and to make an in-depth study of one of them. Clearly it is important to look for patterns between them. Why did they become great civilizations? What did they have in common? In what ways were the different? Why did they end?

Comparing early civilizations: Sumer, Indus Valley, Ancient Egypt and the Shang dynasty

This table is of course not comprehensive. It could be used by a teacher as a guide, in order to ask groups of children to research some of these concepts themselves. This could be organized in various ways. The findings could then be used to create a collaborative table for class discussion of the questions above. Answers need to refer to sources as well as make hypotheses. Or the table could be used by the teacher to plan a breadth study of the four civilizations. Older children could be given this table as a basis for discussing the connections between these civilizations.

- Did these civilizations all grow up near a great river? Was that important? Why? What was the climate like?

- What was similar about their agriculture?

- Could they grow crops so successfully that not everyone had to work on the land to survive? What happened to the surplus?

- What happened to people who left the land?

- How were they able to make luxury ornaments?

- What common metal did they all make and use?

- What was common about the way they moved their goods around for trade?

- How did these changes affect their societies?

- Did they have similar houses? If so why?

- Why did they all need a calendar?

- Did they have similar beliefs?

- Why did they all develop writing and mathematics?

- Why did they develop music?

- Did they all have strong armies? If so why?

- Was there anything similar about the way they were ruled? If so why?

- Were there similarities in why these civilizations ended?

Activities to explore a chosen civilization in depth

Children could then decide which civilization they would like to research further and discuss activities for doing so. For example, if they decided on Ancient Sumer, perhaps working in groups, they might decide to make a map of the area today, and in about 2,200 BCE, in order to connect the Sumer civilization with countries in this region, which we know about today. They might make a plan of a farm (*agriculture*) in the Sumerian Empire and models of irrigation techniques (*technology*) and a farming year (*calendar*). They could make a model of a ziggurat (*artefacts*), find out what Ancient Sumerians seemed to care about and thought, through studying their gods and goddesses, (*beliefs*) create images or 'pipe-cleaner' models of the inhabitants of a Sumerian town, saying what each of their roles was, and model the brick *houses* of the town they lived in (pipe cleaners can be obtained online), or make a model of the dock in the town with Sumerian model boats (*transport*). The possibilities are endless and could generate much historical enquiry. Parker Heath (2015) gives an excellent outline of Ancient Sumer and questions to investigate. (See also – a fascinating child-made animation of the Indus Valley Civilization – at www.harappa.com/video.)

Links between these ancient civilizations and today

If, as it is has been argued, that it is important to make connections between past and present (to see ways in which we are connected with the past), and also connections between different places in the past, Palmyra is an interesting example. Palmyra (in Syria) was at its apex in the third century BCE, and related to the Indus Valley, Sumer and Egyptian civilizations. It was a merchant republic where trade routes crossed, the only city between the Euphrates and the Mediterranean. Arabia, Persia, Hellenism, the Orient and the West all came together in Palmyra, dealing in incense, myrrh, pepper, ivory and pearls, Indian and Chinese cotton and silk (a third of a kilogram of Chinese silk was worth tens of thousands of eggs or 6,000 haircuts!). But in 2015 the remains of Palmyra 'were blown up by Isis in 2015, because it was venerated by westerners whose culture includes a love of historical monuments and a curiosity for the beliefs of other people' (Veyne 2017).

The Iron Age in Britain

The Iron Age can be compared with the previous societies. It is also very interesting to compare it with Table 8.5 about Roman Britain. How long was Britain part of the Roman Empire? In what ways did being part of the Roman Empire change Britain for most people? Why? Was this good for Britain?

What changed between the Stone Ages, the Bronze Age and the Iron Age in Britain, and what did not change? Why not? How does the duration of each period compare? Why are they different? Did they end in the same way as the four ancient civilizations? Table 8.6 is a starting point for considering the similarities between the Anglo-Saxon and Viking civilizations. How much did they have in common? What might be the implications of this? How much of the Roman culture in Britain continued in Anglo-Saxon England? Why? How much had Britain changed since the Iron Age? Since the Bonze Age? Since the Stone Age? Does this tell a story of constant progress? In what ways? What changed most and what changed least? What would an Early Saxon settler make of the society his descendents became part of? Which period contributed most to progress? Is progress inevitable? These are some of the questions to discuss. There are not always 'right answers'. Discussion of similarities and differences between societies, cause and effects of changes, must cite the evidence for a point of view; how do we know? Or is it a hypothesis? If so, what is it based on?

What other questions arise, for you and for children, when you start looking at these 'Big Pictures'?

The Anglo-Saxons and the Vikings

Please refer to Table 8.6.

TABLE 8.3 Recorded achievements of four ancient civilizations, linked to key concepts

Concepts	Ancient Sumer	Indus Valley (or Harappan Civilization)	Ancient Egypt	Shang Dynasty of Ancient China
Time	In approximately 2,200 BCE–1,750 BCE. Sumer became part of the first-ever empire created by Sargon of Akkad, a region just north of Sumer	3,300 BCE–1,700 BCE 'Mature Period' 2600 BCE–1900 BCE www.harappa.com/video	3,100 BCE–32 BCE	1,600 BCE–1,046 BCE
Place	Between Tigres and Euphrates in Southern Mesopotamia, modern Iraq; incorporated parts of modern-day Iran, Syria and Turkey	Modern Pakistan and North/North West India	North Africa around the Nile River (Modern Egypt)	Centred around the Yellow River in North East China
Agriculture	Intensive agriculture and irrigation (sheep, goats, cattle, pigs; wheat, barley, chick peas, millet, garlic, lettuce, mustard); same irrigation techniques as in Egypt	Excavation revealed oldest ploughed field crops: flood plain agriculture, probably dams to store water, reservoirs in coastal regions (east) stored rainfall (dates, peas melons wheat, barley, peas mustard, sesame, pulses, cotton)	Sakia and shaduf for irrigation Emmer wheat, barley Vegetables and fruits grown in gardens Made clothes from linen dyed, for example with indigo or saffron	Cows, sheep, horses, chickens, millet, corn Expanded irrigation systems
Artefacts	Ziggurats, religious figurines – www.youtube.com/watch?v=dxUAtvLy7_w – www.youtube.com/watch?v=msTtqGfOQkc – www.youtube.com/watch?v=NbNqcKoJYhU – www.youtube.com/watch?v=5sM6u91Qplc	Terracotta toys: animals and carts with moving parts; board games, ivory counters and dice, beads; jewellery; bronze weapons, ornaments www.nationalmuseumindia.gov.in /departments-jewellery-gallery.asp?lk=dp11 Cotton cloth woven Elaborate ornaments, jewellery, bronzes, pottery www.bbc.co.uk/guides/zcsbr82	Artefacts: carved jade and stone, bronze ritual vessels and weapons, glazed porcelain and woven silk	Excellent bronzes, jade carving, silk, embroidery, china, lacquer painting developed as industries

continued

TABLE 8.3 Continued

Concepts	Ancient Sumer	Indus Valley (or Harappan Civilization)	Ancient Egypt	Shang Dynasty of Ancient China
Beliefs	Each city had its own god or goddess and a ruling priest (or priest king). Gods included: – Ur – Nanna, the Moon god, Lord of Wisdom, Lord of Destiny – Uruk – Inanna, Lady of the Sky, Queen of Heaven, goddess of love, fertility, and war – Eridu-Enki, the high god of water, intellect, creation, medicine and wisdom, and the inventor of civilization. Temples built in honour of Gods on top of a ziggurat (www.history.org.uk/primary/categories/760/resource/8214/ancient-sumer) Belief in afterlife as descent into underworld: not pleasant.	Little evidence of beliefs to go on, no lavish tombs found with goods for an afterlife. Statue of so-called Priest King (named thus by archaeologists) may have religious motifs. Great Bath, Mohenjodaro may have been place for elite religious ceremony. Elements of Hinduism may have derived from Indus Valley civilization.	Pharoah believed to have divine power. Many gods. Over 1,000 gods. Temple rituals. People could also interact individually with gods. Afterlife and funerary practices. Lasted 3,000 years. Sun god Ra, Creator god Amun, Mother goddess Isis. Pyramids. Story of Jaguar god worshipped by the Maya, and Helios, of Ancient Greece. Three civilisations at different times in different parts of the world and they all have similar gods and stories. How do you explain that?	Believed in a supreme god Di and subsidiary spirits, ancestor worship, afterlife, oracle bones – bones and priests read cracks – ground down to make traditional medicines. Animism (everything has a soul) and shamanism (can communicate with spirit world) and ancestor worship.
Trade	Wealth and success from trade. Weavers and potters sold to traders, who travelled the rivers Tigris and Euphrates and over Safross mountain to Zagross and Afghanistan by donkey.	Possibly first people to grow cotton. May have traded it in Western Asia. Farmers brought food to cities. Traders brought materials to make luxury items e.g. beads, gold, silver, gem	Trade along Nile and sometimes eastern and western deserts and Mediterranean. Traded gold, papyrus, linen, grain.	Around Yellow River and Yangste. Did not trade internationally – avoided foreigners. Traded items made by artisans and sculptors. Jade , marble, woven silk, porcelain tableware,

	Trade through Persian Gulf and across sea to Indus Valley.	stones; took finished goods to trade in other cities. Imported chert (flint), lead, tin and copper from across the whole region. Cedar wood from Kashmir.	Received cedar wood from Lebanon, ebony and ivory from Africa, lapis lazuli from Afghanistan, incense, myrrh, oils from Punt, gold from Nubia and copper and iron leather, slaves, ivory and timber from Central Africa via the River Nile, oil and horses from Lebanon.	bronze items, ink painting on silk. Bronze used to make chariots, vessels, weapons and instruments. Pottery. Bronze armour. Mass produced bronze.
Transport	Boats probably with wooden planks, raised stern and prow and cotton or reed sail. Excavation revealed oldest dock. Overland by pack animals. Probably invented wheel.	Bullock carts and boats – cabin in middle, rowed, probably sails; probably same style of boats as used today for shallow waters.	Boats from papyrus and later wood. Huge cargo boats sailed in Mediterranean; could carry 500 tons of stone for pyramids. Temples often connected to Nile by man-made canals. Donkeys.	Waterway transport. Wheeled vehicles.
Social hierarchy	The social structure of the Sumerians was decidedly different from other societies of that and later times. Stratified: gentry government officials, priests, wealthy landowners, trades, middle class merchants, lower class and slaves.	A ruling elite may have included priests and warriors, possibly local kings. Warriors, traders, skilled craftworkers, merchants, minor officials, farmers, unskilled workers.	Hierarchy: Pharoah Viziers Priests Soldiers Craftsmen Slaves. First to invent organized labour.	Hierarchy: King Military nobles Priests Merchants Craftsmen Peasants
Calendar	Based on moon and sun.	We do not know.	12 months of lunar year grouped into 3 seasons that coincided with 4 seasons of the Nile.	Based on sun and moon.

continued

TABLE 8.3 Continued

Concepts	Ancient Sumer	Indus Valley (or Harappan Civilization)	Ancient Egypt	Shang Dynasty of Ancient China
Attack/ Defence	In order to control irrigation many rivalries and battles. Divided time into minutes and seconds.	Dominated the area and archaeologists disagree about how peaceful it was or whether there was any or much warfare. There is disagreement about whether walls were fortifications or mark social divisions. No evidence of heavy warfare infrastructure but metal weapons may not have survived.	See video: www.ancient.eu/ Egyptian_Warfare	Shang Kings could muster 1,000 troops whom they led themselves.
Houses	Sun-dried brick, faced onto courtyards, flat roofs for extra living space, doors had hinges and keys, wealthy had 2 storeys.	Large and small houses had rooms arranged around a central courtyard. There were no windows onto the main street to keep out dust and noise; side windows let in light and air. Some had two floors. Stairs led to the upper floors and roof. Walls were probably covered with mud plaster.	Bricks from mud and straw. Nobles' villas by Nile, faced with white lime stone, painted white with coloured decoration; some had 30 rooms, often gardens and pools. Peasants, small house with courtyard, ramp to front door and to second or third storey and onto roof. In town ground floor for business.	Built houses. People built fire-pits in the centre of their round houses, and they were probably nice and warm even in winter because the earth made good insulation against the cold. They smoothed and plastered both the walls and the floor, to keep them clean. In summer they moved to tree houses – safe from animals and snakes.
Music	Played lyres and type of oboe. www.youtube.com/watch? v=wSX-xHE-CqU	No evidence survives of musical instruments other than drums in a procession depicted on a small seal, and terracotta bird-shaped whistles	For song and dance in religious rituals and all aspects of everyday life. Stringed (lyres, harps, lutes), wind (flutes) and percussion instruments (rattles, drums, bells). Professional musicians. Wrote lyrics for songs.	The Shang enjoyed music and played ocarinas, pipes, drums, chimes, cymbals and bells.

Settlements	Society organized into cities. These cities were largely independent from one another, although they had to co-operate.	Over 2,000 settlements found, mostly near Indus and Ghagga Hakra Rivers. Cities: include Harappa and Mohenjo-Daro (World Heritage Unesco site). Gateways into cities. Cities built on grid plan, N/S in Mohenjodaro oriented to stars, a separate walled "citadel". Sewage system.	Cities surrounded by administrative area along Nile for trade. Workers villages near temples and pyramids.	Walled cities along the Yellow River. Agriculture in villages. Irrigation.
Writing	First writing. c. 400 literary works written in cuneiform on clay tablets in the Sumerian e.g. Sumerian King List, a valuable source of evidence, the Epic of Gilgamesh about a legendary king of Uruk (a city of Sumer), hymns, parables and letters. www.history.org.uk/primary/categories/760/resource/8214/ancient-sumer	Indus script first in India. Undeciphered, therefore little known of Indus. Thousands of inscriptions found, never more than 26 signs long, usually on seals, clay sealings with reverse impressions of packaging, pottery, tools. 400 basic signs identified. May have been written on palm leaves or birch bark which did not survive.	Hieroglyphics (pictures stood for words) means holy writing. Write on papyrus with sharp reeds dipped into ink. Made 'paper ' from papyrus, (reeds). Writing: hieroglyphics. There was a huge library in Alexandria containing 500,000 books, founded in 290 BCE.	Writing on cattle and tortoise shell bones (oracle bones); also wrote history of dynasty on bones. Writing on silk but none survived. These characters provide a record of the Shang people's fortunetelling, and their belief in and worship to god and their ancestors.
Inventions	Agriculture, wheel, sail boats, chariot, mathematics, irrigation, schools, astrology, the plough, the arch.	2/4/8/16 etc. with upper decimal standardization of weights and measures. Geometry of streets. Copper alloy bar for measuring (ruler). Maths, bricks conform to ratio 4:2:1.	Astronomy, medicine, language, architecture. Mass-produced patyrus. Black ink, brightly coloured inks and dyes. Mathematics: measurements based on body parts to measure land and buildings. Decimal number system based on 19 fingers, multiplication and division.	Developed bronze casting. Yoke, harness, spoked wheel, mathematics: Chinese rod numbers, possibly combination of horse, chariot and composite bow made of animal sinew, horn bone, and wood (small and powerful abacus.

continued

TABLE 8.3 Continued

Concepts	Ancient Sumer	Indus Valley (or Harappan Civilization)	Ancient Egypt	Shang Dynasty of Ancient China
Public buildings	Sumerian ziggurats were enormous temple complexes which also contained offices, workshops and treasuries. Sumerians believed that their gods lived in the temples and descended to earth down their stairs.	No temples, palaces can be positively identified but 'Great Bath' Mohenjodaro considered to be for elite religious ceremonies.	Pyramids, temples. Little remains because mud and sandstone disintegrated. www.ancient.eu/Egyptian_Architecture/	Built public buildings. Also defensive walls and towers out of wood and mud. With increasing wealth and growth of cities 2 luxurious palaces were built with taxes from farming population; also temples.
Rulers/ government	Believed early kings had supernatural powers (e.g. in the Epic of Gilgamesh, monsters guarded the gates to world of the dead and the dead became ghosts. From 2530 BCE had written law code. Council of elders (most wealthy) in cities.	No evidence of supreme ruling Kings, but some small statues found in Mohenjodaro may belong to a ruling dynasty.	Kings and Queens/ Pharoahs. Government and religion inseparable. Pharoah chose vizier (2nd in command), chief treasurer and commander of the armies. Governors in local areas.	Rulers: high priests as well as military rulers (king/priests). Emperors. Lady Fu Hao was a Shang dynasty queen and military leader who died c1200 BCE. She led an army of 10,000 men. Her tomb contains the remains of 16 slaves and six dogs who were sacrificed when she died.
Settlements	Each city was ruled by a king, although only one king was supreme at a time. Largely independent but did co-operate.	Remains of over 2000 cities, sites including large cities discovered (e.g. Harappa first cities – city states – continually rebuilt until they looked like hills). Cities built in grid system, with sewage systems. Most people lived in villages.		Large, walled towns which grew into a huge cities (e.g. Erlitou).

| Reasons why each civilization ended | Empire was destroyed by raids from neighbouring hill peoples. In about 1750 BCE. the Semitic Sumerians moved north and their culture ended. | Theories suggested (and still challenged and debated by generations of archaeologists):
 – invasion of Indo-European peoples
 – climate change
 – changing river patterns
 – external trade crisis
 – political crisis within elite. | Closure of the last pagan temples in the sixth century BCE?

 Last appearance of the ancient hieroglyphic script?

 Fall of the ancient religion in the face of Christianity?

 The Greek Kingdom of Ptolemy ruled Egypt until 30 BCE, when, under Cleopatra, it fell to the Roman Empire and became a Roman province. | Last king, Shang Zhou, was defeated because his own people rebelled against his tyrannical rule. His own troops and slaves joined the Zhou tribe attacking in the last battle. |

TABLE 8.4 Concepts underpinning all societies: the Iron Age in Britain 800 BCE–43 CE

Agriculture	Grain stored in granaries or underground timber-lined pits, with offerings to the gods at bottom. Methods changed little until seventeenth century.
	Oats, rye, millet, later spelt and emmer barley. Fields were rectangular organized on a large scale.
	About 100 BCE forests cleared. Simple plough with iron ploughshare. Fields were manured with mast loam. Chalk soil; wells made in chalk (Pliny the Elder 70 CE). Cows, goats, sheep, pigs. When necessary protected in enclosures around hill forts. Dogs for herding and hunting. Farms grew enough for needs, without surplus until Romans in 54 BCE commandeered supplies. After this they traded with Romans; Cunobelinus had wheat ear on his coins. Thousands of farmsteads and successful agriculture for 4,000 years. Population similar size to Domesday.
Artefacts	By the eighteenth century BCE, there is increasing evidence of Britain becoming closely tied to continental Europe, especially in the south and east. New weapon types appeared which were very much like those in Europe, such as the Carp's tongue sword, which have been found in Atlantic Europe.
	Celtic Art and Industry Exhibition, British Museum 2015–2016.
	This exhibition for the first time, recognized that the Celts were not one people but Celtic art and artefacts spread across Europe from Portugal to Turkey and into Scotland, Wales, Cornwall and Ireland from 500 BCE. It is found in the 'Gundestrup cauldron' (Denmark 100 BCE) and in the eighteenth century CE St Chad's Gospels and in Medieval stone crosses.
	Inspired by the so-called 'Celtic' style emanating from La Tene in Switzerland, the smiths produced a wide range of high-quality items, many richly decorated with incised designs accompanied by enameled inlays. These ranged from brooches to prestige objects including torcs (neck rings), shields, helmets, swords and scabbards, mirrors and ornate horse harnesses and vehicle fittings.
	See www.bbc.co.uk/history/ancient/british_prehistory/overview_british_prehistory.
Attack/ Defence	Boudicca: fighting in chariots, not battle formation.
	3,000 hill forts in British Isles, some huge e.g. Maiden Castle and Old Oswestry (Shrops.) Danebury (Hants.) probably for festivals, trade, religious activities etc.
Calendar	Fragments of a bronze calendar found in Coligny, near Bourg, in France, mentions two of the seasonal festivals: Beltane (1 May) and Lugnasad (1 August). Beltane recognizes the beginning of the warm season – a time when cattle are put out to open grazing, while Lugnasad would have marked the hoped-for ripening of the crops.
	Samhain was a transitional period, when the spirits could pass between the two worlds – this pagan tradition still continues in our society today, at Halloween.
Beliefs	Some groups buried dead with grave gods. Precious objects, including jewellery are found in water, probably votive objects. These include animals and humans (e.g. Lindow Man in Cheshire) often in important part of the settlement.
	Weapons and horse trappings have been found in the bog at Llyn Cerrig Bach on Anglesey and many weapons have also been found in rivers, especially the Thames, but also the Trent and Tyne. Some buried hoards of jewellery are interpreted as gifts to the earth gods.
	Texts refer to Samhain (1 November) and Imbolc (1 February). Imbolc possibly represented a time when the ewes began their lactation and therefore a new cycle for livestock. Samhain represented the end of one year and the beginning of the next. It was a time when the grazing season was over and the flocks were culled.
	See https://en.wikipedia.org/wiki/British_Iron_Age

TABLE 8.4 Continued

Homes	Round, single room, of varying sizes with timber or stone wall.
Music	Singing and instruments important. At age 14 Celtic young people would make their own musical instruments (flute, bagpipes, harp, drum strings). Bards (wandering singers, story-tellers, poets) emerged (Strabo IV.4).
Public buildings	Unlike other ancient civilizations no major cities, palaces, temples, pyramids. Could construct large defensive stone buildings where needed (e.g. brochs of Scotland). Massive hill forts and engineering works, but they were of perishable timber (e.g. Maiden Castle).
Settle-ments	Larger farming communities. A very well preserved settlement has been discovered at the site of Chysauster in Cornwall. It was made up of individual houses of stone with garden plots, clustered along a street. Before the Roman conquest in 43 CE large settlements (oppida) appeared in Southern Britain. These seem to have been religious, economic and political centres and centres for producing Iron Age coins. Society was organized as tribes. See www.britainexpress.com/History/Celtic_Britain.htm Dr Amanda Clarke and Professor Michael Fulford (Reading University) and volunteers have been excavating a site in Hampshire, which is changing our idea of Iron Age settlement. At a level dating to a century before the Romans they found seeds of curry plants, mint, marigold and dill. They planted them and in due course they sprang into bloom. These Mediterranean herbs are familiar from Roman sites across Britain but support other evidence that the Atrebates tribe were enjoying a lifestyle which would have been familiar to the Romans when they arrived in 43 CE. An olive stone was also found at the bottom of a well. See www.theguardian.com/uk/2012/jul/31/silchester-iron-age-roman-britain The Britons were developing 'pro cities', vast conglomerations of industrial, religious and governmental activities. Many developed into major cities of the Roman province and of Medieval England (e.g. Colchester, Silchester, St Albans). See www.britishmuseum.org/PDF/british_museum_roman_britain.pdf
Social hierarchy	The tribal leaders in southern England began putting their names on coins and calling themselves 'rex' (king). The Celts were warriors, as evidenced in their grave goods. Traders and craftspeople also emerged, as well as farming communities. In each tribe there were warriors, leaders and trainers and in civil life administrators, priests, tradespeople and most important, farmers and farm workers.
Technology	The Celts migrated from Europe, bringing iron working to Britain. Wheel thrown pottery. Baking in ovens, spinning, weaving, dyeing.
Trade	Phoenician traders probably began visiting Great Britain in search of minerals around this time, bringing with them goods from the Mediterranean and artefacts from Northern Europe across the North Sea. Bronze Age trade links increased trade links with the continent, especially importing swords and daggers. Celtic style artefacts were imported but later were adopted and adapted by the locals. In 2016 a tiny copper coin dated between 300 and 264 BCE was found in Saltford between Bath and Bristol, which has a horse's head on one side and the head of the chief goddess of Carthage, Tanit, on the other. Experts say it came from Sardinia or Ancient Carthage.

continued

TABLE 8.4 Continued

	Saltford was on a major trade route before the Romans came to Britain, on a ford, which was the only place to cross the Avon. This is the only dateable evidence of human activity in the West of England and suggests trade from the Bristol Chanel to the western Mediterranean. Professor David Mattingly, an archaeologist and Roman historian at the University of Leicester, said, 'It's really interesting to have a Carthaginian coin in Britain. Suppose that coin was deposited close to its minting – at the time, there were no coins being used in Britain. It would have been quite alien to people. We are very sure that horses were important at the time so that may have invoked a lot of interest back then. It's a very interesting find.'
	Phil Harding of the Saltford Environment Group, said that the coin is significant because it is one of the oldest coins ever to be found in England. 'Only eight of these have ever been found, always on ancient trade routes,' he said.
	See www.dailymail.co.uk/sciencetech/article-3038594/Britain-s-ancient-connection-Carthage-2-300-year-old-coin-reveals-Mediterranean-trade-route-dating-Iron-Age.html
	The Celts infiltrated Britain between 100 and 500 BCE, bringing with them iron smelting. This had a great impact as, unlike tin and copper, iron was available in many places and fairly cheap, so increased trade.
	From the late second century BCE onwards, south-central Britain was indirectly linked into Roman trading networks via Brittany and the Atlantic seaways to southwest France importing Italian wine; imported gold coins are evidence of contact with the tribes of Northern France.
	After Caesar's conquest of Gaul, a thriving trade developed between southeast Britain and the near Continent wine and olive oil amphorae and pottery. Strabo, writing in the early first century AD, lists ivory chains and necklaces, amber gems, glass as articles imported to Britain. Exports were grain, cattle, gold, silver, iron, hides, slaves and hunting dogs. This trade probably thrived as a result of political links between groups in Southeast Britain and the Roman world.
	See https://en.wikipedia.org/wiki/British_Iron_Age
	By 20 BCE there was growing trade between south east Britain and the Roman world and after Caesar conquered Gaul in 50 BCE this increased.
	See www.bbc.co.uk/history/ancient/british_prehistory/overview_british_prehistory
	Recent research has revealed how sophisticated Britons' taste in food, and global links were before 44 CE. University of Reading archaeologists have found celery and coriander seeds – used as seasoning – and an olive stone at the bottom of a late Iron Age well, all pre-dating 43 CE. Another well yielded a celery seed from the same period, and several dill seeds dating to c. 40–50 CE. Prof. Mike Fulford said of the finds, 'We take these culinary treats for granted, but over 2,000 years ago trade in these foodstuffs would have been essential – at least for the wealthy tribal aristocracy of Iron Age Britain. A journey to Britain from the Med would have taken several weeks, either by sea around the coasts of Spain, Portugal and France, or overland through France.'
	See www.heritagedaily.com/2012/07/iron-age-people-introduced-mediterranean-cuisine-to-britain/48614
Transport	2- or 4-wheeled carts and chariots, pulled by horses.
Writing	Coins were introduced at the end of the Iron Age, so Britons were probably writing for administrative purposes as were the Gauls, before the Roman invasion. See www.britishmuseum.org/PDF/british_museum_roman_britain.pdf

TABLE 8.5 Concepts underpinning all societies: the Roman impact on Britain

Agriculture	No revolution in agriculture. But farming intensified, with bigger markets. For most people daily life continued as before; farming, planting, ploughing, processing crops, managing woodland, flocks and herds, butchering, tanning, spinning, weaving, basket making.
Artefacts	Roman artefacts found in Britain are concerned with: commerce, travel, industry, agriculture, military and writing equipment, domestic life, personal ornament, recreation, medicine, religion, funerals (Allason-Jones 2011), The British Museum Room 49.
Attack/defence	The army was originally a centre of Roman culture but literally went native as it switched to local recruitment. In the third and fourth centuries all the soldiers were British born. Hadrian's wall and forts built in stone. Standing army in Britain of 40,000 troops. The Roman army brought new weapons and ways of fighting. The few troops remaining in 406 were Britons.
Calendar	Lunar and solar. The Julian calendar was the first to consist of 365 days, along with a leap year every 4 years. Names of our months derive from Roman months.
Beliefs	Britons expected to comply with state gods Jupiter, Juno, Mars etc. and with the imperial cult (worship of the guardian spirit of the emperor as a form of loyalty to the state). But it was also the Roman tradition to worship the gods of the conquered (e.g. Sul in Bath, Aquae Sulis) which they identified with Roman godess Minerva, for mutual understanding). Both Roman and British gods were similar (gods of nature, peoples, war etc.). Many native gods came to be worshipped in stone temples, in Roman style. Romans also brought gods from other parts of the Empire and all religions were tolerated except the Druids who co-ordinated all the tribes and so could foment rebellion and Christians. Constantine, crowned Emperor in York, won a battle at Milvian Bridge in 312 CE, declared Christianity the central religion of the Empire.
Homes	Romano-British villas (and towns) were built by Britons using Gallo-Roman interpretations of Italian ideas. Most people continued to live in Iron Age houses, although, from the third century, they were legally Roman citizens. In Wales and the North even British aristocracy not Romanized and pre-Roman life-style continued. The few 'palatial villas' were mostly fourth century. Most villas did not have hypocausts, bath houses or mosaics and most belonged to fourth century. After 406 CE towns and villas in ruins within a generation.
Music	Played at religious festivals and theatre: lyre, pan pipes, tibia, (wind) percussion.
Public buildings	Romans built in stone, in straight lines on a grand scale, bridges, baths, aqueducts, and in cities temples and administrative buildings, town hall (basilica) and courts of justice, public baths, often a theatre and amphitheatre.
Settlements	Developed some Iron Age towns as major cities and established new cities. Added early Roman farmsteads to British farmsteads.

continued

TABLE 8.5 Continued

	Romans probably realized Britons insufficiently like Romans to be changed into successful Roman provincial societies. Small concentrated areas of 'in-comers' (in e.g. Bath and London). Little settlement of immigrant civilians. Soldiers were from many ethnic backgrounds. Incomers outnumbered by Britons 20:1, although these were the dominant ruling elite. We do not know much about life in Roman towns.
	But lifestyle of ordinary farming families changed little, beyond markets for their produce and taxes. Romans encouraged the growth of towns near army bases and encouraged British aristocrats to build town houses; no set style so a lot of variety. But during the second and third centuries they went back to the land about 10 miles from town. Their villas were the centre of a farming, pottery or metalworking complex.
	www.britainexpress.com/History/Life_in_Roman_Britain.htm
	By the third and fourth century, towns had stone walls. Roman towns were built in lowland areas near rivers and fords. British settlements were in highland areas. Special established towns for retired soldiers.
Social hierarchy	Midlands and southern British tribal aristocracies became culturally Roman and made Roman citizens for services to state. Romans set up administrative areas, based on tribal boundaries and British tribal leaders administered Britain within the Roman framework.
	Elite tribal leaders imported.
Technology	Potting, smelting, smithing as before. New technologies in quarrying, mining, glass-making, statues of life-like human figures, surveying, measuring (including time clocks), architecture, engineering, stone-walls, timber buildings, tiled roofs, drains, sewers, roads, bridges, ports, wharves, bigger ships, mining, metal-working, mosaics, wall-painting, new types of pottery.
Trade	Large new trade network. Britons had coins but did not use them to purchase things. Romans brought their own coinage which was the same and could be used anywhere in the empire. Tribal elite imported Roman wine, jewellery, pottery and exported cattle, grain, lead, iron, tin.
Transport	Roman roads were a huge upgrade on British routes. Watling Street and Dere Street still part of our network.
	The Roman road network continued as a skeletal form of communication until the eighteenth century. Official inns and relays of horses at 30–50 km along roads used by Roman officials.
Writing	Britons probably used Roman writing for trade but its use was clearly greater after the Roman occupation.
	Latin which, with Celtic dialects, is thought to be have been spoken in Roman Britain, was replaced after the Roman withdrawal, with Celtic dialects.

Synopsis

The military imposition of a different, fashionable culture on populous, wealthy, native British societies (www.britishmuseum.org/PDF/british_museum_roman_britain.pdf). The lives of most of the British population changed little during the Roman occupation. After 406 ce there seems to have been a remarkably quick collapse of government and institutions, economy and almost all aspects of Roman provincial life. Unlike in France, Spain, Italy there was a lack of clear direct influence in subsequent centuries.

TABLE 8.6 Comparison of Anglo-Saxon and Viking societies

Concept	Anglo-Saxons	Vikings
Place	Saxon tribes from north-west Germany and Upper Saxony. Angles from south-west Denmark, Jutes from central Denmark. They migrated to Britain in fifth century CE. Traditionally, Saxons settled in South, Angles in East Anglia. Jutes in Kent and Hampshire. Gradually formed 7 kingdoms . . .	From Denmark, Norway and Sweden. In Britain they settled in islands off west coast of Scotland and north-west Scotland, parts of Ireland and Wales, Isle of Man, Northumbria, Nottingham, Derby, Stamford, Lincoln (East Anglia, York – Danelaw).
Time	410–1066 CE	Kings of England 789–1066 CE Viking Kings of England: Sweyn Forkbeard 1013, Canute, 1016–1035, Harald Harefoot 1037–1040, Hardicanute 1040–1042, followed by Ethelred's son, Edward the Confessor 1042–1066.
Agriculture	Most people were farmers. Basis of wealth that made England worth invading. 2 or 3 strip fields; one left fallow. Animals slaughtered and salted for winter.	Most people farmers, even if also raiders and traders.
Artefact	Brooches of different types for fastening clothes, pottery, swords.	See www.theguardian.com/artanddesign/ 2014/mar/03/viking-world-british-museum-neil-macgregor-exhibition Silver Valkyrie (collector of the slain), pendant (Denmark), 800 CE. Most of Viking finds demonstrate the vast area they plundered.
Attack/ Defence	Thanes, chain mail, others iron helmet and round shield, spears, swords, battle axes, formation was shield wall.	See www.bbc.co.uk/history/ancient/ vikings/weapons_01.shtml Fast, shallow draught ships which could cross seas and sail up rivers. Fought on foot; largest armies for a campaign may have consisted of 4,000–7,000 men. Spears, swords, battle axes, bows and arrows; shields, helmets for leaders, mail armour.
Beliefs	C. fifth–eighth centuries CE, Anglo Saxons pagan, many gods; believed magic charms, potions, stones would protect them; buried with everyday objects. Gods e.g. wooden, Thor, days of the week; elves, dragons, cult trees, wells. Seventh–eighth centuries kingdoms converted to Christianity.	Worshipped many pagan gods. Chief god, Thor, was god of war, god of magic, poetry, war storms and thunder. Frig was his wife, daughter Freja, goddess of love and fertility. Loki was mischievous trixter god. Odin sent his warrior maidens, the Valkyries to collect dead heroes from battlefield and take to great hall of

continued

TABLE 8.6 Continued

Concept	Anglo-Saxons	Vikings
		Valhalla. Vikings settled in Britain, became Christians, c. 900 CE but continued both religions initially.
Calendar	See www.wuffings.co.uk/OECalendar.htm See www.wyrdwords.vispa.com/heathenry/calendar.html Lunar calendar, every 2 years inserted extra month in the summer sailing season between June and July.	Based around solstices and equinoxes. Year divided into summer and winter. Roman calendar of months and days existed in Iceland but farmers and seamen did not use it until eighteenth century.
Houses	Wooden huts with thatched roofs, earth floors, no windows or chimneys, rich had candles. Poor rushes dipped in animal fat. Thanes' home was larger hut, walls hung with tapestries.	Longhouses, timber, wattle and daub and thatch.
Inventions	Art of world-significance, epic poem, Beowulf, illuminations of Lindisfarne Gospels, intricate metal work.	Long boat, magnetic compass. Ancient Greeks discovered magnetite but Vikings used natural magnetic deposits in their homeland; bone and bristle combs (unlike previous combs), sagas, (which like e.g. Greek epic poems) conveyed oral history, skis.
Transport	See www.ucl.ac.uk/archaeology/research/directory/travel-communication-anglo-saxon-england; www.heroicage.org/issues/8/dobson.html (ongoing research projects) to explore whether water or land transport was better	Land transport important: walk, ride, ski, sledge, carriage where possible, ox cart. Wheel ruts indicate Viking roads.
Music	Horns to summon to feast, sheep and deer-horn flutes, drum with skin, lyre with hollow sound board (e.g. as in Sutton Hoo)	Bone flute, (panpipes, stringed instrument found in York). Evidence in literature that Vikings enjoyed music but little material evidence remains.
Social hierarchy	Thanes (upper class), hunting, feasting, gave followers gifts i.e. weapons; churls, rich or poor, owned or rented land but free; thralls, very hard lives. All lived in small villages, self-sufficient. By eleventh century CE 10% lived in towns, created by wealth.	Nobles (jarls), middle class (karls), slaves (thralls). Gradually strong leaders developed who, in the ninth century, became kings. Slaves, no rights, often taken on raids, put to death when couldn't work. Gradations in other classes and social mobility possible. See www.legendsandchronicles.com/ancient-civilizations/the-vikings/viking-social-classes/

TABLE 8.6 Continued

Concept	Anglo-Saxons	Vikings
		Rank of hero for those who proved themselves in battle.
Settlements	By ninth–tenth century CE, fortified settlements (burghs), were also market towns	The Danelaw people followed Viking laws and lived much as in Scandinavia. Most people were farmers.
Writing	Believed runes had religious meaning. That's why a spell and to spell (put words down in right order) are same word. Writan means to carve runes and redan means to interpret runes. Used runes until became Christians then used Roman writing. Anglo Saxon (or Old English) is the earliest form of the English language.	Written alphabet called runes; alphabet called futhark because it had 6 letters. Believed given them by Odin, were magical and could tell the future. No paper; carved with a chisel in stone or wood. Usually used for poetry (sometimes illustrated with horses, snakes, longships) and to keep everyday trade records. History handed down orally. Groups of runes separated with full stop to make a word. Wrote names on their weapons, on stones to record dead family or friend.

Breadth studies from 1066 to the present

Any of the key concepts could be the focus for the study of a theme or aspect of British history after 1066 or a local history study beyond 1066. This would allow children to make connections between each of the units of the National Curriculum and the present. The theory of historical consciousness, regards as very important in enabling children to see that they are part of a continuum between past, present and future. Themes might be, for example, changes and the causes and effects of changes over time in agriculture (farming), conflict, beliefs, homes, public buildings, settlements and technologies. This really would link all the study units of the history curriculum to our lives today and make the whole curriculum both meaningful and problematized.

Teaching approaches for developing 'The Big Picture'

Cognitive theory, making connections and key concepts

It is argued in Chapter 4 (pp. 53–54) that children learn the concepts of chronology and other concepts related to historical enquiry through constantly revisiting them in new contexts. This is particularly relevant to using key concepts in comparing societies and the similarities and differences between them. Fordham (2017) explains such a process as involving retrieval practice, spaced practice, interleaving, concrete examples and dual coding. (Dual coding is the theory that information represented in memory as a word and a picture is more memorable than simply by a word.) If we find out about, discuss

TABLE 8.7 Framework based on Rogers (2016) demonstrating a very broad pattern of change, prior to exploring the detail and complexity of a study unit

	Bands	Tribes	Kingdoms	Empires	Multinational organizations
How are we organized?	Family groups	Council of Elders	Kings: Egbert Aethelwulf Aethelbald Aethelburt Aethelred Alfred the Great	Sumer Indus Valley Egypt Shang Egyptians Greeks Romans	United Nations European Union Nato Association of South East Asian Nations
How do we get our stuff?	Hunting Fishing Gathering nuts, berries, leaves, roots	Growing crops Domesticated animals	Markets Trade	Factories Mass production	Factories with robots
How do we think?	Food! Water! Survival	Farming A bit of iron-work	Trade makes some people rich; they don't have to work. They can think! They employ other people. They don't have to think!	Some organize Others work	Robots Fewer jobs
How do we move?	Follow the food	Where there is better land for farming	Where there is better land for farming	Trade around the globe	Emigrate to where there is work

and have a visual memory of a key concept in an early study unit it is easily stored in our memory. If we then 'retrieve it' and enlarge it, when we encounter it in successive study units, the concept is strong enough in our memory to allow us to critique and debate it. We know that retrieval is more likely to be effective if it is 'spaced out' rather than done in one block; if it is not retrieved at intervals, it is likely to be forgotten. Psychologists show that we are more likely to remember things if they are 'interleaved'; if we study them in different contexts, at intervals, and if they are presented in new ways with concrete examples and images. The more pupils are asked to reflect on and articulate a new concept and to link new ideas to existing ideas, the more likely it is remembered. (There are examples of this in Chapter 12, p. 235.) A good idea may be to link key concepts through telling them as part of an ongoing story.

Making initial connections between concepts through narrative

Initially, children may learn to identify, connect and explain changes, as a chronological, sequential narrative. They may do this by telling a story, or perhaps telling stories focused on different themes: changes in farming, in beliefs, in homes and in technology, based on a timeline. They may learn to integrate time vocabulary concerned with duration, causes and effects into their narratives. Or they may sort images from different periods into sets, perhaps also based on key themes/concepts, perhaps with Venn diagrams showing overlaps, continuity as well as changes between periods. These approaches will involve interpretations and may raise questions. These will lead into more problematic questions. What interrupts a long period when nothing changes; climate change, new technologies, migration bringing new beliefs, new technologies and trade? Who is affected by change and who is not? What stays the same when other things change? What changes quickly and what changes slowly? Do changes lead to progress?

Moving from 'low resolution' to 'high resolution'

Rogers (2016: 59–76), a secondary school history teacher, drawing on the work of Shemilt (2009: 167), said that he came to realize how important vocabulary is to explanation in history and for moving from 'low resolution' (a very broad, stereotypical understanding of changes over time) to 'high resolution' (in which children learn more detail, more complex ideas and begin to understand that change is a complex). Table 8.7 is based on the framework Rogers introduced to help pupils to explore very simple, broad patterns of development across the whole of history in order to connect the present with the past. (He drew amusing little images in each square, which I have replaced with words.) This could be a useful, broad-brushstroke framework to introduce at the beginning of a topic, to remind children of the 'Very Big Picture'. Rogers says that, after introducing this framework, he recognized the need to build in more time to explore terminology in investigating a period in more detail. Rogers likens this process to moving from a blurred Google Earth view into a gradually, increasingly detailed view of a particular place.

'The Big Picture': Britain and global connections

The National Curriculum requires children, at Key Stage 2, to learn about 'changes in Britain from the Stone Age to the Iron Age'. They should also 'develop chronological understanding of British local and world history', noting 'connections, contrasts and trends over time'. If we are to see Britain in relation to global history and to look for connections, patterns and trends in the ways in which societies develop, it is important to investigate Britain's global connections. If the Stone Age to the Iron Age unit is studied early in Key Stage 2, it might be considered useful to return again to the global patterns and vast time scale of prehistory later, when children can grapple with large number calculations, and in the meantime to make them aware that these periods occurred at different times around the globe, which were sometimes connected and usually in the same sequence.

Tables for structuring discussion about global links in a unit

This section aims to facilitate making local, national and global connections between Britain and other societies. Table 8.8 shows the times and sequence in which the Stone Age occurred around the globe and Table 8.9 shows selected global connections, trends and patterns in the Bronze Age. A study unit showing links between and other parts of the globe can be used to:

- discover that Britain, like every country, never changes in isolation;

- look at the connections between places over time in order to understand the reasons for these connections;

- discover the key factors that cause connections between places, and their effects, for example population changes and the wish to move to a country with more opportunities, competition for food and materials and to consider the effects of these changes (e.g. new trade, introduction through trade of new ideas, skills, beliefs and values).

Prehistory: connectivity, trends and patterns

The following section on the Stone Age is intended to provide recent research which will stimulate the thinking of adults, beyond the stereotypical, some of which they can include in their teaching in appropriate ways.

What are the origins of humans?

In 2013, in caves near Johannesburg Lee Berger John Hawks found bones of a species between 335,000–236,000 years old, named homo Naledi, a small-brained non-human species, who apparently ritually buried its dead may, which other hominid populations, may have actually encountered and who possibly interbred with homo sapiens and could

TABLE 8.8 The approximate times and sequence in which the Stone Age occurred around the globe

Dates	Continent
6,000,000 years ago **60 m**	Early Stone Age in *Europe and Asia* (hominoid groups but no homo sapiens)
200,000 and 100,000 years ago **2 m**	*Africa* According to genetic and fossil evidence homo sapiens evolved to anatomically modern humans in East Africa between 200,000 and 100,000 years ago.
c. 125,000 years ago **1.25 m**	*Africa* Some evidence left Africa for Middle East
c. 100,000 ago **1 m**	Possibly migrated to *China*
75,000 years ago **75 cm**	Possibly migrated to *Indian subcontinent*
50,000 years ago **50 cm**	Reached *Southern Asia*
c. 45,000 years ago **45 cm**	*Europe* Homo sapiens reached Europe (and replaced Neandertal population). Hunter-gatherers who lived 45,000 years ago and most probably originated in the second human migration out of Africa into Europe.
36,000 years ago at latest **36 cm**	*Australia* There was a migration from new Guinea and the Philippines 36,000 years ago and from India 4,000 years ago. This did not prevent them from living isolated in the Stone Age until James Cook arrived in 1770.
c. 18,000–15,000 years ago (dates and routes subject to ongoing research) **18 cm–15 cm**	*Americas* Siberians, considered to be the original ancestors of the American Indians, set foot in the New World. Early theories suggest that indigenous American came from Siberia. People moved from central Asia, through Bering Straits land bridge to Siberia and Alaska. New archaeological evidence suggests that North America was first discovered by Stone Age people from Europe, 10,000 years before the Siberians. European style stone tools found on East coast of America (e.g. flint knife made in France). 8,000 year old skeletons in Florida have European DNA (see pp. 145–146). Recent theories are that they came from Australia.
c. 17,000–1,700 years ago **17 cm–2 cm**	*Europe* Cave art Abstract symbols: 32 main geometric signs used throughout late Paleolithic Europe, spanning 30,000 years – through nomads? Trade? Possibly has origins in Africa and probably precursor of writing of Sumer and contemporary ancient civilizations.

continued

TABLE 8.8 Continued

Dates	Continent
9,000 years ago **9 cm**	*Europe* Early agriculturists who moved into Europe about 9,000 years ago (cereals, animals, tools) (Levant, Iraq, Turkey). Neolithic Europe: Greece–agriculture c. 7,000 BCE, North Western Europe 1,700 BCE, which came from the Middle East.
800,000 years ago **8 m** Continuous habitation c. 5,000 years ago **5 cm**	*Britain* No continuous settlement due to ice ages and flooding of the land bridge with Europe (Doggerland). For example it has recently been shown that cereals were first cultivated in Britain in 4,000 BCE, but this did not last, and Britain again became largely pastoral until the Middle Bronze Age. Continuous occupation in Britain after last Ice Age.
The medium-term plan for the Stone Ages (Table 10.1) suggests illustrating this with a globe or world map and a timeline. A possible scale for a timeline would be 60 m. The distances from the present using a scale of 1 cm represents 1,000 years are shown in bold.	

live on in our DNA. Our origins may not simply be that homo sapiens evolved and crowded out other species, but is actually the result of complex interbreeding (Berger and Hawks 2017). See www.youtube.com/watch?v=d8hGCElDQ54.

The Stone Ages

Table 8.8 shows the approximate times and sequence in which the Stone Age occurred around the globe.

The key points of this table are that:

- the same written symbols were apparently used throughout Europe (c. 17,000–1,700 years ago);

- there are patterns in the sequences of development of humans, tool and weapon-making and agriculture;

- it raises questions about how these patterns spread between Africa, China, Asia, Europe the Americas and Australia.

Information to support Table 8.8

Pre Stone Age connections between Norfolk, Europe and Africa: Further information

Prehistory is dynamic and exciting. New discoveries that change our understanding are constantly being made – and there remain many questions to which we do not know the answers, so everyone is capable of making and defending valid hypotheses reported on a torrent of surprising discoveries. Footprints, 800,000 years old, that appeared in the sand at Happisburgh, Norfolk, now again underwater, which were hundreds of thousands of years older than any other evidence of a hominoid species living outside Africa. They are the footprints of five members of a group who could live in a very cold place long before Neandertalers adapted to the cold. In an exhibition on migration, in the British Museum you can put your foot in their digital prints on the floor and reflect on what it means to migrate (see www.britishmuseum.org/research/research_ projects/all_current_projects/featured_project_happisburgh/happisburgh_footprints.aspx).

Africa and the development of the Stone Age

The Stone Age is thought to have occurred in Eastern Africa roughly 200,000–100,000 years ago. A warm, damp climate in Africa about 125,000 years ago made one group of Africans so good at thriving that they displaced all the other Africans, and over the next several thousand years spilled out into the rest of the world. What made this great leap from Africa to the rest of the globe possible? Language? Collective wisdom? Sharing ideas that comes with widespread change? We are all descended from these people, whatever our skin colour. There is surely enough evidence in these studies to convince us of our connectedness with others, and against this background, to make us curious about how these people from Africa fared in the places around the world to which they moved.

Stone Age connections between Britain, Europe, the Middle East, China and South-East Asia

When we look at Mesolithic people we are looking at ourselves. Their DNA is the same (so much so that a 9,000-year-old skeleton from Cheddar Gorge shows a direct line of maternal descent to a teacher living there). Archaeologists think that farming began in the Middle East, China, India and South East Asia about 9,000 years ago and arrived in Britain as techniques were introduced by Neolithic people migrating from continental Europe (see www.britishmuseum.org/PDF/visit-resource_prehistoric-britain-KS2.pdf).

Stone Age connections with Europe and the Americas

Even more amazing is that new archaeological evidence suggests that North America was first discovered by Stone Age people from Europe, 10,000 years before the Siberians, considered to be the original ancestors of the American Indians, set foot in the New World. Several dozen stone tools identical with those in Europe, dating from c. 19,000 years ago, have been discovered along the east coast of the United States. Previously European-style stone tools dating back 15,000 years have been found on the east coast long after they ceased being made in what is now France and Spain. And last year a European-style stone knife, found in Virginia in 1971, revealed that it was made of flint which originated in France. The archaeologists, Stanford and Bradley (2013) have proposed that Stone Age people from Western Europe migrated to America at the height of the Ice Age by travelling on the ice and or by boat, along the frozen edge of the Northern part of the Atlantic. The area where the ice ended and the ocean began would have been extremely rich in fish and sea birds. Scientific tests on 8,000-year-old skeletons in Florida have revealed a high level of what is thought to be European DNA. Further sites are now being excavated.

However, there is continuing research-based debate, often based on DNA, about the origins of the later Stone Age peoples who reached the Americas and developed into native cultures. The original theory was that, much more recently, about 20,000 years ago, low water levels created a frozen land bridge 620 miles wide, across which peoples travelled from Siberia. A later theory is that if people could cross the Atlantic they could cross the Pacific, by boat, and that South American peoples may have originated in Australia or Polynesia. The interesting question is why were Native Americans so far behind Europe and China in developing metal technologies, writing and the wheel? The Inca, for example, had an advanced society and made monumental buildings with stone tools. They did plant corn and potatoes and had advanced mathematical systems, but unlike in Europe, they only applied them to agricultural planning and religious ceremonies. Why was this? It may be because, unlike in the Old World, they had no contact with more advanced civilizations. They were isolated from competition and stimulus. When the South Americans came into contact with the Spanish in the sixteenth century they were quickly overcome by European diseases. The Arabs and China, via the Silk Road, from 200 BCE onwards, had enormous influence on European technologies.

The Stone Ages and Asia and Australia

Similarly, it was thought, until recent genotyping and archaeological research, that the Aboriginal peoples of Australia remained in a complex Stone Age culture for 40,000 years because of their isolation. Although we now know that there was a migration from New Guinea and the Philippines 36,000 years ago and from India 4,000 years ago, this did not prevent them from living isolated in the Stone Age until James Cook arrived in 1770.

Reflections

This seems quite a good introduction to questions about global interdependence – and isolation. Of course we cannot comprehend such a time scale, although it is important to convey it visually and perhaps kinaesthetically (see pp. 143–144). It certainly puts human history into awesome perspective and demands our amazement at humans' capacity for travel, endurance, innovation and collaboration.

Questions

For Years 5 and 6 there are some challenging, big-number, duration calculations and comparisons. For some questions there are only hypotheses although new discoveries are frequently made. And children often have imaginative and valid suggestions. Others are suggested in the text above.

- Why did the Old Stone Age last so long?

- How did the Stone Ages occur on different continents at different times?

- How did the Stone Age reach North America? Where did they come from?

- Why did Native Americans and Aboriginal Australians not move beyond the Stone Age?

- Did the Stone Age in all countries follow the same pattern of development?

- How did people endure the Stone Age existence?

- What were the impacts of changes on people's lives? Why did changes gradually accelerate?

- What made the great leap from Africa to the rest of the globe possible? Language? Collective wisdom? Sharing ideas that comes with widespread change?

- Where might your Stone Age ancestors be found?

- Why did the Inca and Australians and Native Americans remain in the Stone Age?

- How did Chinese culture reach Arabia and Europe?

We are also reminded that progress is not always continuous. For example, it has recently been shown that cereals were first cultivated in Britain in 4,000 BCE, but this did not last, and Britain again became again largely pastoral until the Middle Bronze Age. This may have been due to climate changes reducing the population but as the authors Stevens and Fuller (2015) ask, this was when Stonehenge and other megalithic monuments were created, so was reverting to being pastoral a bad thing?

Stone Ages in Britain and Europe

Table 8.1 shows changes during the Stones Ages in Britain, with key concepts making connections across the British Stone Ages. The Stone Age in Europe and Asia lasted approximately 3 million years, ending between 6,000,000 and 2,000,000 BCE. Humans probably first arrived in Britain about 800,000 BCE. They had to cope with extreme environmental changes and left Britain at least seven times when conditions became too bad. Britons in the early Stone Age moved between Britain and Europe, between various mini Ice Ages. (You may find these sites helpful: www.britishmuseum.org/PDF/visit-resource_prehistoric-britain-KS2.pdf, www.bbc.co.uk/history/handsonhistory/ancient britain.shtmlesource_prehistoric-britain-KS2.pdf and www.theschoolrun.com/home work-help/the-stone-age.)

Change: causes and effects of changes

Stone Age communication across Europe

I find it extraordinary that Stone Age communication and culture seem to have been common across Europe. Von Petzinger (2016) has found that Stone Age people could communicate with others across Europe over thousands of years. Stone Age people in Britain and across Europe and the Far East shared a symbolic system of communicating. More than eighty carvings of animals, dancing women and geometric patterns have been found on the ceiling of a limestone cave at Cresswell Crags, in Nottinghamshire which are similar to images of stampeding horses and charging bison, left by Ice Age artists across Europe. They may convey graphic information, the first attempt to convey written information. Previously the earliest symbols conveying information were cuneiform scripts in Iraq. Von Petzinger found that these shapes comprise only thirty-two different types of symbol across Europe and remained much the same over tens of thousands of years. The same signs are repeated over space and time; 65 per cent stayed in use over 30,000 years. What is even more amazing is that Von Petzinger suggests that the first modern humans to settle in Europe were already using many of the symbols when they arrived. I find this fascinating because I found one 8-year-old who said that what he would like to know was whether the nomadic Stone Age tribes, who has made the glyphs he was shown, could all read the same signs or whether they had different languages – a very thought-provoking question, to which we now have an answer (Cooper 1991).

Examples of children's work relating to the Stone Ages can be found on pages 20–21.

Questions

- Were Stone Age tools made first in Britain?

- How did people in Britain find out about agriculture? How did people in Britain find out about farming?

- Was the first 'calendar' invented in Britain?

- Was the New Stone Age in Britain peaceful? If not why not?

- Did the Stone Age in Britain end suddenly?

- How did nomadic Stone Age people create a common language of symbols across Europe which lasted for 30,000 years? What did the symbols mean?

- What did Stone Age peoples believe? How did they build Stonehenge and other stone circles. Why?

The Bronze Age: global connections, showing trends and patterns and questions to discuss

Table 8.9 shows global connections during the Bronze Age

Was copper sent to Europe from America?

Bronze is an alloy of copper and tin. Copper for making bronze possibly came to Europe from America in 5,300 BCE. In North America, on the north–west coast, metal-working predates contact with Europeans. One fascinating mystery has come to light recently, which suggests that copper in Europe was of poor quality. In the Stone Age Michigan, in 5,300 BCE, very pure copper was being mined, with evidence for smelting it, from 4,000 BCE onwards. Mining stopped in 1,200 BCE. It is claimed that ten tons of copper oxide ingots of the same unique Michigan very pure copper were found in the wreck of a ship wrecked off Turkey in 1,300 BCE (Hauptmann *et al.* 2002). The structure and composition of ingots from the Ulu Buran wreck in 1,300 BCE suggest that the cargo represents the world market of bulk metal in the Mediterranean and is greater than 99.5 per cent pure copper. Carbon dating of the wood timbers in the pits dates from 2,450 BCE (see http://turkisharchaeonews.net/news/uluburun-shipwreck).

The Bronze Age exhibition in the British Museum seemed to endorse the finding that copper was brought to Europe from North America at this time. It was stated that from about 2,500 BC, the use of copper, formerly limited to parts of southern Europe, suddenly swept through the rest of the continent. The legends of indigenous American legends say that the mining was done by 'light-skinned marine men'. And petroglyphics have been found of a Bronze Age 'bird ship' and of a circle with a cross in it, also seen on a copper oxide ingot, and a Bronze Age petroglyphic of a similar single-line style has been found in Cornwall (Soskin 2009). There are several internet websites relating this account. This one is supported by numerous academic references: https://graham hancock.com/wakefieldjs1/. No doubt it will be contested, but this theory demonstrates how dynamic and constantly thought-provoking and exciting prehistoric history is.

The Bronze Age in Europe

The use of bronze spread throughout Europe and to other parts of the world, by 2000 BCE.

In Europe the Bronze Age began in the Aegean in 3,200 BCE when trade networks imported tin and charcoal to Cyprus, where copper was mined and alloyed with the tin. It gradually spread throughout Europe and was brought to Britain in about 2,100 BCE, probably by the Beaker people migrating from the continent.

The Bronze Age in Japan

In Japan, the Stone Age Yomon period ended in about 3,000 BCE when bronze and iron were introduced simultaneously from China. In Africa, the inhabitants of eastern Niger are thought to have been the first people in the world to smelt iron in about 1,500 BCE. Iron and copper working then spread south to Nigeria and by 200 CE had reached southern Africa.

The Bronze Age in India, Asia and China

Bronze Age technology spread to the Indian subcontinent, through the Indus Valley civilization, beginning in about 330 BCE, when the Harrapa developed new techniques

TABLE 8.9 The Bronze Age: selected global connections and showing trends and patterns

Date BCE	Britain	Europe	Africa	India	Asia	Americas
5,300						Stone Age Michigan: 5,300–1,200 copper mined. 4000 copper smelted. Evidence transported via Turkey to Mediterranean.
4,000					Sumer 5,000–4,100	
3,000						
3,200–2,200		Greece				
3,000–2,400					China: Shang 1,600–1,046	
3,100–1,000			Egypt			
3,000–1,900					Indus Valley 2,600–1,900 from here spread throughout subcontinent.	
before 2,000 BCE 600	Tin mined in Cornwall and Devon. Exported to Europe.				Spread by immigration from Indus Valley across Asia to China and possibly to Shang.	

Date				
3,000	Time of Stonehenge; considerable Bronze Age communication between Britain and Europe; significant import of swords and daggers from Switzerland.			Japan: following Japanese Stone age, the Bronze and Iron Ages introduced from China.
2,500–800	Spread to Britain from Europe probably by Beaker people from Spain, Portugal, Switzerland. British tin in copper smelting brought Britain into Mediterranean economy.			
16,000	British tin exported across Europe. Intense trading culture across Europe.			
1,500			Eastern Niger – iron	
1,000	Evidence of similar domestic and funerary objects found in southern Britain, France, Belgium. Therefore trade.			
1200–1572 CE				Moche culture in Andes (Incas 1000–600 CE)
200 CE		Iron and copper smelting spread to southern Africa from Nigeria.		

in metallurgy and produced copper, lead, bronze and tin. It spread through the Indo-Europe migrations across Asia to China, which some historians argue is within the range of dates of the Shang dynasty, 1,600–1046 BCE.

The Bronze Age in South America

In South America, Native Americans used metals from ancient times but it was hammered using heat, rather than smelted and was only used for decoration. The Moche culture, in the Andes, independently developed bronze, also used for decoration or symbolic purposes (2,000 BCE–600 CE), which was further developed by the Incas.

The Bronze Age in Britain

There is plenty of evidence of Bronze Age communication between Briton and Europe 3,000 years ago, when Stonehenge was still in use, and long before Tutenkhamun. In the early Bronze Age, swords and daggers from the Hallstatt culture (Switzerland) were a significant import.

Archaeologists knew that communities on either side of the Channel were in contact in 1,000 BCE because they had found evidence for similar objects, homes and burial rites being used in France, southern England and Belgium.

Links with Switzerland, Spain and Portugal

The Bronze Age in Britain started in about 2,500 BCE and lasted until about 800 BCE. Tooth-enamel isotope research on bodies found in early Bronze Age graves around Stonehenge indicates that some of the new arrivals had come from Switzerland and were part of a new culture spreading across Europe, the Beaker culture. These people buried their dead individually, not communally, often covered by mounds (tumuli), which can be found on Ordnance Survey maps. There seems to have been peaceful integration because many of the early henge sites were adopted by the newcomers. Most of the Beaker people who came to Britain probably came from what is now Spain and Portugal. The Beaker people refined the skill of smelting metal. At first things they made things from copper, but by around 2,150 BCE smiths had found out how to make bronze, a much harder metal, by combining copper with a small amount of tin. Over the next thousand years bronze gradually replaced stone in making weapons and tools.

Cornish tin and Mediterranean trade

Tin had been mined in Cornwall and Devon before 2,000 BCE. When the role of tin in making bronze was discovered, south-west Britain was brought into the Mediterranean economy. There were large amounts of tin in Cornwall and Devon, which, by 1,600 BCE was exported across Europe. In his *Bibliotheca Historical*, written in the first century BC, Diodorus Siculus described ancient tin mining in Britain. 'They that inhabit the British promontory of Belerion by reason of their converse with strangers are more civilized and courteous to strangers than the rest are. These are the people that prepare the tin, which with a great deal of care and labour, they dig out of the ground, and that being done the metal is mixed with some veins of earth out of which they melt the metal and refine it. Then they cast it into regular blocks and carry it to a certain island near at hand called Ictis for at low tide, all being dry between there and the island, tin in large quantities is brought over in carts' (1939). Cunliffe (1988) suggested that this was Mount Batten near Plymouth. A shipwreck site with ingots of tin was found at the mouth of the River Erme not far away.

Around the twelfth century BCE the great Eastern Empires were in decline and in the late Bronze Age an intensely networked trading culture developed that included Britain, Ireland, France, Spain and Portugal.

The remains of three Bronze Age boats have been found in the Humber estuary and a Bronze Age ship from c. 900 BCE has recently been found near Salcombe in Devon. This ship, was more sophisticated than earlier dug-out boats; it had sails and was manned by fifteen oarsmen. It was importing copper and tin, used to make weapons and jewellery, which was probably sourced from various places in Europe. Probably people and animals were also crossing the channel as well. Wrist torcs and a sword were found nearby (*The Daily Telegraph*, 27.11.2016). Britain's global connections in the Bronze Age are shown in Table 8.9 and key concepts applied ancient Bronze Age civilizations are shown in Table 8.3.

Indicative questions about Bronze Age Britain

■ Following on from the New Stone Age did everyone in Bronze Age Britain live in a settled community?

■ What can we work out, from Bronze Age grave goods, and burial mounds and stone circles about people's beliefs and way of life?

■ In what ways was the Bronze Age in Britain similar to, and different from the four ancient civilizations studied?

■ Bronze Age weapons suggest battles. What might people have been fighting about?

■ How long did the Bronze Age last compared with the Stone Age, with the New Stone Age?

■ In what ways was the Bronze Age similar to the New Stone Age?

■ Were there any differences between the New Stone Age and the Bronze Age apart from making bronze weapons?

Connections between the achievements of Ancient Greece and the Western world

This section reflects on connections between Ancient Greece, Ancient Rome and the global world. There are no tables identifying key concepts linking Greece and Rome or linking Greece and Rome with other earlier societies or with the modern world. If you have been persuaded of the advantages of doing this, you and or your pupils, can construct you own, as suggested in the section on comparing ancient civilizations, above.

Connections between Ancient Greece and today

The 'study of the life and achievements of Ancient Greece and their influence on the Western world' is a study unit in the National Curriculum. Connections between Ancient Greece and Today is the subject of part of the Historical Association's Study Unit www.history.org.uk/primary/categories/216/resource/6791. This gives detailed instructions on how children can compare and contrast their schooling with education in Athens and Sparta and how they can compare contemporary modern buildings and government with language, buildings and government in Ancient Greece. The Olympics could be another comparison. And there is an opportunity to include discussion of 'British values' in relation to some of these themes.

Probably children can discuss the ethics of slavery in the context of slaves in Ancient Greece with greater detachment than a discussion of the transatlantic slave trade. Slaves were taken for granted by many societies then so was it then acceptable – or are there ethics beyond what most people think at a given time? How will people in future regard our treatment of workers in developing countries who provide, for example, many of our clothes? (Sprigg and Sullivan 2013: 65–68).

Connections between Greek life and achievements and their influence on the Western world

The aims of the Key Stage 2 curriculum state that pupils should establish clear narratives within and across periods of study, noting connections contrasts and trends. The aims of the curriculum include understanding how and why contrasting arguments and interpretations have been constructed. Ancient Greece is traditionally seen as 'The Cradle of Western civilization'. Its legacy is seen as democracy, the law (citizens were chosen at random to sit in the courts), athletics, the arts (theatre, architecture, sculpture and philosophy), mathematics and science. There is a connection today with these achievements, since they were 'rediscovered in the Renaissance' and made fashionable through the enlightenment. So are there contrasting interpretations of the influence of Ancient Greece?

MacIntyre (2016: 86) points out that Aristotle's reflections on ethics, politics and philosophy were written for the Athenian elite 'and would have made his social, political and moral thought politically irrelevant to the vast majority of humankind'. He viewed women, slaves, workers and non-Greeks as 'unable to function well as human beings, by developing and exercising the powers of rational agency in a political society'. From the seventh to the eighteenth century, the term 'democracy' would have been regarded as mob rule. Our notion of democracy has been slowly reformulated from that of Ancient Greece. It could be argued that the roots of our inclusive ethics and morality and concept of equality, lie in Christianity.

If we are seeking to make links across places as well as time in the current curriculum it is interesting that the Greeks according to Hughes (2017) claimed that they founded Byzantium in the seventh century BCE, but the Thracians and Phoenicians founded it long before that. Hughes points out, there is a competing influence on Western Europe, from Byzantium (Constantinople), partly through Christianity. From Istanbul culture we have forks, the Nicene Creed, drum majorettes (a version of Ottoman military marches), swearing an oath on the Bible and booze (*bloza*). Istanbul, she says, was the city that in the sixth century formulated the basis of modern European (although not English) law, thanks to Justinian's Law Code. And the Byzantine influence was spread through its multi-faith, multi-ethnic territories by road systems that connected the world from Basra to Bulgaria. There were dragomans, (Ottoman diplomats and translators who arranged contracts and treaties) in many Western countries. Greek influences then filtered through Roman and Byzantine civilizations and so back to Western Europe in the Renaissance, through a very indirect route and through young aristocrats on the European Grand Tour in the eighteenth century.

The Roman Empire and its impact on Britain

The aims of the National Curriculum state that pupils should discern how evidence is used to make historical claims and discern how and why contrasting arguments and interpretations of the past are constructed. Many information books may give a distorted picture of Roman Britain, suggesting that the Romans in Britain had an impact on the way Britain was placed under one administration for the first time, although this was run by the Celtic tribal aristocracy. It was peaceful because it was connected by roads used by a large defending army, although this came to consist of British soldiers. Trade flourished and the tribal elite benefited from this. Initially they lived in Roman-style cities, but later moved outside the cities to villas, which were usually small industrial complexes. But the way of life, for the majority of people, changed very little. It has been argued that Roman historians described the Britain they conquered as primitive, but actually it consisted of populous, wealthy native British societies in which large towns were emerging, and the Roman occupation consisted of the military imposition of a different, fashionable culture, which did not have any influence beyond 406 AD in Britain as it did in Spain, Italy and Portugal (see www.britishmuseum.org/PDF/british_museum_roman_britain.pdf.)

Connections, trends and contrasts over time: comparison with other Ancient Empires

Clearly the non-statutory examples given for this study unit suggest that this unit is intended to cover the impact of the Roman Empire on Britain from 55 BCE to 410 CE. However, if children are also expected 'to note connections, trend and contrasts over time, similarities and differences, and to make informed responses involving thoughtful selection and organization', it is important to compare the Roman Empire with other empires (including Sumer, the Indus Valley, Shang and Egyptian Empires). Rome wanted to conquer Britain because of its natural resources, metal, corn and pearls. Was this true of the earlier civilizations discussed above? Is it the motivation of all empires? How important is world trade today? Is it always exploitative?

Was being part of the Roman Empire good for Britain?

Claire (2003) suggests a discussion about whether foreign conquest is always bad for the conquered. While history books emphasize the advantages of Roman rule, recent empires are often regarded critically. Claire points out a number of advantages of being part of an empire. First, there is the importance of the cross-fertilization of ideas resulting from colonization. Claire says that Boudicca's rebellion is usually regarded as 'a good thing' but this could lead to a discussion of when and why it might be right to resist. Claire shows how British tribal leaders who allied with Rome gained much; for example Cogidumnus, the leader of the Atrabates, had Fishbourne palace built for him. Is such collaboration acceptable?

Roman Empire, ethnic diversity and connections with the wider world

Another kind of link to be made between Ancient Rome, other parts of the Roman Empire and Britain today is through the ethnic diversity of the soldiers and non-combatants who manned Hadrian's Wall. Their artefacts show a mix of Roman, native and Romanized cultures. There was a cohort of Spaniard soldiers, of Dalmatian soldiers from Croatia and a cohort from the Lower Rhineland. In the third and fourth centuries CE a unit of Daciand (Romanians) was stationed at Birdoswald. There were archers from Syraia. At Vindolanda there was a mix of Latin, Celtic and Germanic peoples. This indicates the movement of peoples across the Empire. At Housesteads and Chesters there were men from Spain, the Netherlands and Germany and on the east coast there were soldiers from across the Empire and also native British soldiers. After 410 CE many remained and mixed with the local populace.

Roman citizens in Britain

Olusoga (2016) tells us that in Roman garrisons in Britain, there were people from Rome's African provinces and women from sub-Saharan Africa. For example Noticia Dignitatum, a Roman register listing officials at the nearby Roman fortress of Aballava (on Hadrian's wall near Burgh by Sands), records that a unit of Aurelian Moors had been stationed there in the third century CE. They had come from what is now Libya, Tunisia and Algeria.

Black people in Roman Britain

It used to be thought that black people in Roman Britain were all male and were in the army but recently two skeletons of have been identified, using modern technologies, that contest this view. One is 'The Ivory Bangle Lady' of York, a woman of high status and mixed race, living in York in the second half of the fourth century CE, who was buried with elephant ivory bracelets; and the other, 'The Beachy Head Lady' of Sussex, may have been the wife of an official at the nearby Roman villa or wife of a merchant trader (see www.ibtimes.com/face-beachy-head-lady-revealed-roman-era-woman-fantastic-discovery-photo-1553166).

(See www.historytoday.com/paul-edwards/history-black-people-britain.)

Evidence of a multi-cultural society in tombstones

There is further evidence of this multi-cultural and mobile society in tombstones. In South Shields there is a tombstone for a woman of the Catavellauni tribe, who was a slave, then a freed woman and finally the wife of a merchant from Syria. A second tombstone was set up by an Asturian cavalry man for a 20-year-old Moor, called Victor whom he had freed. Ilona Aronovsky (2013) tells us that in the Roman Empire there was no racial discrimination or hierarchy of racism on the basis of colour or ethnicity. This is a product of modern European empires. Barbarism was the name for people who were not Roman or did not live the Roman way of life, but this was open to allies and conquered people across the Empire.

Aronovsky gives as an example the North African Emperor, Septimus Severus (193–211 CE), who was a North African, born in modern Libya, went to Rome with career ambitions, achieved power and married a Syrian woman, an educated woman who encouraged the practice of philosophy.

(An ancient site for exploring evidence of diversity in Roman Britain is www.runny medetrust.org/uploads/publications/pdfs/Runnymede%20Romans%20Revealed%20A %2056pp%20LoRes%20v6.pdf.)

Connections with modern warfare

Stewart (2016: 44–46) tells us that soldiers manning Hadrian's Wall came from what we now call Belgium, Holland and Hungary. There were Aramaic speaking Iraqis and 5,000 Sarmatians. They were nomadic horsemen from central Asia. All these people had previously been enemies.

What is surprising is that the camp in which Stewart recently served was on the Tigris, the other extremity of the Roman Empire from Hadrian's Wall. Most of the camps were built on exactly the same pattern as Stewart's. This is also the same pattern as the one that all of the forts of the Roman Empire were built on. And whereas the garrisons on Hadrian's Wall imported fish paste from Spain, olive oil from Libya, ceramic dinner services from Gaul, and some Africans even brought their own ethnic cooking pot, Stewart's camp imported hamburgers, cheesecakes and powdered juices from America and Europe. In a nearby camp, Italian soldiers from Naples brought an espresso machine, and Japanese soldiers constructed Japanese baths. All of the tribes represented on Hadrian's Wall had been enemies of the Roman Empire just as the Coalition included nations that had been enemies 60 years before. If you are looking for examples of similarities and differences, continuity and change Stewart provides an impressive example!

Saxon connections with the wider world

The Saxons had connections with Europe through royal links with the Frankish court and to the papacy in Rome – and of course later with northern Europe through the Vikings. Perhaps they had more far-reaching connections. (As Dr Hella Eckhardt of Reading University says, multi-cultural Britain is not just a phenomenon of our modern times. Indeed the skull of a young black girl, living in tenth-century Anglo-Saxon England, has been found buried in north Elmham, in Norfolk: www.yorkshiremuseum.org.uk/collections/collections-highlights/ivory and http://news.bbc.co.uk/1/hi/england/north_yorkshire/8538888.stm.)

After leaving north Germany and Denmark to settle in south and east England in the fifth century CE, the Saxons gradually created seven kingdoms in Britain, then in the ninth century had to attempt to unite against the Vikings. The Anglo-Saxon ninth-century chronicles show that the Anglo-Saxons were still closely connected with Europe through the Catholic Church after St Augustine's arrival in, 596 CE. This was because St Augustine initiated the conversion of southern England to Christianity. This was followed by the gradual conversion of all the English kingdoms. As a result, in the eighth century, the Anglo Saxon's had a mission to convert the Frankish Empire. As a child King Alfred was sent to the Papacy. He was confirmed by Pope Leo IV and, providing evidence that people from Britain frequently visited Rome, streets from this period were named after them. Alfred also had connections with the Franks and with Charlemagne. However most of his time was spent resisting attacks from the Vikings. Table 10.4 (p. 191) illustrates the extent of his journeys in Britain.

In *Primary History* Volume 76, Aronovsky (2017) describes some fascinating ways of making national and international connections, beginning with Anglo-Saxon graves, and also between specific Anglo-Saxon people and their travels in mainland Europe, which are new and exciting. I thoroughly recommend you read this. Wilkinson (2017) describes an equally fascinating study of links between the Anglo-Saxons and nation and international world, based on ink.

Britain, the Vikings and their international links

In looking at the study unit 'The Viking and Anglo-Saxon Struggle for the Kingdom' it is important to be aware of the international presence of the Vikings. The Vale of York Hoard, found near Harrogate in 2007 contains Irish silverwork, Slavic pendants, Islamic coins and Russian neck-rings. The Viking world is criss-crossed with trade routes representing a keen taste for globalization. Necklaces and brooches from Islamic silver, worn by Viking women are inscribed with 'There is no God but Allah'. The Vikings reached North America half a century before Columbus; they penetrated Russia and the Middle East; they sailed down the Volga and across the Caspian Sea to arrive in Samarkand (modern Uzbekistan). In the Mediterranean they reached Muslim Spain and the North African coast and sailed as far as Istanbul.

The Vikings took slaves; a recent test proves that although Icelandic men are of remarkably pure Scandinavian stock, the women have high quantities of DNA from

Ireland and Scotland. However, much of slave trade was with the Islamic world where demand for unpaid servants was particularly high. The Islamic world, however, was not impressed by the Vikings. An Islamic diplomat, Ahmed Ibn Fadlan complained, in 921 CE, that they were 'the filthiest of god's creatures, not cleaning themselves after urinating, defecating or after having sex'. (Year 3 do not need to know this.)

The locality and national and international links

It can be argued that each of the history study units should begin with the locality. The Ordance Survey (OS) map for Ancient Britain (OS 2005) shows the most significant and accessible sites and monuments, from the Stone Age to the Middle Ages, and the Historical Guide to Roman Britain (OS 2001) shows the sites of archaeological finds in Roman Britain. Local libraries and archives and the local branch of the Historical Association may also be good starting points. Census returns since 1801, available in local archives, identify profound social changes, for example the amazing growth of cities from 1821 to 1831, but also individual stories to illustrate the wider trends. But beware of misleading language in census returns. Seamstress is apparently the self-description of choice for most prostitutes; married women calling themselves slaves was part of the protest campaign organized by the suffragettes; and architects were undoubtedly builders (Hutchinson 2017).

The advantages of beginning with the locality

The Cambridge Review (Alexander 2010) states that, 'The locality of the school is an important resource, which fosters relations between children who may come from different backgrounds (p. 69). It takes account of their interests and is well-stocked with stimulating material.' One particular aim of the Review is celebrating culture and community. Submissions to the Review refer to loss of community, and study of the locality is a way of responding to this need, for cultural and social as well as educational reasons. The Review argues that celebrating the culture of a community can help regenerate communal life and an education in which mutuality in learning as well as relationships is axiomatic (p. 262).

The locality and identity

In their excellent book on local history, Dixon and Hales (2014) argue that a move is needed from traditional local history in primary schools to one where personal and community history is at the heart of the curriculum, demonstrating how, through this approach, children begin to consider who they are, their backgrounds and how they are contributing to the wider environment. They draw both on theory and on conversations with children that reveal the impact of this approach on a child's personal identity.

Local history should never be seen in isolation

Dixon and Hales (2015) persuade us that local history should never be seen in isolation. Asking questions, such as 'What was my family doing then? What was happening locally? What was significant at a national level?', demonstrate the two-way relationship between local and national history. National history has links to the local story through chronology. And there may well be global links through conquest and empire, migration, colonization, religious conversion and travel. There may be local people who had an international significance and events of worldwide relevance. Local industry and transport might well have links overseas as evidenced by docks, warehouses, mills and refineries and imports of products such as sugar, tea and coffee. Local individuals may have derived their wealth from overseas, such as in plantations or in India. A census or parish records may show birthplaces abroad, or old photographs record people from different ethnicities. There may be current links with twin towns or artefacts from around the world. (My father-in-law returned from serving in India during the Second World War with gifts of Indian brassware – but it turned out to have been made in Birmingham – so beware!) Local parks and even gardens of houses may have an international link through the garden design and the plants. Cumbria is full of rhododendrons which were brought back by Victorian plant hunters from the Himalayas, Tibet, or even from the Apalachian or Caucusus Mountains. There may also be institutions supporting people from abroad or travelling, such as seamen's hospitals. For some areas there are Black History publications, which are also available online at www.officialblackhistorymonthuk.co.uk. And evidence about the past can be found in street directories and street names, especially near docks.

Local, national and global links: diversity and identity

It is argued in the Cambridge Review (Alexander 2010), on the basis of research, that primary schools can and should respect and build on children's non-school learning, experience and capability, that the local component encourages this and that communities have massive potential in this regard (pp. 262–263). The locality of the school is an important resource, which fosters relations between children who may come from different backgrounds (p. 69). It takes account of their interests and is well stocked with stimulating material. The aims of the Review emphasize interdependence, respect, reciprocity and citizenship. One particular aim is 'celebrating culture and community', which gives an explicit steer towards the regeneration of communal life and an education in which mutuality in learning as well as relationships is axiomatic. Submissions talk of loss of community and study of the locality is a way of responding to this need, for cultural and social as well as educational reasons. The Review argues that celebrating the culture of a community will encourage a shared interest in learning and promote good relationships (p. 262).

Making links between Britain and global history in the past makes children aware of the constant interactions between societies throughout history, and perhaps indicates why these have occurred, and the outcomes. Perhaps they can see patterns in these interactions. Sir Keith Adjegbo (2013) points out how these connections impact on people's identities and should be explored. He says that time should be given for children to explicitly discuss themselves, their families, their community and the wider world and why their community is like it is. These are questions which are open to historical investigation and discussion. They are relevant to studying the movement of humans in the Stone, Bronze and Iron Ages and Roman Britain, and particularly in Saxon and Viking times, when there is evidence of the history of communities in place names and recently in DNA. But above all, a local study tracing how aspects of national history are reflected in the locality, or of an aspect of history dating from the period beyond 1066 which is of significance locally, or of a significant turning point in British history, would make it possible for children really to engage in how their communities were formed. 'Personalized learning' Adjegbo says, 'is about a contextualized and relevant curriculum for all students and these issues are relevant, regardless of locality'. Adjegbo suggests that such a topic could be called 'Who do we think we are?' and should 'celebrate and share the unique history of their community and how it relates to the United Kingdom and to the wider world'.

Teaching approaches: local, national global links

Personal and community history

Dixon and Hales (2015) emphasize the importance of putting local history at the heart of the history curriculum. They say and that it should emphasize the particular characteristics of a local community so that children can feel part of it their community and its history. This contributes to their sense of belonging and identity and encourages them to contribute to their community. They provide evidence of the success of this approach.

Avronsky (2013) quotes Malorie Blackman (2013), Children's Laureate during the debate on the Government's 2013 draft history curriculum proposals for England, who said that it's very dangerous to make it seem as if history is the province of a certain segment of society. History should belong to and include all of us. The curriculum needs to appeal to as many children as possible or a number of them could become disenchanted with education because they feel it's not relevant. Avronsky says that focusing on diversity through history enables children to learn to think critically, as historians; to make sense of Britain's past and that of the wider world and how it has shaped the present. Diverse histories motivate children to identify with and share their own histories and be moved by them. 'This', Avronsky says, 'puts common humanity into stories which have social, economic, cultural and political dimensions.' She gives examples of the variety of family histories found in some classrooms.

■ Children place on a map where their families have come from. For example in a class project in Brent, families had come from the Welsh Coalfield in the 1930s to seek work in the new industrial factories of West London and medical care for their children. East African Asians came to Britain as refugees, including family with ancestry from a royal line. Children shared painful reasons for migration as refugees or asylum seekers with children from a settled background.

- In schools in the area of the Yorkshire textile industry after World War II there were families of Jewish refugees and of Poles, Ukranians and Lithuanians from Tsarist Russia, who came to work in the garment trade.

- In port cities there have always been settlers: Arab seamen in Tyneside from World War I, Chinese communities in Liverpool and East London, Somalis in Butetown, Cardiff from the 1880s, Sylheti seamen in East London.

- Irish people have come to Britain since the nineteenth-century famine.

- In the 1950s people came from the Caribbean to work in transport and hospitals.

- A longitudinal study of migration and settlement focused on people who moved to Britain to work in former industries began with Celtic and Roman Britain.

People in London from the Romans to the present

The Museum of London has developed numerous, dramatized characters to reflect the 500 nationalities, 300 languages and fourteen major faiths of London's inhabitants and to make history relevant to everybody, ranging from Romans to 1980s dockers. www.museumoflondon.org.uk/Schools. Schools outside London can get in touch with these characters through video conferences (www.movinghere.org.uk). In addition there is an outreach show comparing modern and Roman London and discussing how almost everyone has family stories of migration. A skeleton comes to life to tell her story and the drama includes a black animal trainer who imports wild animals from Africa and transports them across the Empire.

History through connecting classrooms

Diana Excell (2013) describes the Bradford *Connecting Classrooms* project in which three schools in Britain are linked with five in Pakistan. The Indus Valley civilization was part of modern Pakistan. Schools exchanged their studies representing diverse aspects of famous people in Peshawar and Bradford. In each primary school, pupils created and shared local heritage trails. These included recent history but went as far back as the Bronze Age.

Connections, chronology and timelines

Bracey (2016) produced a useful resource to help children to construct a timeline from 60,000 BCE to 2,000 CE. Lomas (2016) has a map and timeline with significant dates for the Vikings in England from 793 to 1035. Parker Heath (2015a) supports her article on Ancient Sumer with a map and a timeline showing significant dates in the Sumer civilization from 3,500 to 1,500 BCE (2014) and Karin Doull, supports her article, 'Teaching Ancient Egypt', with a map and timeline from 3,000 to 30 BCE. Children need a long timeline, covering 60,000 BCE–200 CE, and to understand scale, in order to understand how the more detailed timelines for different study units relate to it. And ideally they need the opportunity to make their own timelines, related to things they have personally researched and also perhaps timelines for depth studies within a breadth study. The Historical Association online Continuing Professional Development on chronology is helpful in understanding more about the complex concept of chronology (www.history.org.uk/primary/categories/787/module/1743/chronology).

Discussing 'The Big Picture'

Dawson (2009a) claims that if pupils can tell a story with links across time this gives them a sense of real achievement and says that from the beginning children should understand that this is what they are learning to do and that they should be introduced to 'the big picture' to start with. Dawson (2008) says that a depth study may be introduced as a story in one sessions, as a hypothesis to be reformulated through depth studies and that depth studies show the interconnectedness of events within a study unit, as well as 'get inside the minds of people' who lived in different periods. In Cooper (2014b, pp. 92–94), Dawson suggests headings for investigating daily life in different periods, in order to make connections and discuss change, similarities and difference, causes and consequences, in the same way as key concepts have been suggested as a structure for making links in this book. The same chapter (pp. 91–108) describes a Year 6 case study comparing timelines for the themes of beliefs, agriculture, houses and transport, from 4,500 BCE to the present; the questions children engaged with a proforma for note-taking; and the ways in which their findings were communicated in a variety of ways through for example PowerPoint® presentations and television interviews. Ian Dawson's website (2009b) gives helpful examples of different types of timelines, time-lines for Key Stage 2, activities for using timelines on creating and using timelines, on timelines to develop a sense of duration, timelines for making connections, human timelines, 'Big Picture' timelines, generational timelines linked to past events (www.thinkinghistory.co.uk/ActivityKS/ActivityKS2AllList.html topics). Always the purpose of the timelines is to raise questions and discussion, to clarify and to make connections.

This chapter has considered ways in which we can help children to progressively build a big picture of connections between societies globally and over long periods of time. The following three chapters discuss how we can plan a history curriculum which enables them to do this in increasingly complex ways, and monitor and evaluate their progress.

PART

Planning, assessment and recording

9

Whole-school planning

Although Part 3 of this book is divided into three chapters, whole-school planning, medium- and short-term planning and assessment, it must be remembered that planning and assessment are interdependent. Therefore the chapters are cross-referenced and should be read as a whole. If you are a student teacher, you will need to discuss the whole school plan for history and where your work fits into it, with your mentor or the history co-ordinator.

The planning and assessment cycle, as a strategy used throughout the school, is explained. The chapter discusses the importance of and reasons why the teaching staff of the whole school should be involved in contributing to a shared understanding of:

■ the purposes and aims of the National Curriculum for history (2013) and what they are enabling children to achieve by the end of Key Stage 2;

■ the government's guidance on *Promoting Fundamental British Values* (DfE 2014) and consider ways in which this is relevant to learning history;

■ how their own school philosophy can be implemented as part of the history curriculum.

It then argues that the whole teaching staff need to discuss the sequence of the National Curriculum study units, across Key Stages 1 and 2, and between Key Stages 1 and 2 and Key Stages 2 and 3. The chapter refers to the ways in which connections can be made between units studied, through a conceptual framework. There are detailed examples of how this works in practice, based on research. Time management is discussed.

Whole-school collaborative planning for history

Although the process of whole-school planning and strategies for assessment and recording children's progress for history will be led by the history co-ordinator, it is important that this is a collaborative process in which all the staff participate, sharing their different

TABLE 9.1 Whole-school plans linking to medium-term plans and lesson (or short-term) plans

School philosophy values and ethos	Head teacher and governors interpret these to meet needs of community.
Whole-school curriculum plan	National Curriculum content, interpreted to focus on the local area and its resources.
Subject policy and long-term school plans	Outlines the areas to be covered in each year and term linked to the whole school assessment strategy.
MTP/theme/topic plan	Focusing on area of subject specified in long-term plans, identifies how the skills, knowledge and understanding will be taught in logical progression, usually over half a term. Summative assessment opportunities are identified.
Individual lesson or 'short-term plans'	Specific lesson content, learning outcomes, differentiation and assessment details. Individual plans based on assessments from previous lessons of children's achievement and teaching and learning strategies.
Modified from Professional Studies in Primary Education, H. Cooper ed. (2014:70)	

levels of experience and knowledge of teaching history and of local and other resources. Everyone has a stake in developing the best possible history experiences for children throughout the school, for supporting and delighting in their progression – and themselves enjoying participating in enquiries and new knowledge, in evaluating, modifying and developing their own teaching and the children's 'history experience' throughout their primary years. Table 9.1 shows levels of planning and the stages at which teachers can interpret the statutory curriculum to reflect the philosophy and needs of their school.

Process of whole-school planning

Teachers need to consider how, as a school, they will integrate the three frameworks for teaching and learning in history: the purposes and aims of the National Curriculum for history, the integration of 'British Values' and the integration of the school's philosophy, into the history curriculum. In particular they need to consider how they will plan to ensure that children develop 'a chronologically secure understanding of British, local and world history, establishing clear narratives within and across the periods they study'.

The National Curriculum

The National Curriculum states that the purpose of studying history is to 'inspire pupils' curiosity to know more about the past. Teaching should equip pupils to ask perceptive questions, think critically, weigh evidence, sift arguments and develop perspective and judgment'. In order to achieve this, the aims of the curriculum are that pupils should understand the methods of historical enquiry, including how evidence is used rigorously to make historical claims and discern how and why contrasting arguments and interpretations of the past have been constructed.

Yet The Historical Association Primary Survey (Historical Association 2016) found that 20–48 per cent of schools reported that there was inconsistent coverage of progression in planning. The survey suggested that schools are aware of and are addressing the issue but are not always sure that they are doing it in a way that will enhance chronological understanding.

Focuses of the 2013 curriculum

Two important new focuses run through the 2013 National Curriculum. First, there is a strong emphasis on children being able to engage with chronology and time concepts and, leading on from this, there is an emphasis on making connections within and across periods and cultures, making connections across time and place. The Historical Association Survey (2016) found that children's understanding of history was episodic rather than fitting a large narrative. It might be helpful to discuss and share strategies for making connections between study units and links between Britain and the wider world, with reference to strategies suggested in Chapter 8.

Your school philosophy

Perhaps your school's philosophy should come first, for it is what you, your colleagues, parents and governors – and perhaps pupils – have created, and fervently believe should underpin the life of the school. Langdale School in Cumbria, for example, says on its website that 'The school ensures that it maximizes its unique location to support children's learning (especially Outdoor Learning), and to help learning to come alive. This might be through the history curriculum, when learning about the Vikings, artwork in the local gallery and studio in Cylinders Wood . . .' (www.langdale.cumbria.sch.uk/).

School philosophy may also include pedagogical principles, for example the importance of visits, working with families and community and the use of a variety of teaching strategies to challenge, motivate and involve all learners, teachers as facilitators and children as learners. Examples of a school's philosophy for history sometimes include a commitment to using a range of sources of information, handling artefacts, visiting museums, first-hand experiences from visitors, listening to stories, interviewing friends and family, using drama and film, working collaboratively to ask and answer historical questions and deep personal studies.

History and values education

There is an expectation that learning British values should be an aspect of the history curriculum. This may sound contentious, but British values, set out in the Prevent Strategy, revised in the Prevent Duty Guidance (HMSO 2015a), and reflected in Spiritual, Moral, Social and Cultural Development (DfE 2014) are:

- democracy,
- the rule of law,
- individual liberty,

- mutual respect and

- tolerance of those of different faiths and beliefs.

While promoting values should not be the purpose of history education, as was thought in the nineteenth and early twentieth centuries, it is a fact that, throughout our history, many groups have been fighting for these values, which were hard won and have emerged out of centuries of conflict.

British values need to be explained in the context of history

Michael Maddison (2016) who was, from 2008 to 2015, National Lead Inspector for History Education, explains, 'if the values are not explained in the historical context from which they evolved, young people will not readily be able to understand why they are so much a part of our lives'. He says that within the inspection framework inspectors may, for example, ask, 'How well does your work in history contribute to the school's focus on British values?' or 'How well are pupils made aware of the importance of what they are studying in history to an understanding of the world in which they live today?' 'Although', he says, 'drawing up an audit, and thinking about these things with your colleagues will not provide you with all the answers.' Ofsted School Inspection Handbook (DfE 2015) makes several references to the teaching of British values. These opportunities might involve the making of laws, starting with Anglo-Saxon laws and the value of and reasons for this; the extent to which people had individual liberty to make choices about their lives; mutual tolerance; and some say in how they were governed. A teacher in a London school, who has pupils with parents from eighteen countries in his class, argues that British history, including Boudicca and the Anglo-Saxons, is relevant to them (Peal 2017). He argues that history should lead the way in fostering integration, and that his ambition is to 'equip each pupil with an understanding of the country in which they live'. The values described as 'British' are certainly not uniquely so, and you may consider that it is not the purpose of history to teach values. However, it is the role of history to compare and contrast the values central to different societies, and the reasons for them.

Key Stage 1

Opportunities to discuss the ongoing development of 'British Values' may occur when learning about the individuals and events selected to teach at Key Stage 1: the Peterloo Massacre or Suffragettes, for example.

Key Stage 2

At Key Stage 2, there could be opportunities in a local study unit, to find out about a local philanthropist, Elizabeth Fry in Norwich, for example. Changes in laws promoting individual freedoms and tolerance might occur in 'Tracing a theme over a long period' for example the changing power of monarchs or an aspect of social history such as crime and punishment.

Discussion of values in earlier British history

Values of different groups, in the British study units might be discussed, compared and explained. We do not know much about Iron Age values. You may – or may not think it appropriate to consider the values that lie behind Iron Age ritual sacrifice (see www.youtube.com/watch?v=X3HMNdbZOhI and www.youtube.com/watch?v=wL UtsjFGMyIatch).

But it might be interesting to compare the reasons for Roman values, Anglo-Saxon values, Viking and Christian values and possibly compare the values which underpin religions in different ancient societies. The Via Romana lists the values all citizens are expected to aspire to: for example, dignity, tenacity, gravity, humanity, truthfulness and the public virtues, for example, freedom, justice, peace [sic] and courage (www.nova roma.org/nr/Roman_virtues). In Anglo-Saxon culture the values set out in Beowulf are bravery, generosity, vengeance, loyalty, chivalrousness and fairness, explained at https://prezi.com/cykukij1tkyx/anglo-saxon-cultural-values/. Anglo-Saxon England became Christianized in the seventh century. The 'noble virtues' of the Vikings were courage, truth, honour, fidelity, discipline, hospitality, self-reliance, industriousness and perseverance. These are explained at http://thewisdomwarrior.com/2010/09/17/the-nine-noble-virtues-viking-values-for-the-warrior-lifestyle/.

Individual liberty and the rule of law

The Early Anglo-Saxon laws' attempts to be fair in allotting punishment could be explored (see Table 9.2). The legal reforms of King Alfred, which evolved from the codes of previous rulers, from the Bible and from tenants' 'common burdens' of military service, fortress work and bridge repair could lead to discussions about the importance of law and responsibility to the community.

Planning the sequence of study

Planning for progression in thinking

Bruner's work on progression (1963) suggests that the history study units can be taught in any order, as long as they are structured so that the processes of historical enquiry, the key concepts, questions and methods of answering them which lie at the heart of the discipline are tackled from the very beginning, then in increasingly complex ways. He defined the sequence as leading the learner through a series of statements and restatements that increase the child's ability to transform and transfer what has been learned. But he was clear that young children's learning demands serious and rigorous pedagogical expectations. Bruner (1963) said that the younger children the children that we teach, the more serious we must be in how we plan their teaching and learning. Bruner also made it clear that children learn effectively through handling artefacts, site visits (enactive learning) and through discussing images (iconic) as well as through maps and written and numerical sources (symbolic). It is through the complexity of the questions asked of the sources that children's thinking progresses. (See Table 9.2.)

TABLE 9.2 Opportunities to discuss links with 'British values' in the ninth-century 'Viking and Anglo-Saxon Struggle for the Kingdom'

Value	Context
One code of law for all, the 'Domboc'	Longest legislation text in Old English; a combination of religious law and Alfred's decrees, adding to and subtracting from laws of Aethelbert of Kent, Ine of Wessex and Offa of Mercia.
Individual liberty; individual freedom of thought and speech for everyone	*Liberty is connected with freedom of access to information, free thought, personal interpretations.* Alfred made translations and his own interpretations of religious texts. When he became king, education had collapsed and few could translate a letter into English. Texts were translated into English by Alfred and priests, so all could understand them. Continental scholars were imported from the continent and Ireland and Wales. Significant people in lay and religious life gathered around Alfred. After his first visit to Rome he had a vision of a wider world. Bishops and Ealdormenn encouraged others to read works in Old English. Alfred was a scholar. His 'pointer' (for reading lines) is in the Ashmolean Museum. He gave beautiful books to main monasteries.
Mutual respect	Alfred translated books on philosophy. He said what he set out to do was to virtuously deliver authority with wisdom; that he always wanted 'to live honourably, for each man must speak as he can and do as he can'.
Tolerance of others' views, (although he expected the Danish king, Gudrun, to convert to Christianity)	At a meeting on 13th June Asser, (in his *Life of King Alfred*) reports that Guthrun was received by Alfred and given a Christian baptism and received as his foster son. 'Alfred therefore honours Guthrun by becoming his godfather, 'with generous feelings'. This changed his relationship with the Vikings. His daughter Aethefrith was also tolerant. Tolerance was a part of her skillful peace-making process. As wife of the Lord of Mercia she took what she learned from her father to the Mercian court, which also became a centre of scholarship.

The source is the version of the Anglo-Saxon Chronicle in Corpus Christi College. The contexts in which these values are identified are given, to put the values in contexts which link them with evidence.

Considerations in sequencing units

Chronologically?

It may be logical to sequence the study units chronologically, which, arguably becomes increasingly complicated, because there are more recent sources, including written sources. Bruner thought that studying early societies is the best way to understand the nature of societies – the human condition and the continuity of evolution (1963). Nevertheless, although sequencing study units chronologically may seem logical, pre-history and early societies are not necessarily the simplest to study, as shown in Chapter 8.

There are no narratives in pre-history, and no individual characters whose actions have causes and effects on changes, no memorable events. There is little detail to make pre-history memorable and it spans changes over vast areas of time, which are can only be explained by climate changes and by potentially confusing global interconnections.

Local history study and a theme in British history beyond 1066

It could be argued, that in deciding when to teach the local history study, a site significant in the locality, it might be very appropriate in Year 3 – perhaps a continuation of a place, or event studied at Key Stage 1. Whereas a study tracing aspects of national history beyond 1066 might be appropriate later on, maybe in preparation for Key Stage 3, because children have greater incidental knowledge of the past and understanding of abstract ideas. Or does the locality have strong associations with the Stone Age, Bronze or Iron Age, with Roman Britain or Anglo-Saxon and Viking Britain, in which case a depth study might be best following a British study unit. Would one of the ancient civilizations be of greater interest to children to whom they are linked by their heritage, the Indus Valley and Pakistan, Sumer and Iraq or China? Should the ancient civiliza-tions link with the Bronze Age unit for chronological reasons or should they be linked to Greece and Roman Civilizations? What would be the rationale for selecting an early Islamic Civilization, Benin or the Mayan Civilization for a particular year group? Other considerations are the interests and expertise of individual teachers, the proximity, or otherwise, of sites, museums or archives that it would be advantageous to visit, and whether the length of journey would make it most suitable for older children. There are many sequence and selection choices, but it is important for agreeing a rationale for those made.

Planning for key concepts across the curriculum

Chapter 8 discusses how time concepts and the key concepts which run through all societies can be planned for, in order to help children to make connections between the societies ranging over large time spans. If everyone agrees to build key concepts (perhaps selected key concepts) into activities in all MTPs, this will give children a consistent framework for comparing the societies they study in increasingly sophisticated ways.

Teachers also need to agree how chronology and time concepts, which are central to the history curriculum, are taught each year in increasingly complex ways; whether there could be an overarching timeline in a central place in the school to which timelines for individual study units can be linked; how this may be done; and how this timeline can be frequently and actively engaged with.

Single subject or a cross-curricular approach

Inspection evidence has suggested that history is best taught as a single subject. This makes it possible to focus on well-structured enquiry, which encourages independent thinking and learning and develops historical knowledge. However, history is an umbrella subject, which involves all the other subjects. Chapter 8 makes links between history,

English language and literature, mathematics, information technologies and art. It is not suggested that such cross-curricular links should always be made, but when thoughtfully integrated into and referenced in planning they could allow extra time to be spent on history, to the benefit of other subjects.

Whole-school policy for assessment

There may be a school policy for assessment. If so, it is important that this meets the rather specific requirements for assessment in history, which are discussed in Chapter 11.

Conclusion

This chapter has considered whole-school plans and decisions which apply to every age group: how values education relates to history, the sequence of study units, the integration of the school philosophy, how whole-school decisions about chronology and core historical concepts embedded in the study units can help children to make increasingly complex connections across different periods and places. Chapter 10 considers how whole-school policies are developed in MTPs, planning units of study.

Medium-term planning

Chapter 10 discusses decisions to be made in constructing MTPs and translating them into lesson plans.

What is a medium term plan?

MTPs (topic, scheme of work or study unit plans), are crucial to the quality and success of a topic. A MTP takes into account the school philosophy in planning how the aims and content of the National Curriculum will be delivered and assessed, in ways which build on previous knowledge and progress children's skills in historical enquiry.

Doing your own research

In order to plan a topic confidently and effectively, it is important to become familiar with the topic yourself before starting planning. This is definitely not so that you can tell the children all about it; ideally there will be a lot you find out with the children. You are involved in the same process as they are, you can model it – and, it is to be hoped, enjoy it.

But having a broad understanding of the period at an adult level will enable you (and perhaps the children) to select good enquiry questions at an appropriate level, then select activities and resources to explore them effectively. You will find useful websites giving you basic information; others, if you are selective, have good teaching suggestions, and others will give you information about images of a vast range of sources, for instance artefacts available in museums as well as written sources. There will be maps showing sites related to a topic, local, national and international and films and video clips. YouTube often have very pertinent clips. And, of course, look out for recent research mentioned in newspapers and on television (see Chapters 2 and 10). This is important in enabling you to include these dimensions in what you plan. So much to include is daunting if you approach it in a haphazard way, but if you approach your MTP systematically is will be manageable – and impressive.

Teacher professionalism and medium-term plans

I know from experience that there are time constraints, but pre-prepared schemes are like convenience food, not as good as what my students call 'cooked from fresh'. The Qualification and Curriculum Authority (QCA) schemes of work for the previous curriculum (now archived) had a negative effect on teachers' professionalism, ownership and creativity because teachers copied them exactly, rather than treating them as models, assuming that this would make them beyond criticism from 'visitors'. But ready-made plans do not respond to a school's particular circumstances and location, and teachers and children do not feel ownership of them. So it is up to teachers to take responsibility for medium-term planning.

However there are some good planning models available that can be modified to respond to a school's particular philosophy and children's interests and needs. The Historical Association has plans that are pitched at Years 3 and 4 on 'The effects of Anglo-Saxon and Viking Settlement' (www.hid.org.uk/primary/categories/787/news/2122/primary-curriculum-schemes-of-work).

The Historical Association scheme of work for the Stone to Iron Age, also aimed at Years 3 and 4, has plenty of suggestions for hands-on work and useful websites to support it (www.history.org.uk/primary/resource/7537). Other units are on the Early Civilisations in the National Curriculum, significant individuals at Key Stage 1 and suggestions for local history studies, with useful websites (www.history.org.uk/primary/resource/7518).

The Historical Association also publishes numerous exemplar study units from the Nuffield Primary History Project, for example on Ancient Greece, Egypt, Sumer, Ancient Greeks, Romans, Anglo-Saxons and Vikings (www.history.org.uk/primary/categories/exemplars-study-unitsry) and many supporting articles (www.history.org.uk/primary/categories/teaching-methods-leading-primary-history) and examples of teaching and learning history (www.history.org.uk/primary/categories/teaching-methods-leading-primary-history).

British values

The expectation that history education should include references to 'British Values', is discussed in Chapter 9. However you regard the expectation to teach 'British Values', which was designed as part of the Prevent Strategy (HMSO 2015a), it is the role of history to compare and contrast the values central to different societies, and the reasons for them.

Connections between units of study

It is the aim of the 2013 curriculum that children should understand how societies they study relate to each other and notice 'connections and trends over time'. Ways of doing this are discussed at length in Chapter 9. In planning, time needs to be built in to do this, perhaps by reviewing what children remember of periods previously studied and comparing similarities and differences between them at the beginning of a unit of study, specifically being aware of where the unit they are currently studying fits into the larger chronological and geographical narrative. This could involve joint discussions with other classes who have studied the topic previously, possibly followed by a quiz.

Planning for breadth and depth

In addition to making connections between study units, to ensure that the big picture is coherent, it is a good idea to plan for an overview of a study unit then for depth studies within it, to enable children to understand both 'the long arc of development and the complexity of specific aspects of the content' (DfE 2013: 3). A breadth study needs to show the interconnectedness of significant events. Dawson (2008) suggests that a breadth study may be introduced as a story in one lesson; as a hypothesis, to be reformulated through depth enquiries, perhaps exploring the story from a different perspective. For example a depth story about the Stone Ages or the Bronze Age in Britain might imply that these periods were unique to Britain (Table 8.1), while breadth studies could show, not only connections within the study unit, but also how it was connected to the rest of the globe (see Table 8.8). A breadth story about Roman Britain might tell the story in a way that suggests that the Romans had little influence on the long narrative of early Britain (see Table 8.5) but depth studies might suggest otherwise. Or an overview story of the Anglo-Saxons might describe them as barbaric and warlike, but depth studies could investigate their sophisticated cultural achievements. At the end of a unit the two perspectives can be discussed. Originally I had not intended to include examples of MTPs because these need to be designed for specific groups and locations. It is a great strength of the National Curriculum that teachers have almost infinite opportunities for creating their own plans. The following ideas for plans are intended to stimulate your discussion and evaluation. (That's brave of me!)

Draft medium-term plan for Britain in the Stone Age

Although the title of this unit says 'Britain', if we are to take seriously the importance of 'a chronologically secure knowledge and understanding of British, local and world history', 'making connections contrasts and trends over time' (DfE 2013: 3) and 'how Britain has influenced and been influenced by the wider world' (p. 1) we need to see the British Stone Age in relation to world-wide connections. Table 8.1 traces changes during the British Stone Ages, with reference to key concepts. Table 8.8 illustrates global connections. Table 8.2 describes characteristics of the Bronze Age using key concepts. Table 8.9 shows global connections during the Bronze Age. These tables are intended to help teachers to integrate key concepts and global dimensions into planning in ways appropriate for a particular class of children.

A draft MTP for 'Changes in Britain during the Stone Age' is given in Table 10.1. A possible scale for putting the time spans on a timeline is given beneath the table. This MTP shows planning for key concepts and predicted timings. Time allocation is very important because we usually have more ideas than there is time for and it is essential to give children time, both to think, question, investigate, collaborate and discuss and to produce high-quality 'products'.

The sequence of five columns is important: the Learning Objectives (LOs), the activities which will enable pupils to achieve the LOs, how these activities will be organized (this might include groupings and notes on differentiation) and the product (what the children will have to show what they have learned; these might include group discussion and the processes of enquiry, the aspects of historical thinking they will have practised in carrying out the activities). If this sequence is thought through precisely, it forms a sound basis for writing lesson plans and for ensuring that children are using historical enquiry skills in the activities and in the product that results. This is very useful to help focus teacher interventions and formative assessment. A note is also added on links with other subjects. If this is cross-referenced with plans for those subjects it could quantify the time spent on each subject in applying it to history and so explicitly show how added time for history was justified.

(There is also a chapter on creating a scheme of work for the Stone Age, Bronze Age and Iron Age in Nichol (2017: 45–57). This gives you all the information about time, sources and resources to create your own original scheme.)

If the unit is being studied over a term a similar amount of time could be allocated to the Bronze and Iron Ages, or these could be covered in much less detail, or alternatively, the dominant period might be the Bronze and/or Iron Age.

Extremely long periods. The National Curriculum refers to the Stone Age, Iron Age and Bronze Age in Britain, but these are very fertile periods for doing what the curriculum emphasizes: making connections and seeing patterns. And if we are looking at building up a global picture, this period demonstrates our global interconnectedness very clearly as well as the reasons why not all societies continued to develop at the same rate subsequently.

Organizational decisions

This plan specifies combinations of teacher-led, whole-class work, a whole-class site visit, collaborative research in small groups, whole-class presentations and discussion of findings and individual writing.

History enquiry skills

Skills used and formatively assessed during this unit include chronology and time concepts, enquiry, making deductions and inferences from evidence.

Resources

These must be included in a plan. In Table 10.1, resources are given in the activities column.

Key concepts

These are identified in Activity 2.

TABLE 10.1 Draft for a medium-term plan: the Stone Ages in Britain

Context

You are a group of famous archaeologists. You have been asked to plan an exhibition in a museum. The title of the exhibition is: 'How did the Stone Ages change over time?'

This class previously studied . . . introductory questions to make connections with previous study units.

Overview

The Big Picture: the Stone Age (connections between British and world history)

Learning objectives

To know something about, become curious about and ask and answer questions about:

- Stone Age beliefs, technologies, tools and weapons and homes based on sources
- To understand that the Stone Ages occurred, in sequence, at different times around the globe, over an extremely long period of time

Concrete concepts related to *Key Abstract Concepts are in bold.

1a) Introductory video (e.g. www.bbc.co.uk/education/clips/zwhcj6f)

Introductory 'quiz', what do we know/can we guess, would we like to know about Stone Age People from these sources? Show series of images to whole class from the Stone Ages; guess what they are, e.g. stone circles (* beliefs, technology, public buildings) (http://britainexplorer.com/top-ten-stone-circles-uk/) images can be downloaded individually; Stone Age tools and weapons (* attack, defence, tools, weapons) (www.gettyimages.co.uk/photos/stone-age-tools-and-weapons?excludenudity=true&sort=mostpopular&mediatype=photography&phrase=stone%20tools%20and%20weapons) download and expand individual images; what were Old Stone Age houses like? (* homes; technology) Middle Stone Age? New Stone Age (Google Images of Paleolithic/Megalithic/Neolithic houses)

Time: 1 hr

1b) Whole-class, teacher-led overview: Teacher-made timeline (p. 143). World map on white board or in Historical Atlases

Children identify places on map as timeline unrolled

Devise suitable time questions for age group. Devise questions about sequence and pattern of changes

Time: 1 hr

In preparation for this session prepare new 10 m timeline, representing Stones Ages in Britain (scale, e.g. 1 m rep. 1,000 years, see Table 8.8) and mark Paleolithic, Mesolithic and Neolithic periods for classroom wall(s). Discuss and compare with scale of previous timeline. This timeline will be the background for a museum exhibition, with information researched for each period (see Table 9.2)

continued

TABLE 10.1 Continued

DEPTH STUDY

How did the Stone Age in Britain change over time? Local, British, world history connections

	Activity	Organization	Product	Processes of enquiry
PART 1. Visit to a local site. What connection does our place have with the Stone Age? Time: half day **Learning objectives** • To collect information about the Stone Age from a site visit • To differentiate between knowing, guessing and not knowing	Depending on site make notes: what can we know/'guess' do we not know about the Stone Age from this site? • **technology, beliefs, homes, attack/defence**	Whole-class or group activity depending on site	Data collection Clip board notes/ sketches/photos/video in preparation for exhibition	Questioning, differentiating between knowing, 'guessing', not knowing
PART 2. Plenary discussion of visit Time: 1 hr **Learning objectives** • To be introduced to key concepts and use in discussion and in writing • In writing captions to differentiate between what is known, hypotheses and what cannot be known	Share data collected from site visit (photographs notes, drawings). Consider how they might be displayed in the museum and captions. Write captions. Say what it tells you about the site/period, any hypotheses and any questions. Research if necessary.	Whole class **Use taught concrete and abstract key concepts.** Individually write captions for data collected from sit; use key concepts	Museum display exhibits with explanatory captions	Descriptions, facts, inferences, questions about evidence on site, related research

	Activity	Organization	Product	Processes of enquiry
PART 3. How did the Stone Age in Britain change over time? **Learning objectives** • To be able to explain the time scale and the changes between the three periods of the Stone Ages in Britain (pp. 116–119) • To work collaboratively in small groups to research the question, relating it to one of the key concepts • To present the finding for display in the exhibition • To recategorize previous exhibits where necessary <u>Time: 180 min.</u>	Each group prepares a concept map showing changes in their area of research (with references to sources), between Old, Middle and New Stone Ages) (a) What did Stone Age people eat? **(agriculture)** (b) What did Stone Age people make and how? **(technologies)** (c) How did Stone Age people **attack and defend** themselves? (d) How did Stone Age people measure time? **(calendar)** (e) What did Stone Age people believe? **(beliefs; public spaces)** (f) What were Stone Age people's homes like? (g) What was Stone Age people's **music** like?	Group research in school using secondary sources Class works in 7 groups (of 4) as museum staff curating the exhibition. (i) Use: information books, websites, video to create a concept maps for each concept (ii) Independent, paired or groups: labelled drawings, paintings, plans, models, (pottery or other), photographs from primary or secondary sources	Presentation of concept maps Arrangement of labelled products from research in correct sections of class museum	Presentation of findings. **Values education** Discussion: What values would be necessary in a hunter–gatherer society, in order to be successful? *For example:* working together for common aims: to obtain food and water, to keep safe, to share . . .

continued

TABLE 10.1 Continued

	Activity	Organization	Product	Processes of enquiry
PART 4. Assessment Focus of formative assessment of chronology and time concepts	Class quiz: Quick-fire chronology questions	Whole class Divided into 4 mixed ability teams		Difficulty of calculations and time concepts depends on age group
Objective To ascertain what chronological understanding children have and prompt and correct where appropriate for age group.	Write an information page/booklet for museum visitors, giving them key information about the Stone Ages in Britain, or make a Power point presentation, or a story board.	Individual		Differentiatiation between the three named Stone Age periods and relative time spans? Use of key concepts? Differentiation between what is known, hypotheses, not known
Summative assessment **Objectives** Evidence of understanding of differences between 3 Stone Age periods	or a picture story, depending on age-group. Remember to use Key Concepts.			
of their relative time spans Correct use of Key concepts Deductions and inferences from sources differentiating between knowing, hypotheses, not knowing	(Remind children to aim to include criteria in Summative Assessment column where they can.)			
Time: 1 hr (+) Record keeping is considered in Chapter 11				

Links between history and other subjects (See Chapter 8)

Language and literacy

Oracy: Speak clearly, justifying ideas with reasons, asking questions, building on others' ideas, (See Chapter 8) 1a, b, listening, discussion, questioning, using language appropriate to subject: (knowing, guessing, (speculating), not knowing, perhaps, therefore, evidence, Paleolithic, Mesolithic, Neolithic

Reading: Research using information books, and internet

Writing: Write summaries, compare similarities and differences (in accounts, in peers' interpretations. Discursive writing, narrative account, writing in genre from different perspectives (museum curators), give structured explanations

Vocabulary: Key names (of periods), abstract concepts

Mathematics

(See Table 8.1 Years 4–6)

Y4 Understand calculations involving BCE and CE, involving thousands, use variety of scales

Y5 Read, write and compare numbers to 1,000,000, solve comparison and sum problems

Y6 Read, write, order and compare numbers up to 10,000,000, use negative numbers and calculate intervals across zero

Information technologies

Sequencing using electronic timelines; make their own photographs and digital videos; examine artefacts on line

Understand opportunities the world wide web offers. Discernment in evaluating digital content, selecting sources and working with others to analyse and check

Art

Draw artefacts, possibly spinning, weaving, dyeing

Geography

Names of countries and continents, compass directions and tracing routes

Plans for summative and formative assessments

These are given in the table.

Cross-curricular links

Historical enquiries throughout the plan are explored through activities which are integrated with cross-curricular links. These are listed at the end of the plan. Activities to explore historical enquiries are suggested throughout the plan.

As part of a Bronze Age extension, you may wish to include the investigation of the grave of a Bronze Age archer (see Nichol 2017b: 73–77).

The Roman empire and its impact on Britain

Please refer to Table 10.2.

This plan also contains planning for time, a site visit, Learning Objectives, activities, groupings, enquiry skills and assessments. It consists of an introductory breadth study, establishing the growth, extent and decline of the Roman Empire and connections within the Empire and discussion of chronology and time concepts. This is followed by a broad enquiry about what Roman Britain was like in the second century BCE and a depth enquiry of a specific place and people in the first century BCE.

Translating a medium-term plan to a short-term plan

MTPs need to be translated into subsections. These need to be reviewed and modified throughout the study unit; each short-term plan may need adjustment, depending on how long children take, whether some activities are not fully understood and need to be revisited in another context, or whether progress is more rapid than expected or if questions suggest new and relevant activities not planned for. For these reasons some activities may need to be differentiated or extended. Flexibility is essential, rather than ploughing through plans, just because you spent a long time writing them. I am calling this a short-term plan because there is no longer an expectation that 'a lesson' lasts 1 hour; rather it is a small part of a larger enquiry. It might be linked to lessons on Alfred's law-giving, scholarship and building of fortified burghs as part of an overview of the struggle against the Vikings.

The short-term plan in this section is part of a study of the Viking and Anglo-Saxon Struggle for the kingdom. There is a wealth of support for planning this study unit. There are excellent suggestions for resources and planning on the historical association website www.history.org.uk/primary/categories/exemplars-study-units. If you are interested in researching Iron Age ritual burials, go to Nichol (2014: 41–44). There is a fascinating section on reading an Anglo-Saxon poem about the end of Roman Britain in Nichol preparing children to writing a poem in the same genre (2014: 27–32). The poem can be found at www.elfinspell.com/PrimarySourceRuinedCity.html.

TABLE 10.2 Breadth and depth studies for the Roman Empire and its impact on Britain

BREADTH STUDY	Enquiry skills
Enquiry: How did Britain come to be occupied by the Romans; what was Roman Britain like?	Understanding of:
(a) Whole class look at the growth of the Roman Empire, identify emergence of key cities, consider extent of Trade routes in Roman Empire and what was traded. Focus on third-century Britain (http://resourcesforhistory.com/map.htm#gsc.tab=0). Time: 30 min. (b) Make a timeline for Roman Britain (50 BCE–500 CE) (c) www.historyonthenet.com/roman-britain-timeline-2/: pairs of children given event and its date from this timeline and asked to research it and write 3 sentences about it on a card. Fix cards to timeline. (d) Discuss using dates and time concepts; comparing duration of Roman Britain, between incidents. Focus on the third century CE and how long Romans had been established in Britain by then. Time: 40 min. (e) Visit to a local Roman site: record as plan, photographs, video, sketches, notes. What can we find out, guess, what would we like to find out Time: Half a day	– British, local, world history – duration of Roman Britain – key events in Roman occupation of Britain – impact of Romans on a local area
DEPTH STUDY 1	
Context for enquiry: Cassius Dio was an historian who lived in Rome (c. 164–235 CE). He has invited a group of his most trusted friends to find out what the province of Britannia is like, for his next volume on the Roman Empire. You are members of this research group. You travel all over Britannia collecting information for Cassius Dio. **Enquiry:** What evidence can we find out about this distant province for Cassius Dio to put in his History of the Roman Empire? Deciding on the information to collect: Whole-class discussion with teacher to pool knowledge of Roman Britain, then teacher and pupils decide what to investigate and why. (This gives the researchers ownership of the enquiry). Children work in small groups. Time: 30 min.	

continued

TABLE 10.2 Continued

Enquiries	What pupils will do	Organisation	Products	Enquiry skills
How do we get there?	In each case research the answer from information books and internet. Each group records their findings in notes, (in present tense), as if discovered from visits and interviews.	Small groups	Each group presents information for Cassius Dio in prose.	Make connections and contrasts between British, local and world history.
Is it a peaceful place?				
Is Britain defended? Where? Why? How? (**attack/defence**)			They may, in role as Cassius Dio's information gatherers, offer their own opinions on the information, expressed in first person as I think . . . (e.g. 'the gladiators fights I saw were thrilling' followed by description.)	Ask and answer valid historical questions.
Shall we inspect some military camps?				Respond with thoughtfully selected, relevant information.
What are the cities like? (**settlements, public buildings, religious buildings**)			Each set of findings should be accompanied by careful plans, maps or illustrations as appropriate.	
What are the native British like? (**Homes**)			A visitor, in role as Cassius Dio, receives the reports which are read to him, in turn, in his villa back in Rome.	
Are there gladiators in Britain?			<u>Time</u> 90 min.	
Will there be somewhere comfortable to stay? (**Homes**)				

DEPTH STUDY 2

Context for enquiry: Claudia Severa. The wife of Aelius Brochus, commander of Briga fort (now Chesterholme) near Vindolanda and Prefect of the ninth cohort of Batavians, invited her friend Sulpicia Lepidina, wife of Flavius Cerealis, the commander of a neighbouring fort, to her birthday party on the third day before the Ides of September (13th) between 97 and 93 CE. We have the first example of a Roman woman's signature because her invitation was preserved on wooden tablet 291 (http://judithweingarten.blogspot.co.uk/2013/08/a-literate-lady-in-vindolanda.html)

'I give you a warm invitation to make sure that you come to us, to make the day more enjoyable for me by your arrival. Give my greetings to your Cerealis. My Aelius and my little son send their greetings. I shall expect you, sister. Farewell, sister, my dearest soul, as I hope to prosper, and hail.'

Enquiry: Based on evidence, what might Claudia's party at the fort on Hadrian's Wall have been like?

Enquiries	Activity	Organisation	Product	Skill
What would Claudia's life have been like living at a fort on Hadrian's Wall?	Research life on Hadrian's wall at the end of the first century CE. Include labelled plans of a fort Julia might have lived in. www.bbc.co.uk/history/ancient/romans/vindolanda_01.shtml	Small groups	Combine research in an information leaflet, e.g. 'Claudia Severus: The Life of a Fort Commander's wife on Hadrian's Wall'; or 'My Wife Claudia Severus' by Aelius Brochus.	Research and select and organize valid responses.
From the evidence, what sort of a woman do you think Claudia was?	Consider Claudia's letters to her friend. What do you think she was like? www.futurelearn.com/courses/hadrians-wall/0/steps/5092			
What might she have worn at her party, what hair style, what jewellery and perfume?	Why do you think this? What might the missing parts of her 2 other letters have been about?			
How might the husbands of the two women dressed, normally? For the party?	Accompany writing with labelled illustrations. www.therthdimension.org/AncientRome/RomanFoodDrink/romanfooddrink.htm			

continued

TABLE 10.2 Continued

Enquiries	What pupils will do	Organisation	Products	Enquiry skills
What might Claudia have served at her party? Can you find out more about Aelius Brochus or Flavius Cerialis?	Research army dress of a Fort Commander, and likely off-duty dress. Include labelled illustrations. How many soldiers might they command in a fort? Can you find out more about Flavius Cerialis? http://vindolanda.csad.ox.ac.uk/exhibition/people-1.shtml Does this tell you more about Claudia and her friend? Time Detectives: How Archaeologists Use Technology to Recapture the Past https://books.google.co.uk/books?isbn=0684818280 http://vindolanda.csad.ox.ac.uk/exhibition/army-8.shtml			

Formative assessment focuses: Do children understand the extent and time scale of the Roman Empire and key events during the Roman occupation?

Summative assessment: Can children ask valid questions and answer them using primary and secondary sources by selecting and organizing their findings about selected aspects of life in Roman Britain?

Cross-curricular links for breadth study and depth study 1 and 2

Language and Literacy: Breadth study, select and organize information, write reports

Mathematics: Breadth study c, f, time calculations

Digital technologies: Breadth study b, d, g. Depth study 2, research Hadrian's Wall, access Claudia's letter, write a report on the fort or an imaginative account of Claudia Severus, research Claudia's appearance and write labelled description, research the fort and make inferences, research lives of fort commanders

Art and Design: Breadth study g, sketch books to record information, clay sculpture, drawing recording their experiences, evaluate and analyse creative works, model making

Geography: Breadth study a, b, locate countries in Europe and key cities. Depth study 1 (How do we get there?) Europe and key cities, maps, globes; is it a peaceful place (possible ambushes); physical geography of Britain, locations of military camps and rationale, making sketch maps, plans for reports

TABLE 10.3 Lesson plan for the Viking and Anglo-Saxon struggle for the kingdom of England (local, national, international connections)

Enquiry: Was King Alfred a great military leader?

Context: you are a television producer making a film 'Alfred the Great'.
In-depth study: Was King Alfred Great?

Learning objectives

- To have a geographical and chronological understanding of the outcomes of the sequence of battles between King Alfred and Aethelfled and the Vikings (Danes) 870–918 CE
- Establish a clear narrative of the period
- Make deductions and inferences based on primary (and secondary) sources
- Understand why and how contrasting interpretations of the past are created

Enquiry	Activity	Organisation	Resources	History enquiry skills
PART 1 Was Alfred a great military leader?	*Whole class*: Watch extracts from BBC TV programme with Michael Wood: King Alfred and the Anglo-Saxons: a) Alfred of Wessex, b) The Lady of the Mercians (Aethelfleada, Alfred's daughter). This can be accessed online. The videos discuss the attacks and defeats of the Saxons and the Danes. (i) Teacher, in role as news reader, reads bulletins (i.e. the notes taken from the Anglo Saxon Chronicle, quoted in the videos (Table 10.4). Children, as TV producers, responding to each bulletin, mark on a map the places where King Alfred fought battles and where his daughter fought battles. Make a note on the date, place and outcome of each battle. (ii) If any of the battle sites is nearby research it further at the local record library or online.	Whole class Working individually, write captions and dates for battles as bulletins read. Whole class > small groups > opposing pairs (Alfred/ Aethelfreda) Selected debating panel + whole class audience	Video clips Pre-prepared, individual outline maps of Britain with battle sites marked. Notes from Anglo-Saxon Chronicle (Table 10.4) Videos (BBC 2016)	From primary source (Anglo-Saxon Chronicle) and video account based on this, identify connections between local and national history and the Viking world. Research from secondary sources: ask and answer questions Thoughtful selection of relevant information

continued

TABLE 10.3 Continued

Enquiry	Activity	Organisation	Resources	History enquiry skills
	(iii) Discuss Alfred's successes in battle, compared with those of his daughter. Note points to argue for Alfred and for Aethelfleada.			
	(iv) Argue, in opposing pairs, whether the title 'Great' is appropriate.			
	(v) Formal television debate following the film, on the motion: King Alfred's leadership against the Danes did not justify the title 'Great'.			

Links with other subjects:

Geography: Pupils should extend their knowledge and understanding beyond the local area to include the United Kingdom and Europe; enhance locational and place knowledge; use apps, atlases, globes, digital mapping

Language and Literacy: Spoken language and listening, reading, justify ideas with reasons, negotiate, evaluate, build on ideas, give well-structured explanations, speculate, explore, hypothesize, debate; write summaries.

Note: Take a long view. Four subsequent Kings of England were Vikings

It is also important to take a long-term view: there were four Viking kings of England after King Alfred; Sweyn Forkbeard, 1013, King of Denmark, his son Cnut 1016–1035, Harald Harefoot 1037–1040 and Hardicanute 1040–1042.

- How significant were Alfred's and Aethelflaeda's victories in defeating the Vikings?
- Alfred commissioned Asser to write the Anglo-Saxon Chronicle, so it is not unbiased.

The last English King was Edward the Confessor, the son of Aethelred (the Unready) and Emma of Normandy and grew up in Normandy. His half-brother was Hardicanute who died after a drinking party in 1043 and Edward became King of England. In 1066, on Edward's death, the Witen named Harold Godwinson Edward's successor. Edward the Confessor had exiled Harold's brother Tostig, the Earl of Northumbria 1065. So when Harald Hardrada, King of Norway laid claim to the English throne and invaded in Northumbria he was joined by Tostig. King Harold, the new King of England, defeated and killed them both at the Battle of Stamford Bridge, but had to immediately move south as William Duke of Normandy, another competitor for the throne, had landed at Pevensey, on the south coast. He was one of a group of Vikings who had conquered Normandy in 911 CE. Ironically, after William conquered England by a 'toss of the die', the dominant culture in England became Norman, not Viking.

TABLE 10.4 Summary of key battles King Alfred and his daughter Aelfraeda fought against the Danes

Date	Note from Anglo-Saxon Chronicle	Alfred's travels to fight	Who won: Danes/Saxons
870	King of East Angles killed by Danes. Danes attacked Wessex at Reading. Alfred (and brother King Ethelred) was defeated. On the Ridgeway 5 tracks met. Alfred met Danes over the ridge. (Alfred's father, King Ethelread, stayed in tent.) In April King Aethelread died. Alfred became king at 22.	Reading	Alfred defeated
871	Danish armies caught up Anglo-Saxons at Ashdown. Alfred attacked. Danes fled. (On E/W Ridgeway around a thorn tree.) Exact place not clear. Ashdown thought to be ancient name for Berkshire Downs. Research suggests near Newbury. Alfred attacked 'like a wild boar'. He broke Viking line. Chased them back to Reading. Ethelred died. Alfred became king. Vikings withdrew from Reading but took up residence in London. (Alfred probably paid them to leave. Hoards of gold, dating to 1871–1872 Viking occupation found in London).	Ridgeway (5,000-year-old track from Wiltshire along Berkshire Downs to Thames) Reading	Alfred and brother Ethelred victorious: both sides experience great losses Alfred won
873–874	Viking Army in Northumbria and East Midlands was divided into 3. One part moved to Repton in Debyshire during this winter, dug in defences, then shared out land, settled, ploughed. Remains of Alfred's army returned to Wessex.	Alfred in Wessex	Vikings settling in Derbyshire
876	Danes attacked and occupied Wareham in Dorset. Alfred blockaded them but couldn't defeat them so negotiated a peace. Blockade fleet defeated by storms Danes swore on 'holy ring of Thor'. Danes broke their word, killed hostages and slipped away to Exeter in Devon. Danes withdrew to Mercia and made attack on Chippenham at Christmas. Most people killed but Alfred escaped to Athelney, between Burrowbridge and East Lyng, in the Somerset Levels.	Wareham, Dorset Alfred in royal stronghold of Chippenham	Peace but Danes remained. Alfred defeated
878	In spring Alfred built fort on the Marshes at Athelney (you can see the causeway where his fortress was). From here he launched the salvation of Wessex. Slag from furnaces where	Ling Athelney (near Bridgewater Somerset)	

continued

TABLE 10.4 Continued

Date	Note from Anglo-Saxon Chronicle	Alfred's travels to fight	Who won: Danes/Saxons
c. 880	Alfred's army forged weapons (sword blades, spears and chain mail) has been found there. Over 7 weeks the men of Somerset came to him. They made camp at Eyley Oak by Warminster, hidden in the monkey puzzle trees of Eyley Wood. We can still see fortification and vessels for prayer. There were 3,000–4,000 men and horses.	Warminster	Alfred won
	At dawn Alfred's army moved to Edington, Wiltshire, under Salisbury Plain; Anglo-Saxon royal estate there. There they attacked Guthrun and the Danes. (You can see the line of attack in field today.) The battle was brutal. Alfred won and destroyed the pagan army with great slaughter. Alfred pursued the survivors to Chippenham – they surrendered. A peace followed with a meeting on 13th June, with Guthrun, who received Christian baptism. (Scandinavians wanted to buy into European culture. They needed to settle and integrate and to do this they needed to live by the rules of Christianity.)	Battle at Edington, (Wiltshire, near Salisbury Plain) Danes surrender at Chippenham (Wiltshire, 13 miles east of Bath)	
	Treaty of Wedmore divided Kingdom of Mercia between Alfred's and Gudrun's kingdoms. This extended Guithrun's Kingdom to East Anglia (The Danelaw). Aldred had half Mercia and control of London.		
885	Danish raid on Saxon city of Rochester, where they built a fort. Alfred marched on them and they fled.	Rochester, Kent	Alfred won
886	Alfred reclaimed and rebuilt London and left it in hands of his son-in law. Alfred acknowledged as king (except by Vikings, in the North East). Alfred's daughter Aethelflaeda married the King of Mercia, Aethelred. Mercia and Wessex became one. Bede's idea of the English people had come true.	London	Mercia and Wessex combined by marriage of Alfred's daughter to Aethelred, King of Mercia.
890s	Further Viking attacks but c. 994 Danes in England retired to Northumbria or East Anglia or retired to the Continent.		
899	Alfred died. Alfred's son Edward was his heir. Land still torn apart by war. Will Anglo-Saxon Kingdom survive?		War follows Alfred's death

TABLE 10.4 Continued

Date	Note from Anglo-Saxon Chronicle	Alfred's travels to fight	Who won: Danes/Saxons
902	The Vikings controlled land from the northern Fens to Devil's Dyke in Cambridgeshire. The Danish King Yorik struck into Wiltshire. Edward (Alfred's son) responded, burning land in Fens. The battle was a bloodbath. King Edward issued a withdrawal but the Kentish people refused and met the Danes at the battle of Place, Cambs. The Danes won but lost King Yorik. Kentish nobles were wiped out but Danes lost more. Edward was forced to make peace. He met the Danish leaders in Buckinghamshire on route from Mercia into Danelaw by the River Ouse. Edward bought peace with silver and treasure. Edward squeezes money from starving people to pay army (snow etc.)	Between North Fens and Devil's Dyke. Battle at Place, Cambs. Edward met Danish leaders in Buckinghamshire and bought peace with silver and gold.	Danes won
907	Chester was regained and held between Vikings and Welsh.		
910	Forces of Mercia (Aethelflaeda – her husband now an invalid) and Wessex (Edward, Aethelflaeda's brother) attacked by Viking army from Northumbria, in Mercia; intercepted at Wednesfield (Wrekin). Overwhelmed in a storm of spears on the road running by the canal between Wolverhampton and Bridgenorth, in the fields of Woden. The fighting ended at Tettenhall near Wolverhampton, which gave its name to the battle.	Mercia attacked by Northumbrian Vikings. The Wrekin, Wednesfield Battle of Tettenhall (or Wednesfield, Woden's field).	Great victory for Mercia and Wessex; thousands of Danes killed
911	Aethelred died in 1911 and Aetheflaeda ruled Mercia ('The Lady of Mercia'), a unique event in Medieval history. She was accepted as king in her diplomatic and international role.		
917	Aethelflaeda bravely led the army in attacking a Danish base at Derby. The Mercian army broke into town. The army accepted Aetheflaeda as their leader in battle. In Anglo-Saxon heroic poetry there is a bond between lord and his warriors for unswerving loyalty.	Derby Aethelfleada led the Saxon army	
918	Danish army in Leicester, Northumbrians and York said all submitted to Aethelflaeda, the Lady of the Mercians. June 918 Aethelfleda died in Tamworth, buried in Gloucester. Anglo-Norman chroniclers such as William of Malmesbury described her as powerful; the delight of her subjects, the dread of her enemies, a woman of enlarged soul.	Tamworth	Danes in York, Northumbria, Leicester all submitted to Aelfleada of Mercia and Wessex

Useful sources for comparing different interpretations of the arrival of the Anglo-Saxons and the reasons for them are:

Gildas, mid-sixth century Welsh monk, says Roman influence still strong. But he saw the Britons as weak and the Saxons as wicked and bellicose. *De Excidio Britannia*, Sections 18, 23–24 (www.tertullian.org/fathers/gildas_02_ruin_of_britain.htm)

Bede (2008), *Ecclesiatical History of the English People*, Book 1 Ch. 15 p. 26 by now the Gemanic settlers have firm root but Bede's account, based on Gildas, identifies invading tribes and focuses on the need to convert invading pagans (https://en.wiki source.org/wiki/Ecclesiastical_History_of_the_English_People/Book).

There are various ways short-term plans can be set out, but it seems a good idea to write them in a way that they can be clearly explained to the children. It ensures that you are using language which is clear to them and to you. Children feel secure, and, one hopes, motivated if the structure of a session is explained. They need, first, to talk about what they have already learned, then hear what they are expected to learn from this lesson sequence, the specific activities which will enable them to learn it, how they will be grouped for these activities and which adults will be working with them. And they need to know how much time they will have for each part of the lesson and ways in which, at the end of the lesson, they will be have an opportunity to demonstrate what they have learned, enjoyed or found difficult. This will inform your plans for the following session.

Table 10.3 is a short-term plan for a depth study related to the struggles of King Alfred against the Vikings.

It has been long and widely claimed that King Alfred was great, for reasons indicated at the beginning of Chapter 1. And there are reasons why he may be regarded as great, although he was not so regarded in Anglo-Saxon times or by the Normans. So this enquiry addresses a central point; the way we learn to see the past and why, whether and how it is related to the truth. This study is based on three videos (BBC 2016), which are based on one of the Anglo-Saxon Chronicles. The videos are very highly recommended for making the period of conflict between the Anglo-Saxons seem real and significant. The rationale for the teaching plan is that it is based on evidence about the battles of King Alfred and his daughter, Aelflaeda (Tables 10.3 and 10.4), which is supported by the videos. It raises awareness of the vast area over which King Alfred was being challenged by the Vikings, and it is possible for anyone living near to one of the battle sites to visit it and perhaps identify the battle site from the evidence. When considering whether King Arthur was greater than his daughter Aethelflaeda, you may be influenced by recent research that shows that some Viking Warriors were women (Hedensternia-Jonson *et al.* 2017).

Chapter 11 considers in more detail how children's learning can be monitored, assessed recorded and communicated to others.

Assessment, monitoring and recording pupils' progress

Perhaps the most important aspect of assessment to promote progression is that the children are clear about what they are supposed to be learning from any activity, whether it is discussion, making a model or writing. All the time I was at school and at university, admittedly not recently, I had no idea why I sometimes got A+ and sometimes B. In those days, there were no marking criteria and assessment depended on individual tutors' judgment. But there was no shared idea of what they were looking for. That is no longer the case and it is important, if children are to progress, that they know what they are aiming for and what they need to do next to achieve it.

Assessment is important

There are many reasons why some form of assessment is necessary. It provides information about pupils' progress and the next stage of learning for children themselves, their present and subsequent teachers, their parents and school leaders, governors and Ofsted inspectors, who all have different, but valid reasons for knowing how children's thinking in and knowledge of history progresses. Each school will have its own assessment policy, stating what should be assessed, how and when. Therefore the curriculum must include an assessment system that enables schools to check what pupils have learned and whether they are on track to meet expectations at the end of each Key Stage and to report regularly to parents.

Why no National Assessment Levels?

The Final Report of the Commission on Assessment without Levels (HM Govt 2015b) gives practical reasons for removing level-based assessment, which apply across the curriculum. 'Removing levels', it says, will allow teachers greater flexibility in the way they plan and assess pupils' learning. It explains that the levels distorted day-to-day formative assessment, because teachers focused on getting children across the thresholds (levels), rather than ensuring that they had secure-knowledge and understanding of the programmes of study. The levels were used as a best-fit model, which meant that pupils could have vast gaps in their knowledge and understanding but still be placed at a certain level. It was not always clear which aspects of the curriculum a child was insecure in and where the gaps were. Levels also encouraged undue pace and progression onto more difficult work, leaving gaps in children's knowledge and understanding. The document also explains that previous assessment methods consumed a disproportionate amount of teachers' time. *History for All* (Ofsted 2011) and the Historical Association Primary Survey (2016) also showed that primary school teachers did not feel confident in how to assess progression in history. So we should give thanks that, finally, 'the levels' have been abolished as an unsatisfactory means of measuring progress and that it is teachers who decide the best ways to assess what children learn.

Assessment in history is particularly difficult

The hierarchy of levels in historical thinking was not based on research. The *Concepts of History and Teaching Approaches* project (CHATA) (Lee *et al.* 1991–1996) attempted to link patterns of progression in historical thinking to age-related progression. However, they concluded that patterns of progression do not describe individual learning paths, as in ascending a ladder. Children may jump steps. There are numerous variables, which prevent the creation of a hierarchy in developing historical thinking; types of questions vary, sources are of different levels of complexity, the content which questions and sources investigate may be simple or very complex. Children do not perform at the same level in each strand of enquiry, nor in the sub-strands within each strand and patterns varied between schools in different strands. Furthermore, there are some examples of 7-year-old children responding to some questions at a higher level than 12- and even 14-year-old children. And in practice, the strands of historical thinking, asking questions about sources, time concepts and interpretations of accounts, are integrally related, not separated.

It is accepted that the link between teaching and learning is very strong, yet these assessments were not linked in any way to pedagogy. The pupils were given small information booklets before each set of tests. It may also be that, as with Piagetian research, the language used and the emphasis on logic was confusing, since it was not embedded in children's deep learning. Donaldson (1978) showed that when children are interested and the question seems relevant and related to familiar experiences they operate at a higher cognitive level.

The CHATA research into aspects of children's understanding of procedural concepts in history (evidence, time and change, interpretations) and how they apply these to constructing knowledge of the past, revealed that progression in understanding these concepts is rich and complex and that the value of the project may be in giving teachers new ideas about how to teach them. Yet a great deal remains unexplored. So perhaps special consideration needs to be given to how a school policy can be interpreted in assessing children's learning in history.

Findings from research into children's development of time concepts were also conflicting. Hodkinson (2003a) critically examined the development of temporal cognition in the primary school, which was set out in the Qualification and Curriculum Assessment Schemes of Work for the previous National Curriculum for History. He argues that the development of historical time concepts within the National Curriculum and the Schemes were confused, seemed to be based upon few, if any, empirical findings and did not offer an effective approach to children's development of time concepts. Hodkinson's research (2003b, 2004b) suggests that understanding of time concepts is neither hierarchical nor linear and therefore concludes that level descriptors are of little use in assessing children's assimilation of time concepts. The way in which they may best be taught, based on Hodkinson's research, is discussed in Chapter 4.

Nevertheless, the Historical Association has created a hierarchical table for assessment: *Progression in history: a guide* (www.history.org.uk). This is described as a *guide* for schools, from the Early Years to Key Stage 3, despite the abolition of a similar statutory table. This may help you feel secure. But for all the reasons discussed, there is no simple hierarchy and teachers need to feel confident in having an open mind and seeing what patterns emerge, building on what their children can do and understand, in the contexts of their teaching and children's learning. This can be fascinating, but there are no quick fixes. A lot of teachers only paid lip-service to assessing learning using the levels. Some did not even do this. But now teachers have the professional initiative to genuinely explore and reflect on the ways in which children learn in history as a result of their teaching.

Mastery assessment

The aim of assessment without levels is to encourage 'deep' and coherent understanding, rather than superficial learning. The Report of the Commission on Assessment without Levels (HM Govt 2015b) emphasizes the importance of 'Mastery Assessment', which, it claims, denotes deep understanding, through problem-solving and questioning. It is less concerned with differentiation than with ensuring that all children have grasped fundamental, necessary content and skills, assuming that pupils will achieve mastery of each unit of learning before moving on to the next unit. It assumes that all pupils will achieve this level if properly supported. It is assumed that, after 'high quality instruction' pupils demonstrate they have learned what was intended or, if not, that measures are taken to decide what they need to work on in order to do so. This process is assumed to ensure 'deep secure learning for all'. It is claimed that, 'in devising this new approach to assessment schools can make mastery a genuine goal'. The approach was introduced for hierarchical subjects, such as mathematics, where teaching can be reduced to small units. As argued above, the skills of historical enquiry are not necessarily learned in small stages or hierarchical. However, 'Mastery Assessment' *is* appropriate in history in that there is generally no need for differentiated teaching, because historical enquiry skills allow pupils to respond adequately to the same questions in different ways.

Ofsted have no predetermined view as to what specific assessment system a school should use. Ofsted's main consideration is whether the approach adopted by a school is effective. They will be looking to see that it provides accurate information, showing the progress pupils are making. The information should also be meaningful for parents, pupils and governors.

Some essential points to remember about assessment

Assessment should not be daunting! The key purpose of assessment is to improve children's historical knowledge and thinking. You only need to keep succinct and manageable evidence of this. And remember that progress is not, as the levels targets implied, linear, so be honest about what children can do. Their understanding may be richer and more complex without constantly demonstrating new skills. As Byrom has said (2013), we should picture progress as a climbing frame rather than a ladder; not only do we go up rung by rung, we often have to go down in order to go up. In assessment using levels to provide evidence of progress, teachers had to assess by tiny increments, which did little to promote progress. The focus of history is enquiry and so it is rational to suggest that we should assess progress based on how well children respond, overall, to an enquiry topic.

Burnham and Brown (2004) suggest that the climbing frame is ours to make, and that we should be thinking about what progression is in history, about how pupils move forwards in historical thinking and knowledge, about how best to move particular pupils forwards, in relation to the areas of knowledge and thinking we would like them to advance into next.

Formative assessment: what is it?

Evidence for Excellence in Education: where have all the levels gone? (NFER 2013) says that, 'The most interesting part of assessing without levels is the suggestion of a greater role for schools in the formative assessment process; schools will be able to introduce their own approaches to formative assessment to support pupil attainment and progression'. This suggests an opportunity for schools to have greater involvement, controls and input into the shape and structure of assessment. 'The connections between teaching, learning and assessment which teachers can forge in the classroom to create the right conditions for developing pupils' understanding' is an important factor in raising pupils' achievement (Loughland and Kilpatrick 2013). So a considered focus on formative assessment is important in progressing children's learning and teachers can control it. Welcome to professional liberation!

Formative assessment is part of what teachers do continuously, through asking questions and observing how pupils go about activities, to check to what extent children have learned what was planned. To take their learning further they may make suggestions, challenge, or offer clues and or plan activities to consolidate knowledge and understanding. Ofsted attach much importance to formative assessment. The Commission on Assessment without Levels (HM Govt 2015b) makes it clear that a school's aims for assessment should be achieved without excessive workload and recognize the importance of formative assessment. Formative assessment is intended to inform teaching and learning. It need not be recorded but *must* be acted upon. Ofsted does not expect to see an extensive collection of marked work.

Formative assessment: how to do it

Classroom ethos

It is encouraging that the type of classroom ethos in which formative assessment flourishes is typical of most primary classrooms. It has been argued in Chapter 6 that good history teaching and learning is essentially creative and the criteria for creativity include being curious, identifying problems and asking questions, imagination, risk-taking, acting individually and collaboratively, making connections and requiring knowledge. Jones and Wyse (2004: 5–6) say that in creative lessons there is a different kind of relationship in the classroom, one which is not about an authoritative figure who holds all the resources and power, but one based on respect, trust and above all enquiry. This requires, as Lucas (2001) suggests, a classroom ethos in which learners are given and set themselves goals, negative stress is limited and feedback enhances self-knowledge, self-esteem and motivation. Learners learn to live with uncertainty; teachers cannot have all the answers but offer structures and processes for thinking, which requires confidence from both teachers and learners, respect for individual learners and their interests.

Clarke (2014: 7) emphasizes the importance of classroom ethos, in which pupils are involved in planning, and after their enthusiasm has been aroused children and teachers co-construct the success criteria, which have explicit objectives. They share examples of excellence, and feedback during lessons comes from both the children and the teacher. Elliott (in Knight 2008) explains that if children have to meet learning objectives which are externally imposed and which they were not involved in creating this does not lead to excellence but to predictable outcomes. Excellence is more likely to be demonstrated by imagination and creativity and result from ownership of learning, motivation and self-evaluation because learners are constantly reflecting on the process of learning. Formative assessment should be based on a specific context and specific advice, controlled by the teacher, not by 'levels' (Knight 2008). In history, formative assessment must take account of the overall picture, not focus on minute changes. Learning in this way is claimed to be part of a process of constructing identity. But I think primary teachers always knew that these are the ways in which we take children's learning forward and are pleased to have it more generally appreciated.

Figure 11.1 shows the cyclical nature of planning learning objectives, based on reflection on pupils' prior achievements, planning differentiated activities to enable them to achieve the learning objectives, reflecting on their engagement and misconceptions when completing the activities, assessment of to what extent children have achieved the learning objectives, through formative assessment: observation, discussion, marking, self assessment or testing. After evaluating pupils' achievements, some evidence of pupils' attainment is briefly recorded on the lesson plan and informs the next lesson plan.

Formative assessment can be done through questioning, discussion and observing children working, as well as by assessing 'products', resulting from these activities. We have discussed the reasons why there are no clear hierarchies in developing the skills of historical enquiry and why prescribed statements of 'levels' were unsatisfactory. Attainment at the end of each Key Stage states simply that students are 'expected to know, apply and understand the matters skills and processes specified in the relevant

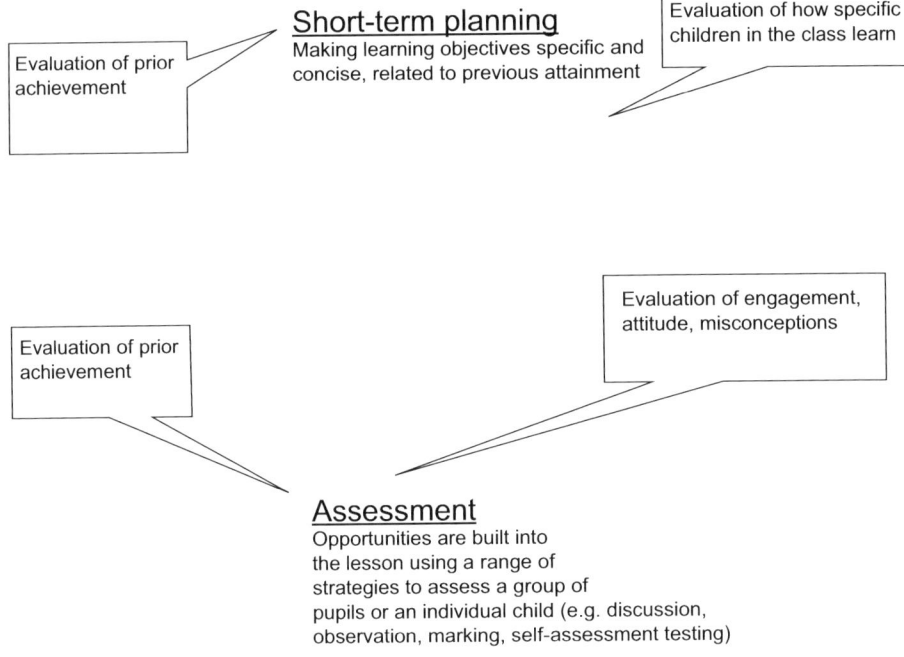

FIGURE 11.1 The teaching and assessment cycle.

field of study (DfE 2013: 2). Sally Burnham (Burnham and Brown 2004) writes brief comments on pupils' work and records for herself in a notebook how she will tweak the next session, if necessary, for a group of pupils. This she finds both 'pupil-focused and history sensitive'.

Formative assessment at Key Stage 1: what skills are we looking for?

At the end of Key Stage 1, children must have an understanding of chronology and time concepts, of how historical sources are used and that there can be different interpretations of the past. The ways in which they should do this are specified.

Time questions

- Use common words and phrases relating to the passing of time.

- Know where the people and events they study fit within a chronological framework.

- Identify similarities and differences between ways of life in different periods.

Historical terms

- Use a wide vocabulary of historical terms.

- Understand a coherent narrative: causes and effects.

- Ask and answer questions, choosing different parts of stories to show they know and understand key features of events.

Understanding sources

- Understand some of the ways in which we find out about the past.

Understanding interpretations

- Understand some of the ways in which the past is represented.

Teaching Key Stage 1 children about how we find out about the past can be assessed in a variety of contexts, usually through questioning and discussion. Clearly it is best to plan discussions which focus on one or two of these aspects at a time, especially initially, and keep a note of what is discussed, so that children are introduced to and learn how to discuss all of them. The following examples show how teachers have done this in different contexts.

Formative assessment at Key Stage 1: how do we do it?

Story

At Key Stage 1, children should be taught about changes within living memory (this is probably best learned initially and by talking to older people), events beyond living memory, the lives of significant individuals, national or international and significant local events, and they should have some awareness the different periods in which they occurred. Children love stories which really happened to people and about real events. Stories provide good key opportunities to continually formatively assess the key process of historical enquiry over a range of time and places.

Indeed Farmer and Cooper (1998: 35) see story as the essence of history teaching. Stories are important in children's cognitive development, for they do not listen passively. They are called upon to create new worlds through powers of imagination, which extend their first hand experiences and their perceptions of the world. Bage (1999) examined the ways in which stories can make historical narrative richer and easier for children to analyse. Egan too (1986: 2) says that story-telling reflects a basic and powerful form in which to make sense of the world and should be at the centre of planning for young children. In addition, a selection of local, national and international stories about past times introduces children to the intellectual and cultural traditions of the society in which the stories occur.

Questions about time through stories

Time questions involve finding out:

- when the story happened, using time vocabulary, how the time of the story was different from today and how it was the same;

- what the key events were, and in what sequence, what caused an event to happen and what happened as a result.

Primary History 67 (Cooper 2014a) sets out, in more detail, historical questions to ask in reading and telling stories. Questions about time include time language such as, before/after, now/then, old/new, questions about sequence and probability words perhaps, probably. Who can tell me the story? What do you think will happen next? They involve questions about cause and effect: why do you think that happened? and about motives: why do you think she/he said/did that? They may be questions about similarities and differences between 'then' and 'now': do we wear these/do this today? Why not? What do we have today instead? Why?

Questions about interpretations in stories

Children can compare versions of stories in different books and explain how they are similar and different and discuss why. They can consider why stories about past times or local places talked about by visitors may be different.

Artefacts sources and time

Questions about artefacts may also be encountered either in stories (windmills, haystacks, flat iron and candlesticks) or in further investigations, perhaps prompted by stories, about farms and markets, journeys, houses/homes, as well as by handling old artefacts or visiting old buildings. How did they use this? What is it for? Do we use this today? Why not? What might it have been like use the old artefact? What is it like to use the (equivalent) today? What caused us to change?

Pictures: sources, time and interpretations

Pictures, 'iconic representations of knowledge' (Bruner 1966), offer powerful ways of representing the past, whether they are illustrations, paintings, video clips or photographs. Children can explain what is happening in the picture, what the significant features are, the sequences of events, the causes and effects of events, what they think happened next and so talk about the passage of time. They can make inferences about past ways of life (Harnett 1998: 71) using time vocabulary – and this can reveal any misconceptions, which teachers can address. Contrasting illustrations, different photographs of the same person or place, introduce discussions about why interpretations of the past may be different.

Harnett (1998: 73–84) gives examples of how teachers can promote discussions of pictures, offer encouragement and make appropriate interventions. She shows how listening to children's talk enables teachers to assess children's current knowledge and use it as a base for extended learning. A teacher may encourage children to look more closely at particular features of a picture or to consider their significance. They might suggest alternative ways of viewing the pictures (perhaps through a magnifying glass) or might intervene to provide children with additional information and further sources to help their investigation. Group work, in particular, is most effective when children are clear about the purpose of the activity and what they are trying to achieve and they need to learn this from whole-class discussions.

Arnheim (2004) suggests how we can help children to look at a painting. He says that first we ask children to describe whole picture, then to explore details before we ask whether the picture tells a story, what might have happened before and afterwards and why and discuss the picture as an interpretation, perhaps in comparison with another. *Lulu and the Flying Babies* (Simmonds 2017) illustrates how children can imagine themselves transported into a painting.

Oral Sources, time, change and interpretations

Older people talking about their pasts and about changes within living memory are, of course, telling their own stories, or histories. Suggestions about choosing interviewees, organizing interviews which will focus on historical questions and following up interviews are given in Cooper 2002: 89–101. Redfern (1998) explains how many aspects of the past can be understood through oral history at Key Stage 1: the cultural diversity of societies, the experience of minorities. He points out that older people can talk about times long before they were born, through oral tradition.

Oral history invites questions involving time concepts and considering different interpretations.

Planning and assessing enquiries about local history and about artefacts

A local visit might be related to a visit from an older local person, or to an event beyond living memory. Possible questions related to a local site or building are given in Cooper (2002: 116–122). For example, having observed various aspects of an old house, children discuss how the building has changed and why, how people used to light and heat it and cook in the past, how many people probably lived there, how the rooms may have changed. Strategies for sequencing questions about artefacts and pupils and progress in answering them from Year 1 to Year 2 are given in Cooper (2002: 112–122).

Play

There are numerous examples of case studies in *Exploring Time and Place Through Play* (Cooper 2004) which explain how teachers helped children to set up play areas related to stories and how they intervened, sensitively, to challenge and extend children's ideas, to make formative assessments. This book was a response to the Researching Effective Pedagogy in the Early Years Project (REPEY) (Siraj-Blatchford *et al.* 2002), which was developed to identify the most effective strategies and techniques for promoting learning in the Early Years. The study found that 'sustained shared thinking' and open-ended questioning were essential in extending children's thinking. The adult is aware of and responds to the child's understanding or capability in the context of the subject and the activity in question, the child is aware of what is to be learned (what is in the adult's mind) and both contribute to and are involved in the learning process. The REPEY study found that the most effective learning took place when teachers modelled dialogue and activities, which could be followed by free access to an 'open environment'. Freely chosen play activities provided the best opportunities for adults to extend children's thinking. Case studies in *Exploring Time and Place through Play* (Cooper 2004) investigate this process, through play about kings, queens and castles (Robson 2004: 40–51); making an 'ancient hut' in the home corner (Moore 2004: 65–76) (lots of polarized differences between 'then' and 'now'!); and constructing a time capsule to visit other times and places (Yates 2004: 77–91).

Play about a local monument

Bicknell (1998) describes role play about Robert Peel inspired by a local monument, the Peel Tower, a feature familiar to the children, which commemorates him in his home town of Bury, near Manchester. Following a visit to the tower children made a collage and models of it, which involved much language, in which Bicknell was aware that they were framing questions and interrogating their own experience in search for an answer and using 'because'; language was becoming a tool for thinking. Children's language in role play areas is more developed and mature than in a normal classroom context.

Play about Florence Nightingale

Harnett and Whitehouse (2016) describe play about a real person who lived in a time beyond living memory, the ubiquitous Florence Nightingale, stimulated by a parent who worked as a nurse talking about her work today. The teacher observed the children's decision making: how they selected their own rules, key decisions made by individual children about how the hospital should be run and the story developed. She describes how the children were highly motivated, spending time looking for different props (Florence's lamp was a small cardboard box with a hole in it and her pet tortoise). The children suggested new scenarios which might have occurred and acted out the different scenes. The teacher noticed how children used their prior knowledge of nurses' work, how they solved problems, for example how they could cook the patients' food, 'cos they didn't have cookers . . .', how they resolved how to contact the doctor 'cos there was no telephone' and how they used the past tense as they described what they were doing.

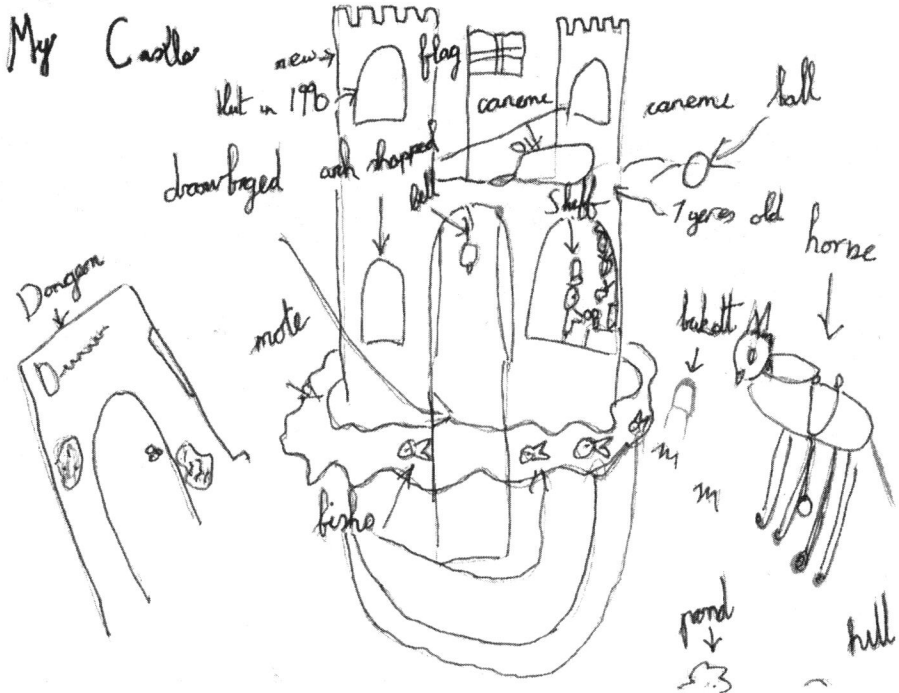

FIGURE 11.2 Initial fantasy image of a castle.

Products

A three-day project with Years 1 and 2 (pp. 205–207) on a visit to a local castle produced evidence of considerable progression in historical understanding. Figure 11.2 shows the kind of fantasy images of a castle children drew on the first day of the project.

True, Figure 11.2 is not the work of the same child as Figure 11.3 but it does indicate the vast amount all the children learned about the castle during the week from primary and secondary sources.

Recording progress

It has been said (above) that it is not necessary to keep extensive records as evidence of children's progress and 'Mastery Assessment' reflects that everyone has learnt the essentials of the learning aims that were planned, but that, in supporting learning through formative assessment, teachers will inevitably also respond to individual differences.

Products: reading, writing and models

There will be some products, as in the Kendal Castle project, which exemplify progression. And of course children at Key Stage 1 can read and write, as Charlotte

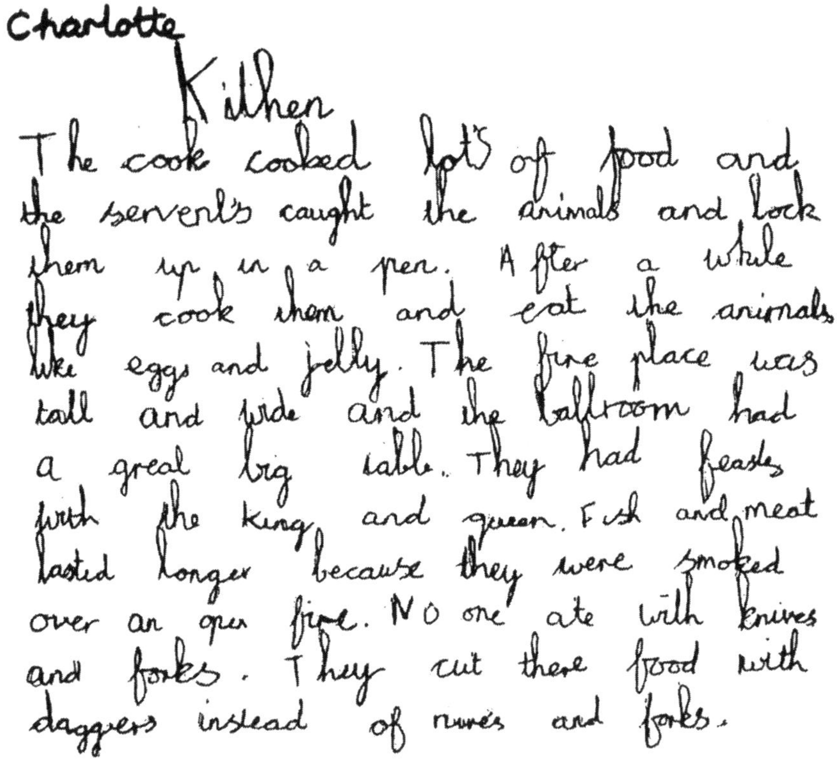

Charlotte

Kithen

The cook cooked lot's of food and
the servent's caught the animals and lock
them up in a pen. After a while
they cook them and eat the animals
like eggs and jelly. The fire place was
tall and wide and the baltroom had
a great big table. They had feasts
with the king and queen. Fish and meat
lasted longer because they were smoked
over an open fire. No one ate with knives
and forks. They cut there food with
daggers instead of nives and forks.

FIGURE 11.3 Section of an information board made by a group of children on day three of the project.

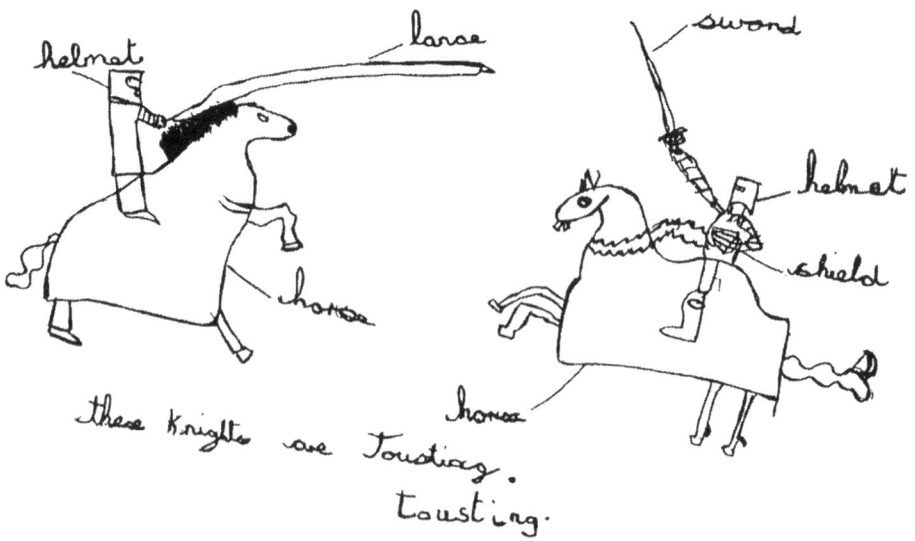

FIGURE 11.4 Samantha's findings about knights from information books.

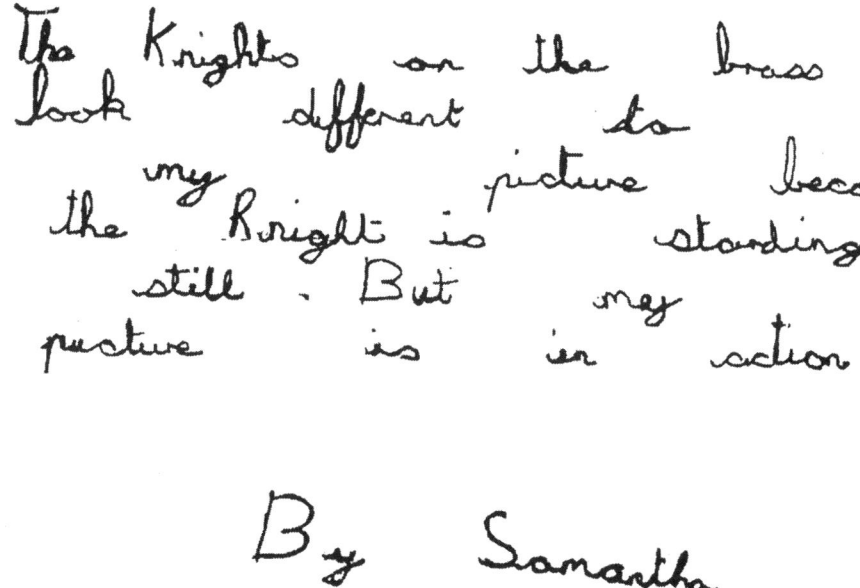

Samantha

The Knights on the brass look different to the my Knight is picture becc the my Knight is standing still. But my picture is in my action

By Samantha.

FIGURE 11.5 Samantha's comparison between her drawing and the brass effigy.

demonstrates. After making a brass rubbing of a Medieval knight, she decided to find out more about knights when they were alive, from information books and to record what she found out. Figure 11.4 shows what Samantha found out about knights from information books and Figure 11.5 compares her drawing of knights, when alive, and the brass effigy.

Gemma can word process and write an account of the visit her class made to a toy museum, and how she was interested in the differences between her toys and toys in the past (see Figure 11.6).

Key Stage 1 children can write questionnaires and count and also deal with the measurement of time, showing and changes over time (see Figure 11.7).

Interestingly, the current National Curriculum does not appear to expect children learning about time and changes to begin with their own lives and experiences or require them to have any understanding of measuring time, but this is where most early years practitioners would start.

Records of pupil talk

Nevertheless, much of the evidence of learning and progression at Key Stage 1 is oral. For example, a record can be kept of children's discussion of pictures shown on an

OUR TRIP TO BETHNAL GREEN
TOY MUSEUM.

On Wednesday, 14th June, we went on the
coach to the toy museum.
The coach driver took us to the wrong
museum. We had to go on the underground
When we got to the toy museum James had
a nosebleed.
In the museum we saw old toys:
Trains, cars, dolls, games, soldiers,
puppets, doll's houses, boats, teddy bears,
horses and theatres.
We found out that old toys were made from
wood and our new toys are made from plastic.
WE found out that dolls were made out of
wood, wax, china, clay, paper and plastic
lots of old dolls had real hair.
We had a talk about old toys—it was very
interesting.
We were tired when we got home.
                    A Story by Class 7.

Gemma

Toys

My grandprents would
have played with
hoops and ropes

FIGURE 11.6 Gemma's account of a visit to the Bethnal Green Toy Museum.

1 When did I first have our first tooth?
   I had my first tooth at five months old
2 When did I first Walk?
   I first walked at 9 Months.
3 When did I first dress our selvs?
   I first dressed at 18 months
4 When did I First read a book?
   When I Was 4 years old
5 When did I First draw?
   When I Was 2 years old
6 When did I Start to write?
   I Started to write when I Was 4 years
7 When did I have money?
   When I Was 3 years old
8 When did I Know my numbers?
   I knew my numbers when I was 4 years

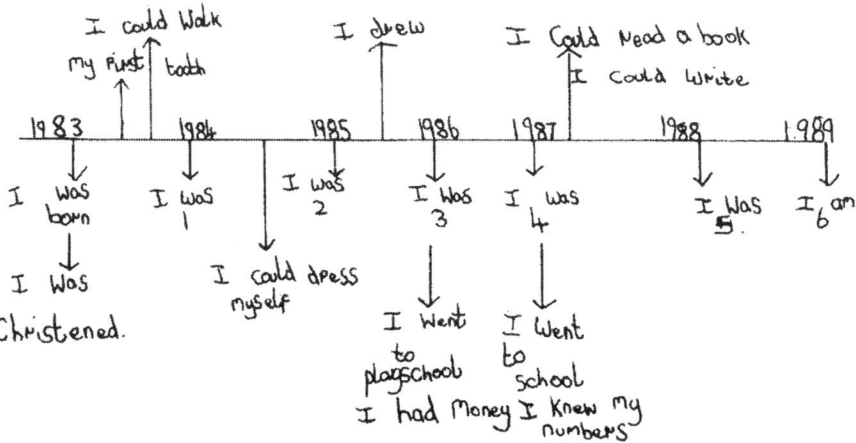

FIGURE 11.7 A questionnaire for parents was used to make a timeline.

electronic white board, comparing differences between 'then' and 'now', initialling their answers. This can be compared with a similar, annotated class discussion much later. Each discussion can be printed and used to evaluate each individual child's progress.

Another simple way of recording thinking is to take photographs of children engaged in history activities, mount them on a large sheet of paper and annotate the photograph with children's comments and the teacher's interventions.

The two approaches could be combined to record children's developing understanding through play. Photographs of key moments in a role play situation could be photographed and their comments recorded either as notes or on the white board. Extracts from oral discussions about past times with visitors could be recorded or scribed to accompany photographs of them and perhaps images and objects that accompanied their talks and images. Discussions of artefacts or a local visit could be similarly annotated, either on the white board or mounted on paper. Children could be involved in making these records. They will, no doubt, fascinate parents – and any other visitors – and involve the children in understanding their learning and reflecting on their own progress – metacognition.

Summative assessment at Key Stage 1

Everyone should be able to explain, to 'a visitor (Ofsted)' what and who they have been learning about and how we know about the past. Ideally during Key Stage 1 they will use words relating to the passing of time, have some idea of a chronological framework, be able to talk about changes over time and about different interpretations. Teachers will have evidence of progress in children's products; printouts of notes from whiteboard discussions and annotated photographs.

Formative assessment at Key Stage 2

What skills must we assess?

Every aspect of history involves enquiry. At Key Stage 2, children are expected to ask and investigate questions about the past in increasingly complex ways, which involve:

■ establishing clear narratives, within and across periods, based on secure chronology; noting connections, contrasts and trends over time;

■ using appropriate historical terms;

■ addressing and sometimes devising historically valid questions about change, cause, similarity, difference and significance;

■ understand how our knowledge is constructed from a range of sources; and

■ selecting and organizing historical information.

Briefly, children must ask questions about the past and investigate them by selecting and interpreting sources and combining their findings, in order to write accounts of the causes and effects of changes over time based on secure chronological knowledge.

They must learn to do this in increasingly complex ways. In order to do this, teachers, sometimes through discussion with pupils, must plan units of work which will enable them to develop these skills and monitor their progress in doing so.

What might take children's thinking forward?

Challenges to an answer

Why do you think that? How do you know? Are you sure? But have you thought about . . .? Do you all agree? Why not? Why do you have different ideas?

- Cause of an event or a person's or group's action:

    Why do you think that happened? What if . . .? Can you think of any other reasons?

- Result of an event or action:

    Why did that happen? What happened next? Can you think of other reasons? What was the most important reason? Why? What was the effect on people?

- Chronology: When? How long before/after? How long did this last/did this happen quickly/slowly? Why? What changed and what stayed the same?

- Comparing different societies: similarities/differences in. . . .

    What were the reasons? Did they change in the same ways?

- Comparing periods: similarities/differences in

    Was everyone/think like this? Who/what was the same/different?

Answers offering a higher level of response

- Cues or answers using probability words are important: may be, I think, perhaps, what if?

- Cues suggesting, or answers with, numerous possible answers at a higher level than single suggestions, although in a group discussion they may be volunteered by different children building on each other's thinking.

- Answers supported by a reason (because, therefore).

- Higher levels of questions and answers involving time concepts can be found in Chapters 4 and 10.

- Questions about connections over time between societies and about connections between Britain and the rest of the world are suggested in Chapter 10.

Common misconceptions and teachers responses

Children's talk and writing often reveals discrepancies between teachers' learning objectives and children's understanding, which teachers need to be aware of and address. Huggins (2000) collected these interesting examples:

Misunderstanding textbooks

Sarah thought Victorian schools were called Board Schools, because they used blackboards. The teacher provided another textbook to give her further information.

Ralph read that 'from the 1880s the development of the camera meant that many photographs survived'. He thought that 'there weren't any cameras until 1880'. Even when shown photographs in the same textbook dated in the 1860s and 1870s he was not immediately convinced.

Misunderstanding historical fiction

A story about women's lives in the nineteenth-century fishing industry was illustrated by photographs from the period. Some children believed that characters in the story were also real people. The teacher led a literacy lesson on the difference between real and fictional characters.

Vocabulary no longer used

Jane was discussing an old implement for washing clothes, which she was told, was an old dolly. Asked what she thought it was for she said 'to put clothes on and dress up'. The teacher explained how it had been used and found a corroborating photograph.

Limited knowledge

One teacher, introducing a study unit on Benin, used a concept map to find out what children already knew about West Africa. This revealed paucity of knowledge and some prejudice, so she began the topic with modern material on West Africa from a children's educational television series.

Out of school influences

Children encounter many inaccurate views about the past from parents and grandparents' conversations, films, cartoons and drama. This information is useful to know, discuss and to build upon.

Changing attitudes and values

One teacher, discussing a pair of 1970s flared trousers was told by the class that they were old-fashioned. (I gather this is no longer so but I prefer skinny jeans. I digress?

Maybe sometimes old ways of thinking return . . .) Asked if they thought the people who wore them thought them odd, the children said, 'Yes'. So the teacher continued with extensive discussion of images of 1970s fashion, then of fashion over a longer period and the reasons why it changes. This was a useful concrete example to introduce the idea that attitudes and values change over time.

Anachronisms

Scott, in Year 3, suggested that a stone water bottle was probably used in caves, 1,000 years ago, when people had no beds to sleep in.

Time measurements

Many children find it difficult to understand, for example that King Alfred died in 899, which was in the ninth century. BC and AD really require an understanding of negative numbers. One child thought AD stood for After Death. As for BCE and CE . . .

Progressing thinking through whole-class discussion, group discussions, then individual writing about sources

If children learn how to ask and answer questions about sources as a *whole class*, they are able to apply these skills to new material, *in small groups*, which are not necessarily dependent on a teacher and eventually this competence will be translated into *individual writing*. This shows the benefits to progression from peer discussion to individual writing (Vygotsky 1978; Alexander 2008). It also reflects Bruner's (1966) emphasis on learning how to ask and answer questions at the centre of a discipline and the questions Collingwood (1939) identified, to ask about all sources: Do you *know* was it made, how was it used and it meant to the people who made and used it? Can you make a reasonable *guess* (a hypothesis) about it?

The following extract from a group discussion of a slide showing flint hand-axes was audio recorded. Now it could be recorded in note form on an electronic white board and printed as a record of these children's ability to take each other's thinking forward and to make inferences and deductions about this particular source.

– *What do you know from these flint hand axes?*
– They're flint.
– They knew how to make them.
– They used tools.
– Did they trade the flint they had left over?
– They could have cut up wood with tools . . .
– And made other things.
– They must have explained to others how to make them.
– They were intelligent; they had control over their hands – so they must have kept on making them, to replace them.
– No. They could sharpen them like pencils.

- They must have shared jobs – one of them made the handle and one made the blade.
- They would trade the flint for money.
- Skills developed gradually.
- They had to concentrate; they could kill animals.
- They could kill people who threatened them too.
- *What can you guess?*
- They're different shapes and sizes. They might have had different weapons for different animals.
- They might have been found at Grimes Graves.
- Or at the white cliffs of Dover.
- Or on a chalk and flint hill in Kent.
- They might have got the flint from the roots of an uprooted tree.
- Or by digging for it.
- They either lived in the place where they found it or travelled through it and dropped it.
- They might have been nomadic; they travelled around looking for flint to cut down trees and to follow the animals.

Formative assessment through story at Key Stage 2

The rebellion of Boudicca

Moore (2016: 77–85) edited the *Annals of Tacitus XIV* (http://classics.mit.edu/Tacitus/annals.html) describing the beginning of the revolt of the Queen of the Iceni against the Romans. Students heard about the horrific scenes as the Thames estuary filled with blood and spectres as Camulodunum was destroyed and the temple where the Roman soldiers were hiding was stormed, after a two-day siege; how the rebels routed the troops of Petilius Cirialis, commander of the ninth legion; how Suetonius decided to fight a battle and Boudicca committed suicide. Tacitus tells the story very vividly, with lots of detail.

Understanding assessed through making a freeze frame: narrative, causes and consequences

Moore's students then suggested various ways in which this could be understood by Key Stage 2 children and how the sequence of events, the causes and consequences they discussed could be assessed. The story could be retold as a freeze frame by a group of children.

■ The rest of the class could ask the Iceni and Roman people in the freeze frame what was happening, ask the Roman Governor of Britain, Suetetonius Paulinus, why he was in Anglesey when the revolt broke out in eastern Britain, what the Druids were like. They could ask the Iceni and Trivantes tribes people why they had revolted against the Romans. The freeze frame would be dramatic and also could involve everyone in demonstrating that they understood the causes of Boudicca's revolt, the events as they occurred and the outcome, in an emotional as well as cognitive way.

- Other students suggested that children could demonstrate their understanding by producing a 'fact book' with photographs of the places in question and associate these with Tacitus' words.

- They could present the same information as above, but on PowerPoint®, perhaps with some attached video, produce a story board of the events, or a play for assembly.

Formative assessment through drama: similarities and differences over time and interpretations; enquiry – where, why, how?

Dodwell (2017: 136–144) and Nichol (2017c: 149–155) show how history can be assessed in formative ways through a drama based on a local story. Researching the drama requires note-taking at different stages. Dodwell shows, stage by stage, how a drama can be created based on a local story. Children research the differences in place and culture over time. Starting with a visit to the locality they research its history in a particular period. Then they develop their characters, with reference to the period, in order to improvise likely conversations about the event. Finally they create an account of the event by acting out the scenes of the story. The process of researching this event and its context and developing characters who lived at a different time provides plenty of opportunities for suggestions, challenges and interventions by the teacher and evidence of children's increasing understanding of time concepts, of researching and interpreting a variety of sources in order to create an account.

Nichol (2017b: 149–155) gives plans for a simulation to consider in detail how Viking settlements in Britain would have taken place, with children in role as members of warrior families, in a tribe that has sailed to Britain in thirty ships. (This might be in the children's local area if there are Viking place names in the locality.) Discussion of the decisions to be made involve deciding, from a modern map, where to land and how to make your way to a valley on the map which your war band leader has assigned to your family and the other nine families. Where should you settle in order to take over the existing small farms that belong to Saxons? What will you do to ensure communication around this area? Where will you place tracks and bridges over streams? Where do the tracks meet, making the best site for a market, a pagan temple? Where should the Viking fort to control the area be situated? What Anglo-Saxon names will be appropriate for the new farms? Such a simulation involves opportunities for teachers to listen to children's decisions and their reasons for them, to challenge, suggest and give clues.

It might be useful to record a few examples of questions in these categories and how they took children's thinking further. At the end of the simulation it should be possible to conclude that all the pupils had mastery of the question, 'How did the Vikings settle in Britain?'. The final maps children make are the summative products of their thinking.

Summative assessment at Key Stage 2

Summative assessment is for the benefit of pupils, parents, teachers, school leaders and Ofsted and is given to all of these stake-holders in a form that they need for their different purposes. It is the broad overview of what children have achieved, at the end of a unit of study or if this is in line with the school assessment policy, at the end of a year.

The Report of the National Association of Head Teachers Commission on Assessment (NAHT 2014) recommends assessment using objectives and agreed criteria and calls upon head teachers to involve all staff in designing a checklist of descriptive statements of attainment criteria which are short, discrete, qualitative and concrete descriptions of what a pupil can do, which is based on the National Curriculum, assessing formally at the end of each term or possibly each year. Many schemes appear on school websites, which are a return to targets, based on requirements set out in the National Curriculum. But the statements are usually similar to the previous levels, with the same disadvantages. Inspectors have no view about the form of summative assessment, except that, at the end of a Key Stage, all children should demonstrate that they have achieved the National Curriculum attainment targets.

Since there is no agreed pattern of progression in learning history, and indeed there may never be one, schools now have the opportunity to create their own assessment scale, based on examples of pupils' work, evidence of progression and teacher assessments. This needs to be based on how children are working towards each Key Stage attainment target. Each year teachers could write a brief synopsis of ways in which each strand has been taught in their class, with some examples of the range of levels at which it has been achieved, together with some examples of formative assessments that progressed understanding, as discussed above. As children progress through the school and the end of the Key Stage looms larger, it will be clear if any gaps need to be plugged and emphasis put on these.

The summative statements and supporting examples for each year group could be collated and reviewed annually to ensure that progress toward the end of Key Stage statement was appropriate. Teaching approaches which seemed particularly successful could be shared and used more widely. Teachers and children will have ownership and control of this and therefore a stakeholder's interest in it. Importantly it will arise from what children have achieved, rather than fitting what they have achieved into a prearranged pattern which has no research basis.

Pupil self-assessment and peer assessment

A personal checklist

Since, as explained above, assessment in history is different from in most subjects, children might keep a booklet through Key Stage 2, with a page for most of the aspects of historical enquiry, in the simplest language, which they experience each year, each statement followed by some examples (e.g. I can use a timeline . . . I know the reasons why some things happened . . . I can tell you the differences between different times in the past . . . I can tell you some things that did not change for a very long time . . . I found out things about the past from different sources . . . I can use a globe/world map to show you how people in the past travelled between distant places . . .) This would be useful for the teacher as a record of differentiation, to the child as evidence of building on existing skills and to what they know and can do to parents.

An annual exhibition

In one of the schools in which I worked one way of demonstrating examples of progression in history over Key Stage 2 was an annual exhibition for children, parents and visitors, showing a variety of different examples of work in history from each class, illustrating use of sources, of time concepts and understanding of interpretations, with brief notes from the history co-ordinator about the ways in which this was done.

Written self assessment

Older children can write their own summative assessments at the end of a topic. Nichol (2014: 14–19) suggests that the writing process has three phases, preparatory, expressive and formal, which are involved in pupils being able to write reflectively and discursively. He says that in the preparatory and expressive phases, children build up a reservoir of information, evidence and arguments, ideas, hypotheses and interpretations. They may do this through collecting information from artefacts, maps, plans, diagrams, visual or written sources. In the expressive phase children deepen their understanding by translating knowledge, through looking, speaking and listening, reading and enacting, writing and drawing into a piece of writing. The formative stage of the above activities may include brief pieces of writing, such as labels, captions, annotated images or photographs, plans and discussions, preparations for constructing a drama or responding to a freeze frame. Summative reflective and discursive writing may well come from subordinate enquiries, investigating the big question in a study unit.

There is an enormous number of interesting ways in which writing, during the preparatory and expressive phases and relating to sub-questions in an investigation, can be constructed as a summative assessment. It may be in the genre of a report for a newspaper or a magazine article written by a journalist. It could be an explanation of why a local event happened or a discussion using persuasive writing between two historians with contrasting views or an investigation from the point of view of a private detective. It might a website, an archaeologist's report, a local person giving a talk on the history of the area, a Briton's account of Saxon settlement in his area, a Viking's perspective of invading Britain or a television programme maker's story board. It could be a drama, based on formatively assessed role play or simulation.

If children's writing ability enables them to write their own summative statement, having reviewed with them all the work they have completed during the unit and having been reminded that the key aims of the writing are to demonstrate their use of sources and their understanding of time concepts and chronology, they can write a summative report in one of the genres suggested above that demonstrates what they have achieved. They could even reference it to the information they have collated from previous work. This will be an ideal form of summative assessment for themselves, their current and next teacher and for their parents and 'other visitors'.

A portfolio

For children whose writing skills cannot justify what they have learned to do in history, they may keep a book or folder of their work, all of which was planned to reflect the history skills and content set out in the National Curriculum. They could, for example as a whole class, go through each of the products of their work which they have collected, be reminded by the teacher that they are looking for evidence of what they can work out from sources, of their time calculations and of their understanding of why accounts may differ. They could then write post-it notes in different colours for each of these three aspects of historical enquiry and place them on the appropriate evidence of their having achieved them. The notes might say how each example of thinking in the same strand of enquiry is an advance on the previous one. The teacher could then either write a brief report on each child's summative piece of work or go through the post-it notes in each child's folder and discuss his or her progress. If it is in line with the school assessment policy and most children have progressed in a broadly similar way, it might be sufficient to write a report for the whole class with individual notes on any children outside this broad band.

Children devise their own success criteria to monitor and evaluate their work

Knight (2008) describes a unit of work in which pupils had considerable scope for self-monitoring and assessment, which they found highly motivating. He describes a Key Stage 3 class, but such practice is quite possible with younger pupils. Pupils were shown a video and a collection of relevant information to introduce the project and reminded of the processes of historical enquiry.

Through whole-class discussion the class created success criteria for evaluating their end product. They then chose their own groups and 'thought-showered' their ideas for achieving this, with feedback at the end. They worked on these for the following three sessions. They had to draw up a time-plan, allocate tasks and roles, create a resources list and a draft outline. They designed an exciting variety of end products, for example an argument on a chat show. In the final session they were reminded of their own assessment criteria, then presented their products and were assessed by the class on each of the products. The teacher feedback was through enabling the pupils to reflect on the processes involved and their ability to relate it to other learning situations. It gladdens my heart to read about Year 8 pupils working in a way which I have frequently found successful with Year 5 and 6 children.

Reflecting on the teacher's written feedback

For younger Key Stage 2 children, a teacher could, at intervals, write post-it notes on their 'products' (which might also include a note on any interesting oral responses) and discuss this with them. (I never wrote on children's work because I think this imposes on their ownership of it.) At the end of a topic or year, children could create their own assessment book, putting the post-it notes in sequentially, as 'stickers' with their own comments on how they had progressed, based on evidence in the stickers.

The Historical Association offers good overview guidance (or a checklist) on assessment of history in primary schools (www.history.org.uk/primary/categories/787/module/ 7616/assessment-in-primary-history-guidance).

Transition between Key Stages

Harnett suggests that the 'journey' from Reception to Year 1 takes time, preparation and planning. She suggests that Reception children might collect mementos from their summer holiday and take them as a tangible link to weave into their work in Year 1, using the object to reflect on their oral histories during circle time, and on change, similarities and differences in school life to form a tangible link between the two phases. (www.history.org.uk/primary/categories/787/module/2511/history-in-the-foundation-stage-and-key-stage-1/2544/41-creating-powerful-meaningful-journeys).

It is really important that the teachers of Year 2 and Year 3 share and discuss the children who are transferring to Year 3 in order to share ideas and plan for progression through teaching approaches which make the transition smooth.

Transition between Year 6 and Year 7 is a cause for concern in many cases. Teaching methods often vary considerably and expectations at Year 7 are often too low. Meetings may be organized between a secondary school and the feeder schools, to share planning and examples of pupils' work and ideally to share teaching approaches. As an advisory liaison teacher between primary and secondary schools and, more recently, working on transition projects with schools, there were some startling misunderstandings, not helped by the fairly meaningless level assessments, which were passed between schools with, understandably, little effect. For this reason the Historical Association has articles and websites with details of transition projects intended to smooth the transition process (Wren 2016; Historical Association Transition Resources www.history.org.uk).

One teacher's Key Stages 2/3 liaison strategy

The following is an outline of a project with Year 7 pupils, which could easily be modified for a Year 6 teacher and taken to their secondary schools by the pupils (Carrier 2015). Jay, the teacher, wanted to build on the independent project work which she had observed in primary schools, which involved ownership of learning, questioning, seeing the purpose of an historical question, being able to select sources and working collaboratively with other learners. Rather than begin with an enquiry question, she gave the class a historian's hypothesis. She gave them a pack of differentiated sources, in order to respond to the hypothesis and gave them a choice in how they did this. She structured the enquiry by asking them first to select one primary source of not more than 100 words and discuss it. In the next session they were given one written and two visual sources. They researched these. Finally they created their own writing frames and used them to create their response to the hypothesis. They shared their responses. They evaluated their work in two or three sentences saying what they enjoyed, found hard and had learned, with a proforma saying which sources they had used and to what extent they found them useful. Finally they wrote a letter to the 'historian' about her hypothesis, taking into account their response and those of others.

Teacher liaison

At the very least, Year 6 and 7 teachers could meet and exchange and discuss the MTP they used. Ideally they could plan a joint project for both year groups in the summer term with an enquiry which spanned the Key Stage 2 and 3 curriculum.

Teacher self-evaluation – a checklist: does your practice meet Ofsted assessment criteria?

The good practice which inspectors are looking for is built up through teachers on-going, day-to-day practice. The *Ofsted School Inspection Handbook* (2016) states what inspectors are looking for

- teachers' detailed and relevant subject knowledge, which is communicated to pupils;

- assessment information gathered from looking at what pupils know, understand and can do;

- that is used to plan appropriate learning and teaching strategies which enable all pupils to make good progress;

- pupils who are given and able to respond to useful feedback, written or oral, from teachers.

To make these judgments inspectors consider

- 'evidence gained from observing pupils in lessons, talking to them about their work and scrutinizing their work;

- effective transition between schools;

- pupils' views about the work they have undertaken;

- information from discussion about teaching, learning and assessment with teachers, teaching assistants and other staff;

- parents' views about the quality of teaching;

- scrutiny of pupils' work, with particular attention to pupils' efforts so that they can progress and enjoy learning, how their knowledge, understanding and skills have improved, the level of challenge, (not necessarily "getting it right first time", and how well pupils use teachers' written and oral feedback to improve their understanding'.

Inspectors evaluate the accuracy and impact of assessment by considering how well

- teachers use pupils' starting points and teacher assessment to modify their teaching;

- assessment draws on a range of evidence of what pupils know, understand and can do;

- teachers make consistent judgements about pupils' progress and attainments across a year group and between year groups.

Outstanding teaching, learning and assessment require that teachers

- have deep knowledge and understanding of the subject;

- use questioning to identify and correct misconceptions effectively;

- plan lessons effectively, using good resources;

- and allow time to embed pupils' knowledge, understanding and skills effectively, introducing subject content progressively;

- demand high standards; and

- support struggling pupils.

Conclusion

Chapters 9–11 have considered the implications for planning history at whole-school level, how these policies can be transferred into MTPs and short-term plans and how children's learning can be monitored, progressed and assessed. These suggestions are carefully referenced to related guidance and statutory requirements.

PART

IV

Practitioner research

12

Doing research into the teaching and learning of history

Soon after my book, *History in the Early Years* was published I found a set of undergraduate essays on a table in the history room and started reading the one on top. Clearly one of my colleagues had asked the first-year students to read and critique a book on the teaching of history. I could not avoid looking at this paper, since it was clearly critiquing my book. 'Why do we need to do research to find out what kids think?' it began. 'Why don't we just ask them' . . . 'But ask them what?' I thought. Oh well.

This chapter picks up the themes on research undertaken by practitioners into children's use of historical sources in Chapter 2, (pp. 25–31) into children's understanding of interpretations in Chapter 3, (pp. 36–41) and their understanding of chronology and time concepts in Chapter 4 (pp. 47–53). Many of the studies described are small-scale, others are Master's or doctoral studies. This chapter explains how you, as practitioners, are well-placed to undertake research into children's thinking, drawing on work in your own classroom, as a student and as an experienced teacher (as I did). Your children constantly provide data, in their everyday work, which can be systematically examined.

The chapter begins with the reasons for engaging in research into teaching and learning in history, the progression in knowledge and understanding required for research at the level of an undergraduate dissertation, a Master's degree and a doctoral degree. It then considers the stages in the process of 'doing research' which apply at any level, illustrated by examples from a particular study investigating young children's ability to make deductions and inferences about a range of historical sources (Cooper 1991). This chapter is intended to awaken your interest in research and how it is done. Of course it cannot be a comprehensive guide to research. More detailed information can be found at http://libweb.surrey.ac.uk/library/skills/Introduction%20to%20Research%20and%20 Managing%20Information%20Leicester/page_32.htm.

Why do research?

As a reflective practitioner, having read this book, or as a result of your teaching experience, implementing a curriculum (which, very fortunately, gives little guidance on how you should teach the curriculum or assess progression), probably raises questions, large and small. For there is very little research into how children best learn history and even less knowledge of the research that has been done.

A couple of years ago I was invited to take part in a documentary for Radio 4. I was told that the programme aimed to 'understand what approaches there are to getting 10-year-olds to understand the past'. After an hour-long interview, in preparation for the programme, the producer thanked me for 'giving such a detailed and example-rich account of your research and analysis of these questions'. The resulting programme veered on the one hand, from a school in which children followed an account read by the teacher with their fingers, then answered questions about the text, to, on the other hand, a very simple role play. The producer had understood nothing from the literature I sent him, of the nuances and complexity of understanding teaching and learning in history. This apparently, remains the perception of the general public, who, apparently, found it a very good programme.

Why do research?

Research, at the very least, refines the thinking of a teacher who undertakes it and so the quality of his/her teaching. Action research by practising teachers is both possible and desirable and should therefore be supported and encouraged. It is essential that the broad brushstrokes with which a statutory curriculum aims to paint a map of the past is balanced by small-scale, detailed and carefully focused investigations. Experience suggests that children are interested in detail and in problem-solving. But time for history is limited so we must find the best teaching approaches possible if we are to provide a rich, rigorous and exciting history experience which children can build on throughout their lives.

Research into history education

Dissertation in an honours degree in education studies

For undergraduates studying for an honours degree in education studies a dissertation in their preferred specialism is often required. The benchmarks they must meet to obtain a degree are set out in www.qaa.ac.uk/en/Publications/Documents/SBS-education-studies-15.pdf.

The benchmarks most relevant to an undergraduate dissertation are probably those which help to identify a research question:

- the ability to use a range of evidence to formulate appropriate and justified ways forward and potential changes in practice;

- to analyse educational concepts, theories and issues of policy in a systematic way;

- the ability to use knowledge and understanding critically to locate and justify a personal position in relation to the subject.

Benchmarks which support a review of relevant literature:

- the ability to select a range of primary and secondary sources, including theoretical and research-based evidence, to extend their knowledge and understanding;

- the ability to organize and articulate opinions and arguments using relevant specialist vocabulary;

- understanding of theories and concepts relevant to education;

- articulate their own approaches to learning.

Benchmarks which support planning the methodology and data collection and presentation:

- an understanding of the significance and limitations of theory and research;

- the extent to which learners and teachers can influence the learning process;

Benchmarks which support data collection and presentation:

- present data in a variety of formats;

- collect and apply numerical data;

- use technology to enhance critical and reflective study.

Benchmarks which support discussion and evaluation of data:

- analyse and interpret qualitative and quantitative data;

- process and synthesize empirical and theoretical data, to present and justify a chosen position, having drawn on relevant theoretical perspectives.

You will have encountered all of these benchmarks previously, during your undergraduate course. These benchmarks are Level 6.

Research for a Master's degree

A Master's degree is intended to enable students to focus in greater depth on a particular aspect of a broader subject area in which they have prior knowledge or experience. To achieve a Master's degree students should demonstrate a *systematic* understanding of knowledge and a *critical awar*eness of current problems and/or new insights, informed by their field of professional experience, a *comprehensive understanding of techniques* applicable to their own research or advanced scholarship, *originality in the application of knowledge*, together with *practical understanding* of how to use research techniques. Students should understand how to *evaluate current research* in the discipline, *critique*, deal with complex issues systematically and creatively and communicate their conclusions clearly. They should demonstrate self-direction in planning and implementing tasks (Framework for higher education qualifications degree level 7, QAA 2010, www.qaa.ac.uk).

Research for a doctoral degree

Students need to demonstrate the creation of new knowledge through original research, based on systematic acquisition of substantial knowledge at the forefront of . . . professional practice, demonstrating a detailed understanding of applicable research techniques (QAA 2011, Framework for educational qualifications www.qca.ac.uk).

The research process

What do you want to find out?

In my view, if the research aims to offer new insights into pedagogy, it must take both teaching and learning into account because they interact with each other. This book is full of references to small-scale studies which may stimulate some good areas for further research. Alternatively you may have an interest in finding out about teachers' or students' views, attitudes and values. It is important that you have a genuine interest in your enquiry.

What I wanted to find out

I was really interested in how children might learn to use historical sources.

I had come across exciting new approaches to teaching history using sources (Ballard 1970; Coltham and Fines 1971), followed by Bruner (1963, 1966) and Shulman (1986) who, like Bruner, talked of translating the thinking processes of a discipline into ways young children can learn to engage with them. The possibility of combining my interest in history with my love of teaching young children was intriguing and – as explained in Chapter 1 – unusual at the time.

Deciding on a research question

At any level of personal research, it is important that the research question is very precise and that the scope of your research is very tightly focused and small-scale. This will provide boundaries for focused and relevant reading around the subject. Think in terms of a small group of children, a specific activity and a small number of questions or things to observe. This will reveal rich and meaningful data.

My research question

My questions and sub-questions for my doctoral research could have been investigated, in a modified form, at dissertation or Master's level. It was, 'To what extent can 8-year-old children develop arguments about a variety of historical sources?'

- Can they make deductions and inferences about five different kinds of sources? Is there a difference between written and oral responses?

- Can they use historical concepts; concrete, abstract and superordinate concepts?

- Are teaching strategies significant in progressing children's historical thinking?

Any part of any of these questions would be fine for a smaller study.

What have others written on this subject?

You need to be able to show that you are aware of what has already been written on the subject and what research others have done in order to show, first, that you are building on previous work, not duplicating it, and, second, that there is a gap in what is already known into which your research fits.

My literature review

Focusing on previous work relevant to the question, 'To what extent can 8-year-old children develop arguments about historical sources?' I read about theories of cognitive development (Piaget, Bruner, Vygotsky and their successors), related to deductions from sources and to research with secondary school students, theories of developmental psychology and research investigating concepts of empathy (subsequently a dirty word but that is another story) and research into concept development and its application to children's use of concepts in history.

Research design: collecting your research data

You need to decide what method will elicit the richest data. You may reject quantitative research using numerical and statistical data, in favour of qualitative research, which provides rich or deeper insights, rather than broad, overarching generalities, or you may combine the two. Qualitative research involves interaction with individuals, and qualitative data comes from interviews, focus groups, observations or action research. Action research involves identifying a problem, devising a plan to improve the situation, then observing whether the situation is improving or not. Data might be collected by observing, video-recording, interviews and analytic memos. Case studies may be based on investigating a particular theory by asking a particular question, or exploring a hypothesis, in a complex everyday situation, such as a classroom. Data can be collected in a variety of ways.

An overview of my study

I shall describe my doctoral study step by step, as an illustration of the research process in this context. In this study, history was taught as a dimension of a cross-curricular approach. The study consisted of four units each lasting five weeks, focusing on the

Stone Ages, the Iron Age, the Romans and the Saxons. Each unit consisted of five whole-class lessons, one each week. In each of the five lessons the class discussed an example of a different type of evidence: an artefact, a picture, a diagram, a map and a written source (in the case of the Stone Age a glyph).

The teaching approach was to teach children to feel confident to say what they knew for certain, what they could guess/hypothesize and what they would like to know. In each instance children were also encouraged to say why they thought this; to develop an argument, using 'because', or 'therefore' (Piaget 1926) in order to make further deductions and inferences about the source and to reach conclusions based on both arguments. They were also taught specific concepts (concrete, abstract and superordinate), which underpin all societies (which were discussed and learned as spellings and introduced into the discussions).

In addition, children also made tape recordings in small groups at the end of each unit, discussing what they knew, what they could 'guess' and what they would like to know about each of the five types of evidence but discussing previously unseen examples. The first year, there was an adult present, and the second year, no adult was present.

In another school, a teacher taught the same content using a traditional approach, in order to act as a base-line/foil for the analyses. Table 12.1 shows evidence used in the written and oral tests in the research (experimental) group.

Who will be the subjects of your research?

Depending on your research design, how many 'research subjects' will you have and how will you select them (for particular reasons or randomly)?

The subjects in this study were two experimental groups, taught by the researcher in consecutive years, and one control group taught by a teacher in another school using 'traditional methods'. Each group consisted of twenty children in the 8–9 age group. The groups were statistically compared for verbal and non-verbal abilities.

Ethical considerations

Universities have their own criteria for checking ethical considerations; for example, was everyone told about the purposes of the research, about anonymity, that they could opt out at any point, who will benefit from the research and how it will be disseminated?

How will you analyse the data?

Most qualitative research is analysed using a grounded theory approach. Essentially this means sorting the data, of whatever kind, into categories which each have something in common, using cards for small-scale studies. For example, collecting units from talk or observation, which are all about 'what children know for certain about a source', 'what they can hypothesize' and 'what they would like to know'. Then these cards are grouped into sub-categories, depending on, for example, whether or not they include 'because' and 'therefore' statements. Then they are grouped under types of sources they

TABLE 12.1 Evidence used in written and oral evidence tests

Unit	Test 1 Artefact	Test 2 Picture	Test 3 Diagram	Test 4 Map	Test 5 Writing
1	Slide. Palaeolithic flint hand-axes c. 200,000 BCE Museum of London. Slide 0L91	Slide. Font de Gaume Lascaux. Ray Delvert S. Lot	Stone circle. The Druids Circle. Caernarvon. Stone circles of the British Isles. A. Burle	Map showing site of neolithic artefacts on North Downs	Petroglyphics from 'How Writing Began', Macdonald
2	Bronze helmet (1 BCE) Slide BM	Uffington Horse photos	Little Woodbury. Iron Age house plan Wilts. In Cunliffe, R.K. 1974	Lynchets of Iron Age Fields Butser Hill, Hants.	Strabo 1.4.2. Description of British exports
3	Shield boss found in River Tyne. Slide BM	Detail from frieze of great dish, Mildenhall Slide BM PRB 47	Villa plan Chedworth, Gloucs.	Roman roads across South Downs	Tacitus Annales XII 31–40 Boudicca Revolt
4	Replica of Sceptre. Sutton Hoo ship burial. BM Slide MZ 18	Illuminated manuscript of Harvest made by BM F21985	Plan Saxon church Cirencester	Saxon settlements in Surrey	Beowulf slays Grendel Penguin 1973 trans. 824–838

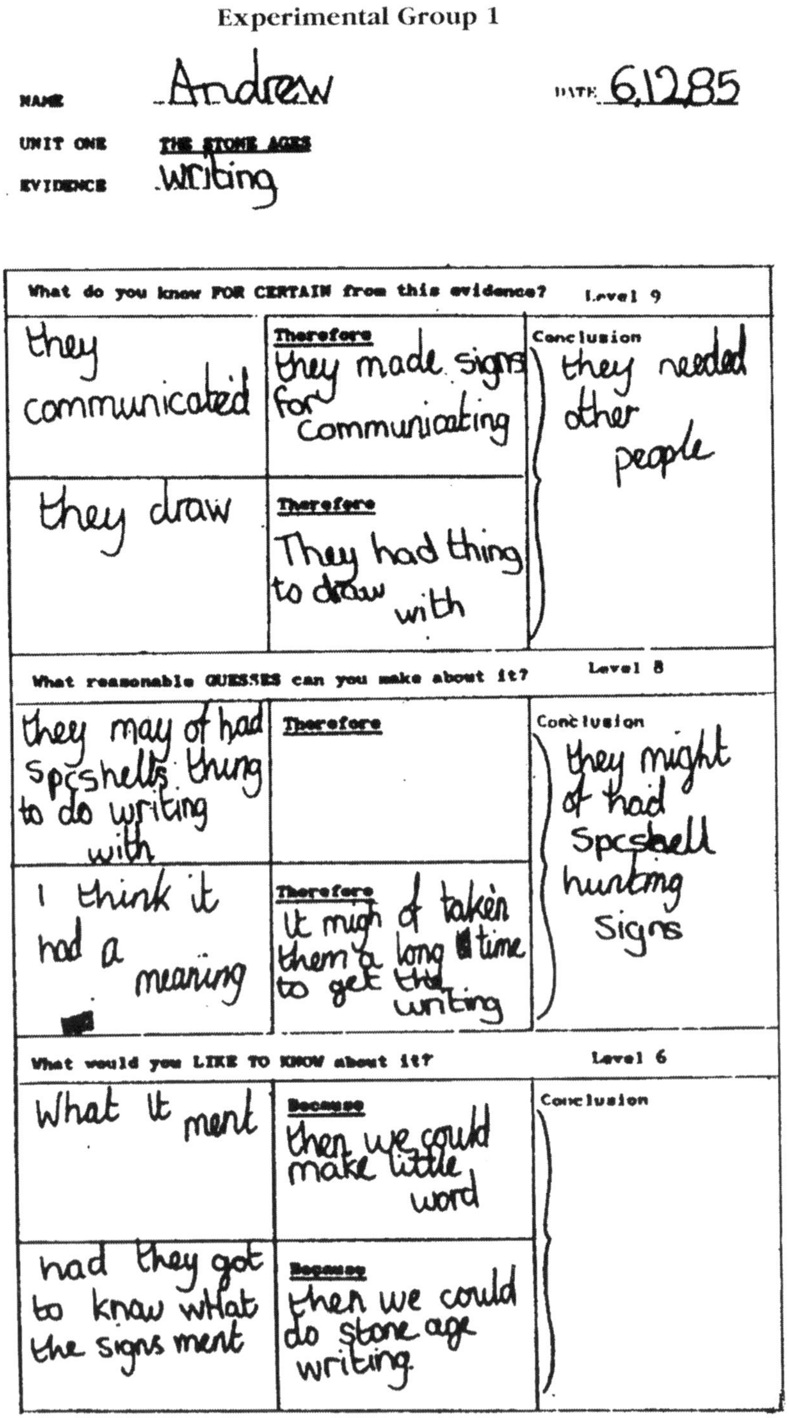

Experimental Group 1

NAME Andrew DATE 6.12.85

UNIT ONE THE STONE AGES

EVIDENCE writing

What do you know FOR CERTAIN from this evidence?		Level 9
they communicated	Therefore they made signs for communicating	Conclusion they needed other people
they draw	Therefore They had thing to draw with	

What reasonable GUESSES can you make about it?		Level 8
they may of had spcshells thing to do writing with	Therefore	Conclusion they might of had spcshell hunting signs
I think it had a meaning	Therefore it migh of taken them a long time to get the writing	

What would you LIKE TO KNOW about it?		Level 6
What it ment	Because then we could make little word	Conclusion
had they got to know what the signs ment	Because then we could do stone age writing	

FIGURE 12.1 Andrew's 'archaeologist's' report on petroglyphics at the end of the Stone Age unit.

refer to. I might have used a grounded theory approach in my study, but it had not been invented.

The method I devised was to give children proforma, which I called an 'archaeologist's report form'. This encouraged them to think at the highest level by filling it in under these sections (Figure 12.1). It encouraged them to differentiate between knowing, guessing (using probability language) and not knowing. It encouraged them to give reasons for their argument (causal thinking; Piaget 1928) and to combine their ideas using an abstract concept (Vygotsky 1966). Each question, since there was still a fashion for quantitative data, was given a number on a scale 1–10, based on previous research into children interpreting data. This made it possible to compare scores for all the answers, for each child for all four units of study for all three groups (analyses of co-variance – do not ask!). I also applied the same categories to the tape-recorded discussions. I compared the instances of children spontaneously using the taught concrete, abstract and superordinate categories during each unit simply by counting them.

The report is structured to encourage distinction between knowing, hypotheses and what is not known. It may appear simplistic, but it includes a complex key concept: 'communicated'. It has conclusions based on thoughtful causal reasoning. And most interestingly, Andrew is speculating about the meaning of what is now understood to be written Stone Age communications which were the same across Europe for thousands of years. Another child said he would like to know if Stone Age tribes spoke the same language, which was prescient for a 9-year-old. (See Von Petzinger 2016; p. 148 in Chapter 8.)

How will you present your findings?

This will be a prose description, in a qualitative study, but it can also be helpful to show the findings as graphs, pie charts or diagrams.

Presenting my findings

Here are some examples of graphs which show some of the findings clearly.

Figure 12.2 shows an example of a graph which shows statistics in a clear simple form. It refers to pupils' deductions and interpretations of sources. The graph shows that the children's scores improved over the four units taught (Unit 3 was not analysed due to shortage of time). It also shows that the children consistently found the easiest question to be, 'What do you know for certain?'. They found valid guesses only slightly more difficult. But they found 'What would you like to know?' the hardest. This is probably because they did not have enough knowledge of a period to know what they wanted to know. This suggests that if children are involved in deciding on enquiry questions, they need some prior knowledge introduced by the teacher to inform their discussion of questions they would like to investigate.

Figure 12.3 contains a great deal of information. It shows progression; scores are higher for interpretations of each type of source over the four units taught by consistent teaching approaches. It shows that scores were slightly different for different types of evidence; initially the scores for the diagram and the map were lower than for the

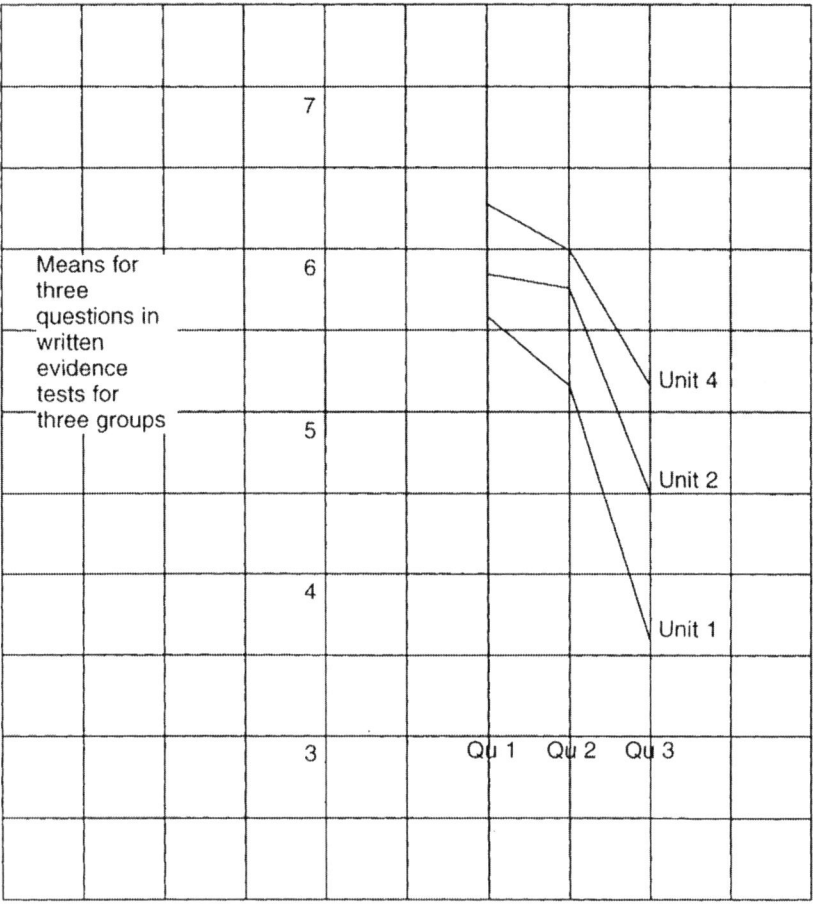

Question 1 What do you know FOR CERTAIN, from this evidence?
Question 2 What REASONABLE GUESSES can you make from this evidence?
Question 3 What WOULD YOU LIKE TO KNOW about this evidence?

FIGURE 12.2 Mean scores for answers in three units of the study and their application to each type of evidence in each unit.

artefacts and pictures, but, surprisingly, that this was not the case with written sources. This is probably because the teaching method is more important than the type of source.

The meanings of relevant concepts were introduced, their meanings explicitly clarified, and used in discussions each week during each unit. Some concepts were concrete (e.g. plough and chariot). Some were abstract concepts, which can not be seen in the mind's eye – groups of things which have something in common (e.g. invent and symbol) Some were superordinate – groups of abstract concepts (e.g. agriculture, power and trade).

Figure 12.4 shows that children had internalized many of these concepts; they enjoyed using 'hard words'. They had made them part of their own vocabulary and could use

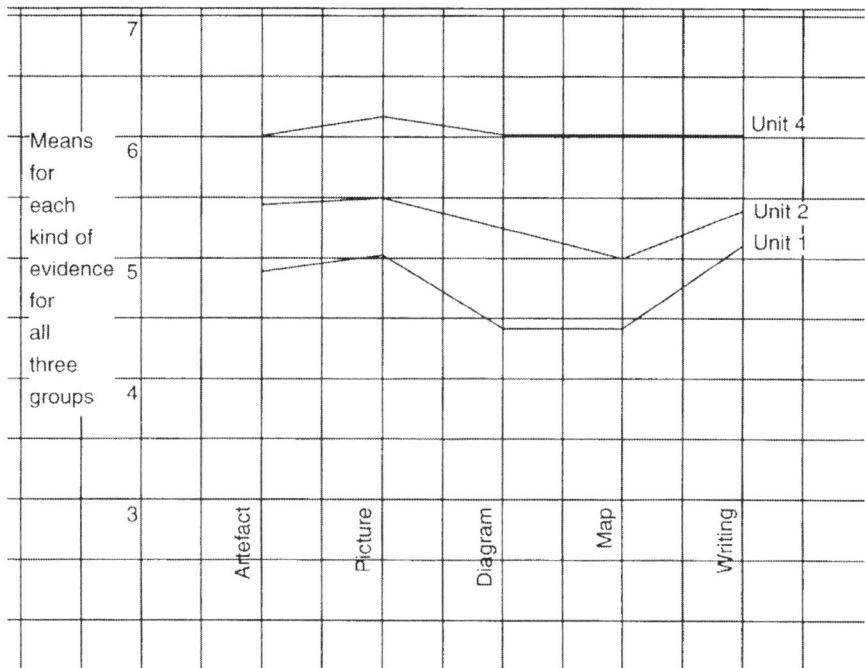

FIGURE 12.3 Mean scores for each type of evidence in each unit.

This bar chart shows how children in both experimental groups retained concepts learned in units 1 and 2 and applied them in their answers to unit 4. The control group used no abstract key concepts.

Concrete		Abstract		Superordinate	
Exp 1	9	Exp 1	34	Exp 1	15
Exp 2	11	Exp 2	29	Exp 2	5
C	2	C	2	C	0

□ represents 1 concept used by Exp 1 group child
▨ represents 1 concept used by Exp 2 group child
■ represents 1 concept used by control group child

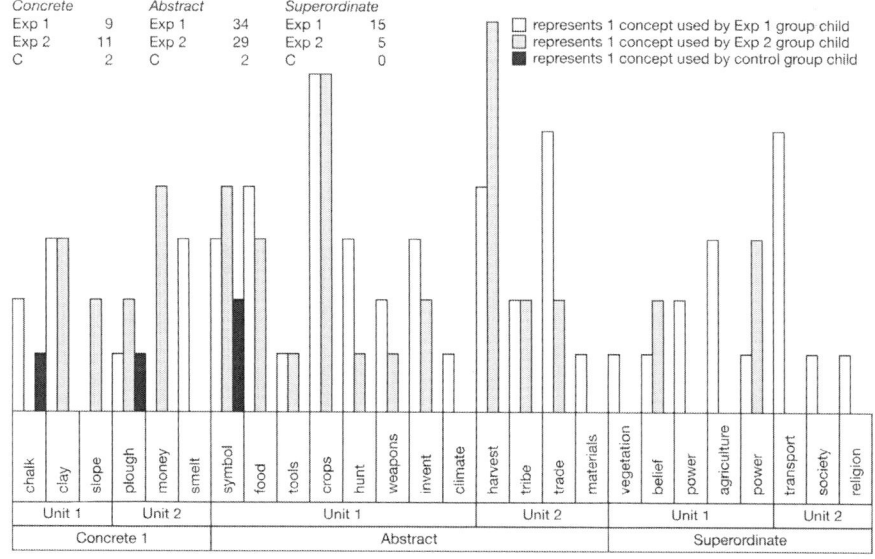

FIGURE 12.4 Children's retention of concepts learned in previous units.

them in new contexts. The bar chart shows that many children used concrete, abstract and superordinate concepts which they had learned to use in previous units in their written answers in Unit 4. Understandably the control group (represented in black) used very few of these concepts because they had not been embedded in their teaching and learning.

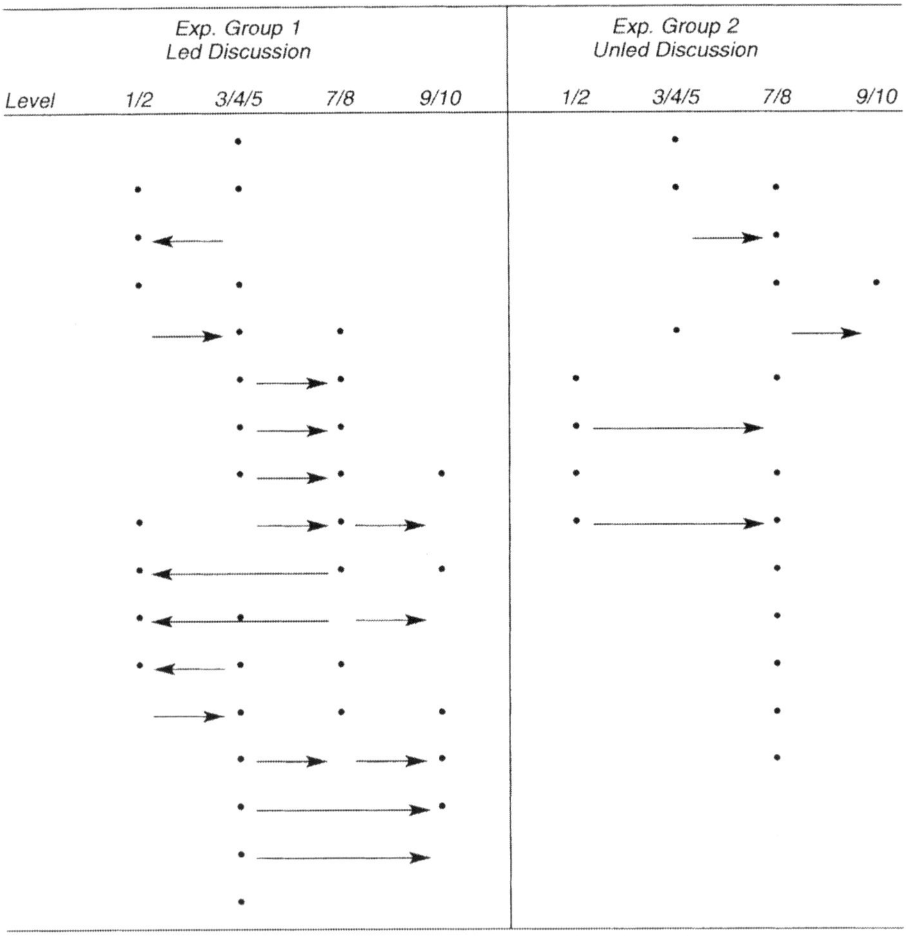

Points made at each level in led and unled discussions

Led Discussion		Unled Discussion	
level 1/2	5 points	level 1/2	4 points
level 3/4/5	13 points	level 3/4/5	3 points
level 7/8	8 points	level 7/8	11 points
level 9/10	5 points	level 9/10	1 point
Total:	31 points	Total:	19 points

FIGURE 12.5 Graph demonstrating that children generate more ideas and reason at higher levels when in a group than working individually.

Figure 12.5 analyses the way in which children corrected points made which the rest of the group agreed were incorrect and how they took each other's arguments forward, generating more ideas than they could individually and sometimes reaching higher levels of argument than they could individually. It also suggests the teacher, in the 'led discussion', enables them to do this by cues and questions. The levels of responses are based on the same scale as above.

A comparison of children's written answers with their recorded discussions found that children made similar points but added rich, but valid, imaginative details in the oral discussion. In discussing an Iron Age helmet seen in the British Museum, a typical written answer was 'They wore it to protect their heads. They had fights'.

But a typical oral answer is 'It's got horns. It looks fierce – like an ox that could kill. Like a Stone Age hunter's deer antlers – to hide in the bushes. The pattern could show what side you were on – so you didn't kill your own men.'

This has implications for assessment in history. A child can almost certainly reveal a higher level of thinking orally. The analysis also shows that by asking questions about sources children gradually learned to consider and attempt to explain the perspectives of people living in other times. The control group, again understandably, did not achieve the same levels on any of the tests because they had not been explicitly taught to make deductions and inferences from sources.

Figure 12.5 is an example of many diagrams which suggest that when there is no teacher present children make similar points about a source, in this case an Anglo-Saxon sceptre, but often express more ideas.

Figure 12.6 suggests that, in discussions with no adult present compared with having an adult present, the points children make are similar but they are more imaginatively expressed. This endorses the findings of the comparison of written and spoken responses. It seems that the presence of an adult is necessary to teach children to reason systematically, but that they reflect more imaginatively and freely when talking among themselves. This suggests that if children are *taught* how to think about sources they can do this effectively in small groups without an adult (Good old Vygotsky 1966).

Finally, Figure 12.7 shows the influence of the inestimable Bruner (1963: 19). Bruner said that children must be asked about carefully selected evidence, so that general principles can be transferred to specific instances, connections made and detail be placed in a structural pattern which is not forgotten, in order to discover regularities in previously unrecognized relations. Here children are transferring knowledge and ways of thinking learned on a site visit to a new context, raising questions about a map describing similar field patterns.

Why do your findings matter?

You need to conclude by stating succinctly what you have found out, how this might fill, or help to fill, a gap in current research, why this is important and who will benefit. You need to show that you are aware of the limitations of your study and what further work you hope it will stimulate.

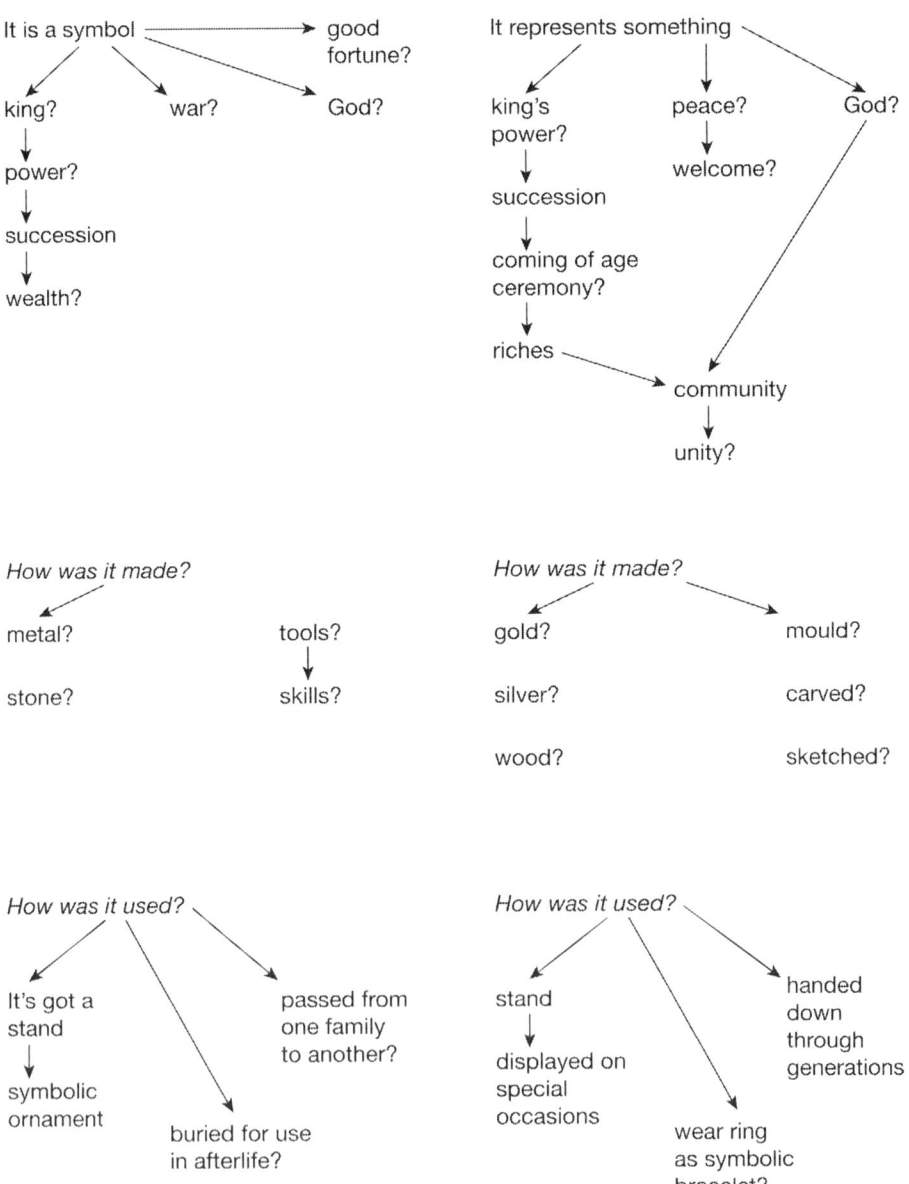

FIGURE 12.6 A comparison of led and unled discussions about previously unseen sources.

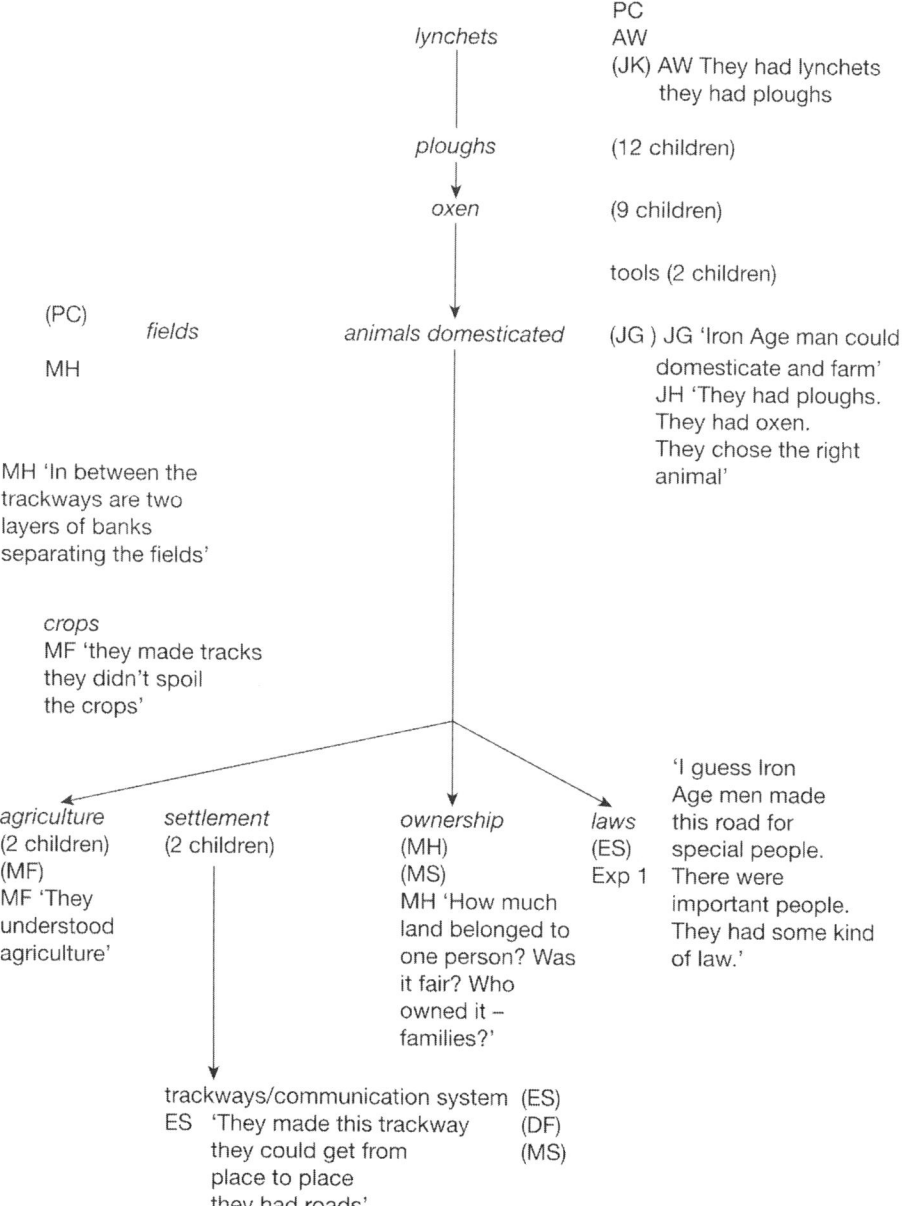

lynchets

PC
AW
(JK) AW They had lynchets
they had ploughs

ploughs

(12 children)

oxen

(9 children)

tools (2 children)

(PC)

fields

MH

animals domesticated

(JG) JG 'Iron Age man could
domesticate and farm'
JH 'They had ploughs.
They had oxen.
They chose the right
animal'

MH 'In between the
trackways are two
layers of banks
separating the fields'

crops
MF 'they made tracks
they didn't spoil
the crops'

agriculture
(2 children)
(MF)
MF 'They
understood
agriculture'

settlement
(2 children)

ownership
(MH)
(MS)
MH 'How much
land belonged to
one person? Was
it fair? Who
owned it –
families?'

laws
(ES)
Exp 1

'I guess Iron
Age men made
this road for
special people.
There were
important people.
They had some kind
of law.'

trackways/communication system
ES   'They made this trackway
they could get from
place to place
they had roads'

(ES)
(DF)
(MS)

FIGURE 12.7 Children were able to transfer their discussion of Iron Age fields seen on a visit to Farthing Down to a previously unseen map of Iron Age field systems on Butser Hill, Hampshire.

What research topics are most relevant for primary history today?

When I did my doctoral research, as explained in Chapter 1, the notion of teaching young children to undertake enquiries based on the discipline of historical enquiry was in its infancy. It seems to me that areas we really need to understand more about now are concerned with helping children to see 'The Big Picture'.

- How can we help children to make connections within and across societies over time? How? What connections can they make?

- How can we help them to make connections between Britain and the wider world?

- If values education is a dimension of teaching history, how can this be done in non-didactic ways? What values? How do children learn to explain the values of a period different from their own? What do they need to know in order to do this? Are the values and attitudes of more recent periods or more familiar societies easier to explain? Can they compare and contrast and explain the values of two different earlier societies?

These are some of questions I have been thinking about in writing this book, but of course the number of interesting questions to investigate about teaching history is infinite. Secondary teachers, I understand, have only recently thought it relevant to relate teaching history to theories of learning . . . (Fordham 2017).

Neuroscience is also now an important new avenue of enquiry.

Conclusion

The examples here were taken from a large study but any of the aspects referred to above could, I hope, inspire a small-scale study. This might be in a different context, perhaps a different period. Data might be collected in different ways, perhaps just focusing on analysing oral or video records. There might be a smaller sample of children or children across a broader age range. You might design a simpler historian's record sheet, which aims, for example to analyse how valid a written source might be, or how valid a panting might be as a source. Who created it? Why? How valid is it? Or an artefact – how old is it? Why do you think so? You may, of course still respond as the student did at the beginning of this chapter: 'Why do research? Why don't you just ask them?' But if you ask them, what are you going to ask them? How are you going to record it? How are you going to analyse what they say? I think you would have to do some research . . . Why not join the British Educational Research Association (BERA) and attend their conferences or the conferences and workshops of the Historical Association (www.history.org.uk). As the heavyweight boxing champion Anthony Joshua said when he beat Wladimir Klitschko, anyone can do it. You just have to dig deep.

Good luck everybody!

References

Adams, S. and Baxter, K. (2006) *The Kingfisher atlas of the ancient world, 10,000 BCE–1,000 CE*, London: Kingfisher.

Adi, H. (2014) *The history of African and Caribbean communities in Britain*, Hove, UK: Wayland.

Adjegbo, K. (2013) 'Identity and connections: history and identity', *Primary History*, 63: 8.

Alexander, R. (2008) (4th edn: 2016) *Towards dialogic teaching: Rethinking classroom talk*. Available online at www.misanortheast.ca/media/7365/lucy__towards_dialogic_talk.pdf (Accessed 3 October 2017).

Alexander, R. (ed.) (2010) *Children, their world, their education: Final report and recommendations of the Cambridge Primary Review*, London: Routledge.

Allason-Jones, L. (ed.) (2011) *Artefacts in Roman Britain: Their purpose and use*, Cambridge, UK: Cambridge University Press.

Andrews, K., Cunningham, A. and Nichol, J. (2017) 'Creativity, King Arthur and the Anglo-Saxon settlement of Britain', in H. Cooper (ed.), *Teaching history creatively* (2nd edn), Abingdon, UK: Routledge, pp. 58–70.

Angevik, M. and Von Borries, B. (1997) *Youth and history: A comparative European survey on historical consciousness and political attitudes among adolescents*, Hamburg, Germany: Korber Stiftung.

Arnhein, R. (2004) *Visual thinking*, Berkeley and Los Angeles, CA: University of California Press.

Aronovsky, I. (2013) 'Diversity history belongs to all of us: diversity in the history curriculum', *Primary History*, 65: 5–11.

Aronovsky, I. (2014) 'Investigating the Indus Valley 2,600–1,900 BCE', *Primary History*, 38: 30–35.

Aronovsky, I. (2017) 'A trail of garnet and gold: Sri Lanka to Anglo-Saxon England', *Primary History*, 76: 22–72.

Ashby, R. (2004) 'Developing a concept of historical evidence: Students' ideas about testing singular factual claims', *International Journal of History Teaching Learning and Research*, 4(2): 44–55.

Ashby, R. and Lee, P. (2001) 'Empathy, perspective taking and rational understanding', in O. L. Davis, S. Foster and E. Yaeger (eds), *Historical empathy and perspective taking in social studies*, Lanham, MD: Rowman & Littlefield.

Asser (1983) *Alfred the Great: Assser's life of King Alfred and other contemporary sources*, S. Keynes and M. Lapidge (trans.), London: Penguin Classics.

Ausubel, D.P. (2000) *The acquisition and retention of knowledge: A cognitive view*, Dordrech, the Netherlands: Springer.

Bage, G. (1999) *Narrative matters*, London: Falmer Press.

Bage, G. (2000) *Thinking history 4–14, teaching, learning, curricula and communities, new directions*, Oxford: Blackwell.

Ballard, M. (ed.) (1970) *New movements in the study and teaching of history*, London: Maurice Temple Smith.

Barton, K. (1996) 'Narrative simplification in elementary students' historical thinking', in J. Brophy (ed.), *Advances in research on teaching, vol. 6: Teaching and learning in history*, Greenwich, CN: JAI Press, 51–84.

Barton, K. and Levstik, L. (2004) *Teaching history for the common good*, Mahwah, NJ: Lawrence Erlbaum.

Barton, K. and McCully, A.W. (2005) 'Learning history and inheriting the past: The interaction of school and community perspectives in Northern Ireland', *International Journal of History Teaching, Learning and Research*, 5(1): 41–49.

Beddoe, D. (1983) *Discovering women's history*, London: Pandora.

Bede (2008) *The ecclesiastical history of the English people*, J. McClure, R. Collins and B. Colgrave (eds), Oxford: Oxford University Press.

Berger, L. and Hawks, J. (2017) *Almost human: An astonishing tale of homo Naledi and the discovery that changed our human story*. Washington, DC: National Geographic.

Bicknell, G. (1998) 'Peel appeal: Talking about the locality with nursery and reception children', in P. Hoodless (ed.), *History and English in the primary school*, London: Routledge, pp. 8–19.

Bloom, B.S. (1956) *New taxonomy of educational objectives*, London: Longman.

Blyth, J.E. (1994) *History 5–11*, London: The Historical Association.

Boulding, E. (1976) *Handbook of international data on women*, Beverly Hills, CA: Sage.

Boulding, E. (1977) *Women in the twentieth-century world*, New York: Sage.

Boulding, E. (1981) *The underside of history*, Boulder, CO: Westview.

Bracey, P. (2016) 'So was everyone an Ancient Egyptian? Developing an understanding of the world in ancient times', *Primary History*, 73: 12–17.

Bradley, R. and Edmonds, M. (2008) *Interpreting the axe trade: Production and exchange in Neolithic Britain*, Cambridge, UK: Cambridge University Press.

Bragg, M. (2003) *The adventure of English: The biography of a language*. London: Hodder & Stoughton.

Bredo, E. (1994) 'Reconstructing educational psychology: Situated cognition and Dewyan pragmatism', *Educational Psychologist*, 29(1): 23–35.

British Broadcasting Company and Wood, M. (2016). *King Alfred and the Anglo Saxons*. Available online at www.bbc.co.uk/programmes/b038118n (Accessed 1 July 2017).

Brown, D. (1991) *Bury my heart at wounded knee*, New York: Henry Holt.

Brown, G. and Wrenn, A. (2004) '"It's like they've gone up a year!" Gauging the impact of a history transition on primary and secondary teachers', *Teaching History*, 121: 5–13.

Bruner, J.S. (1963) *The process of education* (1977 edn), Cambridge, MA: Harvard University Press.

Bruner, J.S. (1966) *Towards a theory of instruction* (1974 edn), Cambridge, MA: Belknap Press.

Burne, J. (1995) 'Sex change for skeleton after feminist enquiry', *Sunday Telegraph*, 15 January.

Burnham, S. and Brown, G. (2004) 'Assessment without level descriptions', *Teaching History*, 1125: 5–13.

Burningham, J. (1992) *Come away from the water, Shirley*, London: Random Century Children's Books.

Byrom, J. (2013) '"Alive and kicking", some personal reflections on the revised National Curriculum 2014 and what we might do with it', *Teaching History*, 153(Supplement Curriculum Evolution Edition): 22–32.

Cambridge Primary Review Trust (CPRT) (2014–2016) *Classroom talk, social disadvantage and educational attainment: Raising standards, closing the gap*, Institute of Effective Education: University of York.

Cannadine, D. (2001) *Ornamentalism: How the British saw their empire*, London: Penguin.

Cannadine, D., Keating, J. and Sheldon, N. (2011) *The right kind of history: Teaching the past in twentieth-century England*, London: Palgrave Macmillan.

Capita, L., Cooper, H. and Mogos, I. (2000) 'History, children's thinking and creativity in the classroom: English and Romanian perspectives', *International Journal of Historical Learning Teaching and Research*, 1(1): 31–38.

Card, J. (2004) 'Seeing double: How one period of history visualizes another', *Teaching History*, 117: 6–9.

Carrier, J. (2015) 'Taking the plunge: Developing independent learning with Year 7', *Teaching History*, 161: 30–36.

Champion, J. (2017) 'What got me into history in the first place?' *Primary History*, 3.

CHATA Project 'Concepts of history and teaching approaches at Key Stages 2 and 3'. A project funded by the Economic and Social Science Research Council, led by Peter Lee. Available online at www.esrc.ac.uk/my-esrc/Grants/L208252006/read (Accessed 5 September 2017).

Chinn, C. (1995) *Poverty amidst prosperity: The urban poor in England 1834–1914*, Manchester, UK: Manchester University Press.

Claire, H. (1996) *Reclaiming the past: Equality and diversity*, London: Trentham Books.

Claire, H. (2002) 'Why didn't you fight, Ruby? Developing citizenship in KS1, through the history curriculum', *Education*, 30: 3–13.

Claire, H. (2003) Dealing with controversial issues with primary teacher trainees as part of citizenship education. Available online at www.citized.info/pdg/commarticles/hilary_claire.pdf (Accessed 5 September 2017).

Claire, H. (2005) 'Learning and teaching about citizenship through history in the early years', in *Leading primary history*, London: The Historical Association, pp. 24–43.

Clarke, S. (2014) *Outstanding formative assessment: Culture and practice*, London: Hodder Education.

Collingwood, R.G. (1924 repub. 2013) *The archaeology of Roman Britain*, Oxford: Oxford University Press.

Collingwood, R.G. (1938, repub. 2013) *The principles of art*, Oxford: Oxford University Press.

Collingwood, R.G. (1939) *An autobiography* (Reprinted 2002), Oxford: Oxford University Press.

Collingwood, R.G. (1946) *The idea of history*, Oxford: Clarendon.

Coltham, J.B. and Fines, J. (1971) *Educational objectives for the study of history: A suggested framework*, London: The Historical Association.

Cooper, H. (1991) *Young children's thinking in history*, unpublished, PhD thesis, London: University Institute of Education.

Cooper, H. (1992) *The teaching of history*, London: David Fulton.

Cooper, H. (1995a) *History in the early years*, London: Routledge.

Cooper, H. (1995b) *The teaching of history in primary schools* (2nd edn), London: David Fulton.

Cooper, H. (2000) *The teaching of history in primary schools* (3rd edn), London: David Fulton.

Cooper, H. (2002) *History in the early years* (2nd edn), London: Routledge.

Cooper, H. (2004) *Exploring time and place through play*, London: David Fulton.

Cooper, H. (2007) *History 3–11*, London: David Fulton.

Cooper, H. (2011) 'Constructivist chronology and horrible histories', *Primary History*, 59: 32.

Cooper, H. (2012) *History 5–11*, London: David Fulton.

Cooper, H. (2014a) 'Why Stories?', *Primary History*, 67: 6–7, London: The Historical Association.

Cooper, H. (2014b) 'Writing about time', in H. Cooper (ed.), *Writing history 7–11: Writing history in different genres*, London: Routledge, pp. 91–108.

Cooper, H. and West, L. (2009) 'Years 5, 6 and Year 7 historians visit Brougham Castle', in H. Cooper and A. Chapman (eds), *Constructing history*, London: Sage, pp. 11–19.

Counsell, C. (2014) 'Using time lines in assessment', *Teaching History*, 157: 54–62.

Craft, A. (2002) *Creativity and early years education*, London: Continuum.

Craft, A. (2005) *Creativity in schools: Tensions and dilemmas*, Abingdon, UK: Falmer.

Craft, A. and Jeffrey, B. (2008) 'Creativity and performativity in teaching and learning: tensions, dilemmas, constraints, accommodation and synthesis', *British Education Research Journal*, 34(5): 578–584.

Craft, A., Jeffrey, B. and Leibling, M. (2001) *Creativity in education*, London: Continuum.

Cremin, T. Burnard, P. and Craft, A. (2006) 'Pedagogy and possibility thinking in the early years', *Thinking Skills and Creativity*, 1(2): 108–119.

Cropley, A.J. (2001) *Creativity in education and learning: A guide for teachers and educators*, London: Routledge Falmer.

Cunliffe, B. (1988) *Mount Batton, Plymouth: A prehistoric and Roman port*, Oxford: Oxford University Committee for Archaeology and Individual Authors.

Davies, D., Jindal-Snape, D., Collier, C., Digby, R., Hay, P. and Howe, A. (2013) 'Creative environments for learning in schools', *Thinking Skills and Creativity*, 8(1): 80–91.

Dawson, I. (2008) 'Teaching across time: planning and teaching the power of time and democracy', *Teaching History*, 130: 14–23.

Dawson, I. (2009a) 'What time does the tune start?' *Teaching History*, 135: 50–56.

Dawson, I. (2009b) *Developing enquiry skills*. Available online at www.thinkinghistory.co.uk (Accessed 5 September 2017).

DCSF (Department for Children, Schools and Families) (2009) *Independent review of the primary curriculum: Final report*, London: DCSF. Available online at www.educationengland.org.uk/documents/pdfs/2009-IRPC-final-report.pdf (Accessed 5 September 2017).

Deary, T. (1994) *The rotten Romans*, London: Scholastic.

Deary, T. (1997) *The cut-throat Celts*, London: Scholastic.

Deary, T. (1999) *The gorgeous Georgians and the vile Victorians*, London: Scholastic.

Deary. T. (2001) *The stormin' Normans*, London: Scholastic.

Deary. T. (2004) *Villainous Victorians*, London: Scholastic.

DES (Department for Education and Science) (1991) *History in the National Curriculum*, London: HMSO.

Dewey, J. (1933) *How we think: A restatement of the reflective thinking to the educative process*, London: Harrap.

Dewey, J. (1958) *Perigee books*, New York: Berkley Publishing Group.

DfE (2008–2011a) *National literacy strategies*. Available online at www.educationengland.org.uk/documents/literacytaskforce/implementation.html (Accessed 5 September 2017).

DfE (2008–2011b) *National numeracy strategies*. Available online at http://webarchive.national-archives.gov.uk/content/20031220221911/http://standards.dfes.gov.uk/numeracy/publications/ (Accessed 5 September 2017).

DfE (2013) *History in the National Curriculum*, London: HMSO. Available online at www.gov.uk/government/uploads/system/uploads/attachment_data/file/239035/PRIMARY_national_curriculum_-_History.pdf (Accessed 5 September 2017).

DfE (2014) Promoting fundamental British values as part of SMSC in schools. Available online at www.gov.uk/government/uploads/system/uploads/attachment_data/file/380595/SMSC_Guidance_Maintained_Schools.pdf (Accessed 5 September 2017).

DfE (Department for Education) (2015) Ofsted school inspection handbook. Available online at www.gov.uk/government/publications/school-inspection-handbook-from-september-2015 (Accessed 5 September 2017).

DfEE (Department for Employment and Education) (1999), 'National Advisory Committee on Creative and Cultural Education', In *All our futures: Creativity, culture and education*, London: DfEE.

Dickens, C. (1853) *A child's history of England*. Available online at https://archive.org/details/childs_history_0801_librivox (Accessed 5 Septembr 2017).

Dixon, L. and Hales, A. (2014) *Bringing history alive through local people and places*, Abingdon, UK: Routledge.

Dixon, L. and Hales, A. (2015) 'What makes good local history?' *Primary History*, 71: 19–24.

Dodwell, C. (2017) 'Using creative drama approaches for the teaching of history', in H. Cooper (ed.), *Teaching history creatively*, (2nd edn), Abingdon, UK: Routledge, pp. 136–144.

Doise, W. and Mugny, G. (1979) 'Individual and collective conflicts of centrations in cognitive development', *European Journal of Social Psychology*, 9: b105–b109.

Doise, W., Mugny, C. and Perret Clermont, A.N. (1975) 'Social interaction and the development of cognitive operations', *European Journal of Social Psychology*, 5: 367–383.

Donaldson, M. (1978) *Children's minds*, London: Fontana Books.

Donnelly, C. (ed.) (2016) *The Oxford companion to cheese*, Oxford: Oxford University Press.

Dorling Kindersley (2015) *What happened when in the world*, London: Penguin.

Doull, K. (2014) 'Teaching Ancient Egypt', *Primary History*, 67: 16–21.

Doull, K. (2016) 'Anglo-Saxon women', *Primary History*, 74: 20–26.

Egan, K. (1986) *Teaching as story telling*, Chicago, IL: University of Chicago Press.

Egan, K. (1992) *Imagination in teaching and learning*, London: Routledge.

Elliott, R.K. (1971) 'Versions of creativity', *Journal of Philosophy of Education*, 5(2): 139–152.

Elton, G.R. (1967) *The practice of history*, London: Fontana Books.

Elton, G.R. (1970) 'What sort of history should we teach?' in M. Ballard (ed.), *New movements in the study and teaching of history*, London: Temple Smith.

Evans, R. (2013) 100 'Academics savage education secretary, Michael Gove for conveyor belt curriculum for schools', *The Independent*. Available online at http://historyworks.tv/news/2013/03/09/history_curriculum_debate_ (Accessed 19 March 2013).

Excell, D. (2013) 'History through connecting classrooms in Bradford and Peshwar, Pakistan', *Primary History*, 65: 39–40.

Farmer, A. and Cooper, C. (1998) 'Story telling in history', in P. Hoodless (ed.), *History and English in the primary school*, London: Routledge.

Ferguson, N. (ed.) (1997) *Virtual history: Alternatives and counterfactuals*, London: Macmillan.

Ferguson, N. (2002) *Colossus: The price of America's empire*, New York: Penguin.

Fildes, L. (1974) Applications for admission to a casual ward. Painting in Royal Holloway College, University of London. Available at www.royalholloway.ac.uk/aboutus/artcollectionandpicturegallery/explore/applicantsforadmissiontoacasualward.aspx (Accessed October 2017).

Fines, J. (2011) 'Powerful pedagogy: teaching principles for 'Doing History' with children – Nuffield Primary History Project', *Primary History*, 57: 20–21.

Foote, P.G. and Wilson, D.M. (1970) *The Viking achievement*, Book Club Associates. Available online at www.abebooks.co.uk/book-search/title/the-viking-achievement/author/foote-p-g-and-wilson-d-m/ (Accessed 5 September 2017).

Fordham, M. (2017) 'Thinking makes it so: Cognitive psychology and history teaching, *Teaching History*, 166: 37–42.

Fry, M. (2005) *Wild Scots: Four hundred years of highland history*, Alloa, Scotland: John Murray.

Fryer, P. (1984) *Staying power*, London: Pluto.

Fryer, P. (1989) *Black people in the British empire: An introduction*, London: Pluto.

Gardner, H. (1993) *Multiple intelligences: The theory in practice*, New York: Basic Books.

Gardner, H. (1999) *Intelligence reframed: Multiple intelligences for the twenty-first century*, New York: Basic Books.

Gerritsen, A. and Riello. G. (eds) (2015) *Writing material culture history*, London: Bloomsbury Academic.

Glennard, J., Mohabir, S., Short, J. and Surman, G. (2016) 'Our Iron Age challenge: Developing historical understanding through building an Iron Age house, *Primary History*, 73: 48–50.

Gombrich, E.H. (1982) *The image and the eye: Further studies in the psychology of pictorial representation*. Oxford: Phaidon Press.

Goscinny, R. (2004) *Asterix in Britain*, London: Orion Books.

Grayling, A.C. (2006) *Among the dead cities: Is the targeting of civilians in war ever justified?* London: Bloomsbury.

Grund, S. (2017) 'Behavioral ecology, technology, and the organization of labor: How a shift from spear thrower to self bow exacerbates social disparities', *American Anthropologist*, 119: 104–119.

Harlow, J. (1996) 'Found: Site of forgotten battle that decided 1066 and all that', *The Sunday Times*, News, 3, 29 December.

Harnett, P. (1993) 'Identifying progression in children's understanding: the use of visual sources to assess primary school children's understanding in history', *Cambridge Journal of Education*, 23(2): 137–154.

Harnett, P. (1998) 'Children working with pictures', in P. Hoodless (ed.), *History and English in the primary school*, London: Routledge.

Harnett, P. (2005) 'Exploring the potential for history and citizenship education with primary children' at the British Empire and Commonwealth Museum in Bristol', *International Journal of History Teaching Learning and Research*, 6: 34–39.

Harnett, P. (2014) 'Teaching about significant people at Key Stage 1', *Primary History*, 67: 37–40.

Harnett, P. and Whitehouse, S. (2016) 'Creative exploration of local, national and global links', in H. Cooper (ed.), *Teaching history creatively* (2nd edn), Abingdon, UK: Routledge, pp. 157–170.

Harnett, P., Whitehouse, S. and Carter, J. (2014) 'It depends on your point of view: exploring different representations of the past', in H. Cooper (ed.), *Writing History 7–11: Historical writing in different genres*, London: Routledge.

Hastings, M. (1979) *Bomber command*, London: Michael Joseph.

Hauptmann, A., Maddin R. and Prange, M. (2002) 'On the structure and composition of copper and tin ingots excavated from the shipwreck of Uluburun', *American Schools of Oriental Research*, 328: 1–30.

Heaney, S. (1999) *Beowulf: A new translation*, London: Faber & Faber.

Hedensteirna-Jonson, C., Kjellstrom, A., Toron, Z., Krzewińska, M., Sobrado, V., Price, N., Günther, T., Jakobsson, M., Götherström, A. and Storå, J. (2017) 'A female Viking warrior confirmed by genomics', *American Journal of Physical Anthropology*. Availbale online at http://onlinelibrary.wiley.com/doi/10.1002/ajpa.23308/full (Accessed 11 October 2017).

Hellen, N. (1998) 'Sex and drugs drove mutiny on the Bounty', *The Sunday Times*, News, 4 January.

Her Majesty's Government (2015a) *Revised prevent duty guidance for England and Wales (2015)*. Available online at www.gov.uk/government/uploads/system/uploads/attachment_data/file/445977/3799_Revised_Prevent_Duty_Guidance__England_Wales_V2-Interactive.pdf (Accessed 5 September 2017).

Her Majesty's Government (2015b) *Commission on assessment without levels*. Available online at https://gov.uk/government/groups/commission-on-assessment-without-levels (Accessed 5 September 2017).

Hexter, J. (1971) *The history primer*, New York: Basic Books.

Hill, B. (1989) *Women, work and sexual politics*, London: Routledge.

Hill, B. (1996) *Servants: English domestics in the eighteenth century*, Oxford: Clarendon.

Hill, B. (2001) *Women alone: Spinsters in England 1660–1850*, London: The MIT Press.

Hill, C. (1980) *The world turned upside down: Radical ideas during the English Revolution*, Harmondsworth, UK: Penguin.

Historical Association (2016) 'Primary survey results 2015'. Available online at www.history.org.uk/primary/categories/rg-survey-results (Accessed 5 September 2017).

Hodkinson, A. (2003a) 'National Curriculum and temporal vocabulary: the use of subjective time phrases within the National Curriculum for History and its schemes of work: effective provision or a wasted opportunity?', *Education 3–13*, 31(3): 28–34.

Hodkinson, A. (2003a) Children's concepts of historical time, unpublished PhD thesis, University of Lancaster.

Hodkinson, A. (2004b) 'The social context of learning and the assimilation of historical time concepts: an indicator of academic performance or an unreliable metric?' *Research in Education*, 71: 50–65.

Hodkinson, A. (2004b) 'Does the National Curriculum for history and its schemes of work effectively promote primary aged children's assimilation of the concepts of historical time? Some observations based upon current research', *Educational Research*, 46(2), 99–119.

Hodkinson, A. and Smith, C. (in press) 'Chronology and the National Curriculum for history: Is it time to refocus the debate?', *Education 3–13*.

Hoodless, P. (1998) 'Children's awareness of time in story and historical fiction', in P. Hoodless (ed.), *History and English in the primary school: Exploiting the links*, London: Routledge, pp. 103–115.

Hoodless, P. (2004) 'Spotting adult agendas: investigating children's historical awareness using stories written for children in the past', *International Journal of History Teaching, Learning and Research*, 4(2), 66–74.

Huggins, M. (2000) '1066 and all that!', in H. Cooper and R. Hyland (eds), *Children's perceptions of learning with trainee teachers*, London: Routledge, pp. 85–93.

Hughes, B. (2017) *Istanbul: A tale of three cities*, London: Weidenfeld & Nicolson.

Hutchinson, R. (2017) *The butcher, the baker, the candlestick maker: The story of Britain through its census, since 1801*, New York: Little.

Jones, R. and Wyse, D. (2004) *Creativity in the primary classroom*, London: David Fulton.

Kang, S. (2010) 'How do Korean nine-year-olds make historical inferences?' *Education 3–13 International Journal of Primary, Elementary and Early Years Education*, 38(3): 243–256.

Kant, I (1989) *On education*, A. Churchton (trans.), London: Kegan Paul, Trent Trubner.

Kenny, A. (1989) *The metaphysics of mind*, Oxford: Oxford University Press.

Klausmeier, H.J. (1979) *Cognitive learning and development*, Pensacola, FL: Ballinger.

Knight, O. (2008) 'Create something interesting to show that you have learned something', *Teaching History*, 131: 17–24.

Kounios, J. and Beeman, M. (2009) 'The aha! Moment: The cognitive neuroscience of insight', *Current Directions in Psychological Science*, 18(4): 210–216.

Kustosdiev. B. (1916) *Shrovetide*. [Painting] St. Petersburg, Russian State Museum.

Langer, E.J. (1997) *The power of mindful learning*, New York: Addison-Wesley.

Lave, J. and Wenger, E. (1991) *Situated learning: Legitimate peripheral participation*, Cambridge, UK: Cambridge University Press.

Leach, J. (2001) 'A hundred possibilities: Creativity, community and ICT', in A. Craft, B. Jeffrey and M. Liebling (eds), *Creativity in education*, London: Continuum, pp. 175–193.

Lee, P., Ashby, R. and Dickinson, A. (1991–1996) 'Concepts of history and teaching approaches at Key Stages 2 and 3', Economic and Social Research Council. Available online at www.researchcatalogue.esrc.ac.uk/grants/L208252006/read (Accessed 5 September 2017).

Letourneau, J. (2005) 'Museums and the (un) building of historical consciousness', QCA Symposium. Available online at www.heirnet.org (Accessed 5 September 2017).

Levin, J. and Nolan, J.F. (2004) *Principles of classroom management: A professional, decision-making model* (4th edn), New York: Allyn and Bacon.

Lomas, T. (2015) 'The Shang dynasty: The co-ordinator's view', *Primary History*, 37.

Lomas, T. (2017) 'Coherence in primary history: What is it and how can it be achieved?', *Primary History*, 76: 8–12.

Loughland, T. and Kilpatrick, L. (2013) 'Formative assessment in primary science', *Education 3–13', International Journal of Primary, Elementary and Early Years Education*, 43(2) 128–141.

Lucas, B. (2001) 'Creative teaching, teaching creatively and creative learning', in A. Craft, B. Jeffrey and M. Leibling (eds), *Creativity in Education*, London: Continuum pp. 35–44.

Lyotard, J.F. (1979) *Post modern condition: A report on knowledge*, G. Bennington and G. Massumi (trans.), Minneapolis, MN: University of Minnesota Press.

McGregor, N. (2012) *A History of the World in 100 objects*, London: Penguin.

MacIntyre, A. (2016) *Ethics in the conflicts of modernity: An essay on desire, practical reasoning and narrative*, Cambridge, UK: Cambridge University Press.

Maddison, M. (2016) 'Fundamental values and history teaching', *Primary History*, 73: 45–47.

Marshal, H.E. (1905) *Our island story*, Cranbrook, UK and London: Galore Park & Civitas.

Mason, C. (1993) *Charlotte Mason's original home schooling series, vols 1–6*. Available online at www.ambleside online.org (Accessed 5 September 2017).

Megill, A. (1994) 'Jorn Rusen's theory of historiography between modernism and rhetoric of historical enquiry', *History and Theory*, 33(1): 39–60.

Messent, J. (2010) *Celtic, Viking & Anglo-Saxon embroidery*, Tunbridge Wells, UK: Search Press.

Montessori, M. (2007/1949) *The absorbent mind*, Radford, VA: Wilder Publications.

Moore, H. (2004) 'Ancient history: things to do and questions to ask', in H. Cooper (ed.), *Exploring time and place through play: Foundation stage – Key Stage* 1, London: David Fulton, pp. 24–39.

Moore, H. (2017) 'Using artefacts and written sources creatively', in H. Cooper (ed.), *Teaching history creatively*, Abingdon, UK: Routledge, pp. 71–86.

National Association of Head Teachers (NAHT) (2014) 'Report on Assessment'. Available online at: www.naht.org.uk/assets/assessment-commission-report.pdf (Accessed 3 October 2017).

National Foundation for Educational Research (NFER) (2013) 'Evidence for excellence in education: Where have all the levels gone?' Available online at: www.nfer.ac.uk/publications/99940/99940pdf (Accessed 5 September 2017).

Nichol, J. (2013) 'Creativity and historical investigation: Pupils in role as history detectives (proto historians) and as historical agents', in H. Cooper (ed.), *Teaching history creatively*, (2nd edn) Abingdon, UK: Routledge, pp. 101–118.

Nichol, J. (2014) 'Genre and children writing history; reflective and discursive learning and writing', in H. Cooper (ed.), *Writing history*, Abingdon, UK: Routledge, pp. 7–11.

Nichol, J. (2017a) 'Creativity, connectivity and interpretation', in H. Cooper (ed.), *Teaching history creatively* (2nd edn), Abingdon, UK: Routledge, pp. 145–157.

Nichol, J. (2017b) 'Creative teaching and learning using prehistoric sources: Changes in Britain from the Stone Age to the Iron Age', in H. Cooper (ed.), *Teaching history creatively* (2nd edn), Abingdon, UK: Routledge, pp. 45–57.

Nichol, J. (2017c) 'The Vikings scheme of work', in H. Cooper (ed.), *Teaching history creatively*, (2nd edn), Abingdon, UK: Routledge, pp. 149-155.

Office for Standards in Education (Ofsted) (2011) 'History for all'. Available online at www.gov.uk/government/uploads/system/uploads/attachment_data/file/413714/History_for_all.pdf (Accessed 5 September 2017).

Office for Standards in Education (Ofsted) (2016) 'School inspection handbook'. Available online at www.gov.uk/government/uploads/system/uploads/attachment_data/file/553942/School_inspection_handbook-section_5.pdf (Accessed 5 September 2017).

Olafson, F.A. (1970) 'Narrative history and the concept of action', *History and Theory*, 9(3): 265–289.

Olusoga, D. (2016) *Black and British: A forgotten history, Chapter 1: Ham's people*, London: Macmillan.

Ordance Survey (2001) *Map of Roman Britain*, Southampton, UK: Ordance Survey.

Ordance Survey (2005) *Historical map and guide to Ancient Britain*, Southampton, UK: Ordance Survey.

Parekh Report (2000) '*The future of multi-ethnic Britain*', London: Profile Books.

Parker Heath, C. (2015) 'Ancient Sumer', *Primary History*, 69: 28–33.

Passmore, J. (1980) *The philosophy of teaching*, London: Duckworth.

Peal, R. (2017) *Making history stick*. Workshop at the Annual Conference of the Historical Association, Manchester, UK.

Piaget, J. (1926) *The language and thought of the child*, London: Routledge.

Piaget, J. (1928) *Judgement and reasoning in the child*, London: Kegan Paul.

Piaget, J. (1932) *Moral judgement and the child*, London: Kegan Paul.

Piaget, J. and Inhelder, B. (1951 repub. 2014) *The origin of the idea of chance in the child*. New York: Psychology Press.

Pinto, H. (2013) 'Challenging children's Ideas on historical evidence by using heritage remains', *International Journal of Historical Learning, Teaching and Research*, 122(1): 121–136.

Plowden Report (1967) *Children and their primary schools*, London: HMSO.

Quality Assurance Agency for Higher Education (QAA) (2010) 'Masters degree characteristics' Available online at www.qaa.ac.uk/Publications/InformationandGuidance/Doctoral_Characteristics.pdf (Accessed 9 October 2017).

Quality Assurance Agency for Higher Education (QAA) (2011) 'Doctoral degree characteristics'. Available online at www.qaa.ac.uk/Publications/InformationandGuidance/Documents/Doctoral_Characteristics.pdf (Accessed 9 October 2017).

Redfern, A. (1998) 'Voices of the past: oral history and English in the primary school', in P. Hoodless (ed.), *History and English in the primary school*, London: Routledge.

Reynolds, P. (1979) *Butser, an Iron Age farm*, London: British Museum Publications.

Robson, W. (2004) 'Kings, queens and castles', in *Exploring Time and place Through Play*, H. Cooper (ed.), London: David Fulton, pp. 40–51.

Rogers, P.J. (1979) *The new history: Theory into practice*, London: The Historical Association.

Rogers, R. (2016) 'Frameworks for big history: Teaching history at its lower resolutions', in *Masterclass in history education: Transforming teaching and learning*, C. Counsell, K. Burn and A. Chapman (eds), London: Bloomsbury, pp. 59–76

Rogoff, B. (1999) 'Cognitive development through social interaction: Vygotsky and Piaget', in P. Murphy (ed.), *Learners, learning and assessment*, London: Open University Press.

Rowbotham, S. (1973) *Hidden from history*, London: Pluto.

Rozensweig, R. (2000) 'How Americans use and think about the past: implications from the national survey for the teaching of history', in P. Stearns, P. Sexias and S. Wineburg (eds), *Knowing teaching and learning history: National and international perspectives*, New York: State University of New York Press.

Ryle, G. (1979) *On thinking*, Oxford: Blackwell.

Samuel, R. (1994 repub. 2012) *Theatres of memory: Past and present in contemporary culture*, London: Verso.

Sarson, M. and Paine, M.E. (1930) '*Stories from Greek, Roman and old English history, Piers Plowman histories'*, Junior book 11, London: George Philip & Son.

Saunders, T. (2004) 'History on your doorstep', *Times Educational Supplement*, 12 March.

Schmidt, M. A. and Garcia, T. B. (2003) *Recriando historias de Campanina Grande do Sul*. Curitiba: Universidade Federal do Parana – Prefeitura municipal de Campanina Grande do Sul.

Schmidt, M.A. and Garcia, T.B. (2008) '*Recriando des Historias de Aroucaria*, Curitiba: Nucleo de Pesquiba em Publicacoes Didaticus', Universidade Federal de Parana.

Schmidt, M.A. and Garcia, T.B. (2010) 'History from children's perspectives: learning to read and write historical accounts using family sources', *Education 3–13*, 38(3): 289–299.

Scruton, R. (1974) *Art and imagination: Study in the philosophy of mind*, London: Methuen.

Sellar, W.C. and Yeatman, R.J. (1930) *1066 and all that*, Harmondsworth, UK: Penguin.

Sendak, M. (2007) *Where the wild things are*, New York: Harper Collins.

Shemilt, D. (2009) 'Drinking an ocean and pissing a cupful: How adolescents make sense of history', in L. Symcox and A. Wilshut (eds), *National history standards: The problem of the canon and the future of teaching history*, Charlotte, NC: Information Age Publishing pp. 141–210.

Shulman, L.S. (1986) 'Those who understand: Knowledge growth in teaching', *Educational Researcher*, 15(2): 4–31.

Siculus, D, (1939) *The library of history: Book V*, C.H. Oldfather (trans.), Cambridge, MA: Harvard University Press.

Simmonds, P. (2017) *Lulu and the flying babies*, London: Anderson Press.

Siraj-Blatchford, I., Sylva, K., Muttock, S., Gilden, R. and Bell, D. (2002) *Researching effective pedagogy in the early years*, (Research Report 356), Annesley, UK: Department for Education and Skills.

Soskin, R. (2009) *Standing with stones*, New York: Thames and Hudson.

Sossick, M. (2011) 'Big time lines, bigger pictures, supporting initial teacher trainees to think big about chronology', *Primary History*, 59: 31.

Sprigge, N. and Sullivan, K. (2013) 'Teaching diversity through drama at the museum of London', *Primary History*, 65: 35–38.

Stanford, D.J. and Bradley, B.A. (2013) *Across Atlantic ice: The origin of America's Clovis culture*, London: University of California Press.

Stevens, C.J. and Fuller, D.Q. (2015) *Did Neolithic farming fail? The case for a Bronze Age agricultural revolution*, Cambridge, UK: Cambridge University Press.

Stewart, R. (2016) *The marches: Border walks with my father*, London: Jonathan Cape.

Strabo (1989) *Geography, volume II: Books 3–5*, H.L. Jones (trans.), Cambridge, MA: Harvard University Press.

Sutcliffe, R. (1974) *The Changeling*, London: Hamish Hamilton.

Sutcliffe, R. (2004) *Eagle of the ninth*, Oxford: Oxford University Press.

Swanton, M. (2003) *The Anglo-Saxon chronicles*, London: Phoenix Press.

Taylor, J. (2016) 'The Stone Age conundrum: making use of a local site to develop historical knowledge of and enthusiasm for the Stone Age', *Primary History*, 73: 26–29.

Temple, S. (2017) 'Using archives creatively', in H. Cooper (ed.), *Teaching history creatively* (2nd edn), Abingdon, UK: Routledge.

The Daily Telegraph (2016) '3,000-year-old shipwreck shows European trade war thriving in Bronze Age' Available online at www.telegraph/earth/environment/archaeology/7238663-year-old-shipwreck-shows-European-trade.html (Accessed 27 December 2016).

The Times (1996) 'Letters to the editor, Dr Olga Asby', 30 December.

Thornton, S.J. and Vukelich, R. (1988) 'The effects of children's understanding of time concepts on historical understanding', *Theory and Research in Social Education*, 126(1): 69–82.

Tiffany, S. (2012) 'History and the digital age, the interactive white board or smart board', *Primary History*, 62: 17–19.

Toynbee, A. 1922 (abridged 1987 by D.C. Somervell) *A study of history* (Vol. I–VI), Oxford: Oxford University Press.

Toynbee, A. J. (1987) *A study of history: Abridgement of vols. VII–X*, Oxford: Oxford University Press.

Treece, H. (1985) *The Viking saga: Viking's dawn, Viking's sunset, Road to Miklagard and Viking's sunset*, London: Puffin Books.

Tyldesley, J. (1988) *Hatchepsut: the female pharaoh*, London: Penguin.

Unstead, R.J. (1953) (reprinted 1961, 1963 and 1964) *From cavemen to Vikings*, London: A&C Black.

Vass, P. (2004) 'Thinking skills and the learning of primary history: thinking historically through stories', *International Journal of Historical Learning, Teaching, Learning and Research*, 4(2): 112–125.

Vella, Y. (2004) 'Assessing history talk in a group', *History Educators' International Research Conference*, St Martin's College, Ambleside, UK.

Veyne, P. (2017) *Palmyra: An irreplaceable treasure*, T.L. Fagan (trans.), Chicago, IL: University of Chicago Press.

Vishram, R. (1988) *Ayahs, Lascars and Princes*, London: Pluto.

Von Petzinger, G. (2016) *The first signs: Unlocking the mysteries of the world's oldest symbols*, New York: Atria Books.

Vygotsky, L.S. (1962) *Thought and language*, Cambridge, MA: Massachusetts Institute of Technology.

Vygotsky, L.S. (1978) *Mind in society: The development of higher psychological processes*, Cambridge, MA: Harvard University Press.

Wedgwood, C.V. (1955) *The King's peace 1637–1641 (The great rebellion)*, London: Collins.

Weldon, G. (2004) 'Thinking each other's history: can facing the past contribute to education for human rights and democracy?' *International Journal of History Teaching, Learning and Research*, 5(1): 62–70.

West, J. (1981) 'School children's perceptions of authenticity and time in historical narrative pictures', *Teaching History*, 29: 8–10.

Wheeler, S. (2006) 'And so the years passed . . .', *Spectator*, 48, 25 March.

White, H. (1992) 'Historical employment and the problem of truth in probing the limits of representations', in S. Friedlander (ed.), *Probing the limits of representations*, Cambridge: Cambridge University Press, pp. 37–53.

Whitworth, D. (2017) 'The new boss of the British Museum—and his to-do list: An exclusive interview with Hartwig Fischer', *The Times*, 21 April.

Wilkinson, A. (2017) 'The gall nuts and lapis trail: What can you tell about Anglo-Saxon trade from ink?', *Primary History*, 76: 28–30.

Wood, E. and Holden, C. (1997) 'I can't remember doing the Romans: The development of children's understanding in history', *Teaching History*, 89: 9–11.

Woods, P. and Jeffrey, B. (1996) *Teachable moments: The art of teaching in primary schools*, Buckingham, UK: Open University Press.

Wren, A. (2016) 'Why bother with transition between history at Key Stages 2 and 3?' *Primary History*, Spring: 26–27.

Yapici Dilek, G. (2010) 'Visual thinking in teaching history: reading the visual thinking skills of 12–17-year-old pupils in Istanbul', *Education 3–13 Educational Journal of Elementary and Early Years Education*, 38(3): 243–256.

Yates, J. (2004) 'Time and place capsules', in H. Cooper (ed.), *Exploring time and place through play*, London: David Fulton, pp. 92–108.

Yorke, B. (1999) 'Alfred the Great and the most perfect man in history', *History Today*, 49(10): 8–14.

Index

Printed in Great Britain
by Amazon

47020857R00151